John Little spent 25 years working as a reporter and producer in television current affairs before becoming a full-time author. He has written eight books, including *Down to the Sea*; *Jem, a Father's Story*; *Christine's Ark*; *Maalika* (with Valerie Browning) and *Catherine's Gift*. He lives with his wife, Anna, on Sydney's northern beaches.

Dr Catherine Hamlin
WITH JOHN LITTLE

The HOSPITAL by the RIVER

Updated with a foreword by The Honourable Dame Quentin Bryce AD CVO
and an afterword on Catherine's story to the present day

MACMILLAN
Pan Macmillan Australia

First published 2001 in Macmillan by Pan Macmillan Australia Pty Limited
This revised Macmillan edition published 2016 by Pan Macmillan Australia Pty Limited
1 Market Street, Sydney, New South Wales, Australia 2000

Cataloguing-in-Publication entry is available
from the National Library of Australia
http://catalogue.nla.gov.au

Typeset in Bembo by Post Pre-Press Group
Printed by IVE

MIX
Paper from responsible sources
FSC® C018183

To my grandchildren, Sarah, Paul, Catherine and Stephanie

Whatever you did for one of the least of these brothers of mine, you did for me.

Matthew 25:40

Foreword

by The Honourable Dame Quentin Bryce AD CVO

I hold in my heart the memory of my first meeting with Catherine Hamlin when I went to Addis Ababa to address the African Union early in my term as Governor-General. We talked long into the evening – just the two of us – about her life in Ethiopia. I wanted to know *everything* about the woman whom I had held in the highest esteem for so long from afar. When I first met Catherine, straightaway I saw shining through the qualities and attributes which have made her one of the most loved and admired women in the world: warmth, energy, humour, optimism, vivacity, empathy, authenticity.

I felt the depth and steadfastness of her faith, the inspiration that led her and her husband Reg, in 1959, to answer an advertisement in *The Lancet* 'Gynaecologist wanted to set up a school of midwifery for nurses in the Princess Tsehai Memorial Hospital in Addis Ababa'. They were following long traditions of Christian mission in their families, reaching back into the nineteenth century; service, accomplishment, selflessness.

I was enthralled by Catherine's storytelling, her strong true partnership with Reg steeped in mutual respect, equality, shared vision, the finest values and intellectual rigour. Together they faced extraordinary challenges that they could never have imagined. 'The fistula patients will break your heart', they were warned. And indeed they did.

Never daunted, guided by God, Catherine and Reg drew on every ounce of their skills, experience, courage, gathering any advice they could as they treated girls in the most desperate suffering, pain, shame, sorrow; women ill, weak, wretched. This would be their life's work, long hours, tough times. Across the decades thousands of women were rescued with innovative surgical procedures, given hope, a new life.

Next morning I visited the hospital. I saw and I listened. My heart sang in that sanctuary of loving and dedicated care. I was enchanted by the vivid turquoise bedcovers, the handmade comforters to go home. The Hamlins' treatment and recovery programs are respected and highly valued by practitioners from around the world who travel there to observe them and to learn. Oh those smiles on every face, the gentleness, the quiet confidence that comes with feeling secure and safe.

As Catherine introduced me to staff, volunteers and patients with her generous engaging manner, always inclusive, always uplifting, I was overwhelmed by what I could see clearly: goodness translated into action day after day. It is a life-changing experience to have the privilege of being in the hospital by the river. Human kindness in spades.

We walked arm in arm in Catherine's garden, a lovesome retreat, with daturas, trumpet flowers near the verandah with wonderful perfume that fills the air and wafts into the hospital in the evenings. There was so much to share as we talked about the road ahead. Catherine continues to carry out the plans she and Reg made to mend, to teach, to prevent, and to find new solutions to stamp out the long neglected and shameful maternal tragedy of the fistula pilgrims.

When Her Majesty Queen Elizabeth II stayed at Yarralumla in 2011, I was thrilled that Dr Hamlin accepted my invitation to join a diverse group of outstanding Australians at lunch. We had a few days together in the beautiful Government House gardens, conversations I will always treasure. We travelled together to Perth for a special event at the CHOGM on women's leadership. Catherine was acknowledged with a powerful standing ovation by people from across the Commonwealth.

It was deeply moving to hear her speak, her strong voice and strong words reminding us that there is still much to be done for thousands of women who every year suffer the agony of obstructed labour and its consequences. 'I could never imagine just living here and not working, it would be unthinkable.'

It would be unthinkable, dear reader, for us not to help.

Quentin Bryce. 2016.

Prologue

I shall call her Enatanesh, a common name in Ethiopia. It is evening. She crouches by the fire burning in the centre of the hut, somewhere out in the country far from the nearest town, preparing food for her husband. Three cows, their entire wealth, stand and chew their cud quietly in the shadows. Outside the hyenas howl.

There is barely enough *wat* to feed them. Enatanesh and her husband break off pieces of *injera* which they use as a scoop. As ever Enatanesh takes the smaller portion, and when the meal is over they are both still hungry. They accept this as normal. A little hunger is better than starvation, which they have experienced all too often when famines ravage the countryside.

There is no light in the *tukul* except for the flames. They cannot afford a lamp. No furniture. The bed is a goatskin spread over a raised section of mud floor against one wall. There are a few blankets, old and threadbare, to keep out the bitter cold of the highland night. The flat clay plate for cooking *injera,* one or two cooking pots, some large clay jars for fetching water from the well half a kilometre away – these are their possessions.

Enatanesh could be fourteen or fifteen, I have seen them younger, but let's say she is seventeen – married for a year and pregnant with her first child.

After finishing the meal they do not stay up. They are exhausted from their long day working the little plot where they grow a few vegetables, perhaps some sugar cane and the *tef* for the *injera*. They have no books. They could not afford such things and, anyway, they are illiterate. There is no radio. Television is unheard of. They build up the fire, check the door to see that the cattle are secure, wrap themselves in their blankets and curl up on the mat to sleep.

In the middle of the night Enatanesh feels her first contractions. She welcomes them but she is also afraid. She knows that childbirth may not be easy. She has heard bad stories. She tries not to think about them and faces the coming ordeal with fortitude. For better or worse it must be endured, for she is a woman and without children she is nothing. She offers a prayer to Christos, the Jesus of the Ethiopian Orthodox Church, to make her labour an easy one.

As she finishes praying she is seized by another contraction which makes her cry out. Her husband mutters in his sleep and rolls over. She does not wake him. He would not welcome being disturbed when he has to be up at dawn. She knows this is something a woman must endure alone.

By morning the contractions are coming at closer intervals. Her husband lets out the cattle and drives them off for the day. Before he leaves he alerts his mother, who lives in the same compound, to come and stand by. The mother is experienced in these matters. She has had ten children of her own, four of them, by the grace of God, still alive. She tells her daughter-in-law to get out of bed and crouch. It will help the baby to be born. All that day Enatanesh squats, straining in agony, but the baby does not come.

Her husband is not an unkind man. That night when he comes in from the fields, he enquires after his wife's well-being. He does not put his arm around her or hold her hand. Such displays of affection would be inappropriate. Still, he is concerned, and his thoughts are for her.

The contractions continue throughout the night. Enatanesh lies in her blankets during the hours of darkness, but every time she drops off to sleep the relentless pain wakes her. Oh please, dear God, let the baby be born soon and give it life.

By morning she is very weak. Her mother-in-law gives her a sip of water and counsels her to squat once more. Her legs are stiff from hours of squatting the previous day, but somehow she manages to crawl out of the blankets and do as she is advised.

The day wears on. It seems the pain will never end. It is constant now. But the baby, obstinately, still does not want to be born. Around noon the *wogesha* comes. He looks grave and gives her a small drink of local medicine. But neither the untrained village 'doctor' nor the mother-in-law can help.

On the morning of the third day the child inside her dies. Enatanesh knows it with certainty. Yet the contractions continue. Four days. Five. In the late afternoon of the sixth day she feels a change. The baby is coming. It is coming. Grimacing with effort, her eyes screwed tight, she pushes. And screams. And the child is expelled – a dead little being who will never know the world. A tear trickles down Enatanesh's cheek. She rolls herself in her blankets and sleeps the sleep of utter exhaustion.

Late next morning she wakes. But what has happened? The bed is wet and smelling. With alarm she sees that she is lying in urine. Her first instinct is to hide the shame. Perhaps if she keeps absolutely still, with her legs together, whatever has happened inside her will heal before her husband comes home. She pulls her knees up and lies on her side. She prays to God to make her whole.

But there is no hiding her condition. Usually the *tukul* is fresh with the smell of burning eucalyptus leaves, but now there is another smell and it is offensive. Despite the difficulty of keeping herself clean, the sorrow of losing her baby and the shame of her condition, she tries to be brave, to greet her husband with a smile and prepare his meals. But it is no use. She is ill, weak and wretched. Soon he moves out.

The long, obstructed labour has left Enatanesh with terrible internal injuries. She stays like this, forlorn and alone for months. Or years. Or a lifetime. She is fit only for work in the fields. The village women shun her. She is abandoned to her shame.

Sometimes in her unhappiness Enatanesh asks, 'Why has this happened?' She believes she is cursed by God for some misdemeanour, and that only a miracle can cure her. She is unaware that far away in Addis Ababa, the capital, there is a place where healing is possible.

Most likely she spends the rest of her life in misery. But occasionally her story ends with joy. Somehow she hears about the hospital. Somehow she begs the fare or persuades a relative to take her on the long, frightening journey to the unimaginable confusion of the capital.

The hospital is quiet and clean, set amongst flowers. People treat her with kindness. She is bathed and experiences the strange luxury of a soft bed with clean sheets. And the miracle she has hardly dared to believe in happens. After a time she returns home, cured, to begin life anew.

In various versions I have heard Enatanesh's story 20,000 times. Each one is part of my story.

Chapter One

Djibouti, a parched and barren republic on the southern edge of the Gulf of Aden, is said to be one of the hottest places on earth. I could well believe it on the day in May 1959 when my husband, Reg, and I and our son, Richard, aged six, sat in a squalid little café on the edge of the desert, waiting for the plane that would take us to Addis Ababa in neighbouring Ethiopia.

Reg and I were both doctors, specialising in obstetrics and gynaecology. In Australia we had answered an advertisement in the British medical journal *The Lancet,* which read, 'Gynaecologist wanted to set up a school of midwifery for nurses in the Princess Tsehai Memorial Hospital in Addis Ababa.' As we were keen to work for a few years in a country short of doctors, we thought this was the opportunity we had been waiting for. Reg enjoyed teaching and his great interest was obstetrics. We applied and were accepted. The contract was for three years. We did not know then that we were embarking upon our life's work.

Facing a two-hour wait, we'd considered taking a taxi to see the town, but the thought of dragging around in that furnace was too daunting so we elected to stay where we were.

I can still remember the baking concrete verandah with a few tables scattered about, the flies buzzing round the stale food which no one had bothered to remove, and above all, the unbearable heat. We sat in the meagre shade of some spindly trees, loud French music blaring from the radio, and surveyed our fellow travellers. The most striking of these was a beautiful Frenchwoman, there with her husband. She was tall, dark-haired and well-dressed, with a large picture hat. Her every gesture was elegant. She did not so much walk as glide. Despite the heat, the flies and our squalid surroundings, she was perfectly composed.

At another table was a sad-looking Japanese man carrying his only luggage – a paper bag – and near him a Frenchman sitting alone. Reg, who was never shy, tried to engage him with his schoolboy French, but he gave a Gallic shrug and spread his hands wide, as if to say it was really too hot to make the effort. At that time, 40 years ago, Djibouti was administered by the French.

The French proprietor of the café – a slovenly looking woman with peroxide hair, wearing a red sack dress – kept popping in and out of the kitchen with scraps of food which she fed by hand to three large hounds chained to a tree. They would devour it avidly, and she would go back inside without troubling to wash her hands, to prepare food.

Some distance away on the tarmac, men were arranging the cargo to be loaded when our plane arrived. Among it was our luggage – clothes, my linen and china, a vacuum cleaner and heaters, a few of Richard's toys, and our medical books. This, we hoped, would be enough to get us started in our new home. The rest, we were assured by the Arab agents in Aden, would arrive later by train.

After what seemed like an interminable time, an aeroplane appeared in the sky and landed on the dusty airstrip. Two Englishmen climbed stiffly out, looking rather drained, and made their way over to the café. We asked where they had come from.

'Addis Ababa.'

'That's where we're going.'

'Well,' they replied, 'the best of British luck. This was the worst journey we've ever experienced.'

There was more waiting while the plane was refuelled and the luggage loaded. At length the co-pilot, a casual American, came sauntering over and told us we were ready. We clambered aboard and arranged ourselves on bench seats that ran down either side of the fuselage. Most of the space was occupied by cargo lashed down to the floor. The door slammed, the engines rose to a deafening roar, and the plane commenced to quiver and shake. Outside, a sandstorm obliterated the view from the windows. Slowly the aircraft trundled forwards then bumped its way at ever increasing speed down the runway and into the air.

As we banked we caught our last glimpse of the sea, laid out like an indigo carpet with a scattered design of islands and reefs, before we turned south-west into the Horn of Africa. We droned on over desert for some time, but it seemed the journey had hardly begun when we landed again at a place called Dire Dawa. Our complement was increased by a few herdsmen with dusty *shammas* thrown over their shoulders, several small children with wide, wondering eyes and a herd of goats that cowered nervously in the tail of the plane.

We bumped across the unmade strip and lurched once more into the air. I suppose the old plane could not fly very high, for I could see perfectly well the land reeling slowly by below. The thermals rising off the searing continent flung us about the sky. Trying to remain on our hard seats was like riding some ill-mannered horses I have known.

Some of the other passengers looked frightened. Perhaps I should have been frightened as well but I was too excited. Richard turned pale and was on the verge of being sick when our good-hearted American invited him up to the cockpit. This took his mind off his discomfort, and he spent the rest of the journey there. The peasant children had weaker stomachs. Before long the beautiful Frenchwoman and Reg and I were holding their heads as they vomited into paper cups. Her husband, kind man, did his best to clean up the floor.

While we were thus engaged, we managed to carry on a conversation over the roar of the engines. The Frenchwoman informed me that her husband owned a large business enterprise in Ethiopia.

'What is it like in Addis?' I shouted.

'In Addis you can survive.' She waved her perfectly manicured hands. 'But Asmara, *c'est la terre belle*.'

We would come to know Asmara in Eritrea before the war made it impossible to visit. And it was, as she said, a beautiful place.

Meanwhile, beneath us the desert gave way to mountains cut by deep ravines. With all that was going on in the cabin, the heat and the violent motion, I was scarcely disposed to appreciate the scenery. Even so I could not help noticing the similarity to our own Blue Mountains in New South Wales. This savage terrain, which makes so much of Ethiopia inaccessible by road, is one of the reasons women cannot get help in childbirth. If only they had access to hospitals, the terrible injuries they suffer would not occur.

Soon the glint of corrugated-iron roofs below showed us that we were over Addis Ababa. The plane began its descent. We touched down smoothly and rolled to a halt near a tin shed.

As we tottered onto the tarmac, giddy and slightly sick, Richard echoed the words of the Englishman, 'Well, that was the worst journey I've ever had.'

We breathed a familiar scent, a mixture of dust and eucalyptus – the smell of the Australian bush. Like much of Africa and the Middle East, Ethiopia has been planted with Australian gum trees. I wonder now if it is significant that my first impression of Addis was of home.

Our fellow passengers and the pilots said their goodbyes. The plane was unloaded, and our heavy luggage placed in the shed. The workers drifted away, and we were left alone. Two weeks previously, we had sent a cable from the ship advising of our arrival, so we were expecting someone from the hospital to turn up at any time. But as the minutes ticked away into a half-hour or more, it was obvious that no one was coming. There was nothing for it but to find our own way into town.

Shouldering our luggage and grasping Richard firmly by the hands, we walked out of the airport and faced our first decision, whether to turn left or right. We chose left and set off along a broken road. Here again we were struck by the similarity to home. It was just after the 'small' rains which usually come in March for about three weeks, and the countryside was green like the south coast of New South Wales. In the distance the hills which surround the city were visible. It was a beautiful setting, and we could see why the city was called Addis Ababa, new flower. But where was it?

We passed heavily laden donkeys being driven by ragged boys and men, herds of sheep and goats and the odd cow plodding along. The few cars had to weave their way slowly among the livestock. Off in the fields were round *tukuls* made with mud walls and conical, thatched roofs. Children ran delightedly to greet us, crying, *'Ferenji, ferenji.'* Foreigner, foreigner.

There was no sign of a town and no hint of a hospital. After a while we decided that we were heading further and further into the countryside.

'Don't worry, Cath,' said Reg. 'I'll take you home next Saturday.'

'We can't go home,' I responded. 'We've only just arrived.' To tell the truth, I was enjoying these strange sights and smells, but it was getting on towards six o'clock. Not having had the courage to eat in Djibouti, we had had no food since six that morning. Richard, especially, was tired and hungry.

We turned round and headed back the way we had come. After walking only a few hundred yards past the airport in the other direction, we came to a big double gate with an arch over the top. On the arch, in English and Amharic, were written the words, 'Princess Tsehai Memorial Hospital'.

Our arrival produced a great flurry among the staff. It seems that our cable had not reached them, and no one was expecting us. In fact it did eventually turn up, two weeks later!

When he heard we had arrived, the medical director, Professor Burrow, came hurrying to welcome us. Professor Burrow was an Englishman, and very soon we were introduced to a Czech surgeon, two Indian doctors, an Irish matron and a number of British nursing sisters, all of whom lived in houses within the hospital compound. In addition there was a remarkable Englishwoman, Margaret Fitzherbert, who had once been the chief gynaecologist at Princess Tsehai and was now working with leprosy patients at a mission hospital nearby.

Dr Fitzherbert was tall, thin and rather gaunt-looking, with a lined face and grey hair. She seemed old but was so lively and talkative that we could hardly get a word in. She had spent many years in Ethiopia as a medical missionary and was dedicated to the country and her work. We were drawn to her immediately because of her vitality and her tremendous love for Ethiopians. She spoke with great enthusiasm about the task which lay ahead of us.

Someone went off to the airport to fetch our luggage, but there was one more hitch. Professor Burrow informed us that the previous gynaecologist had left hurriedly, leaving behind a pile of unpaid bills. Because of this there was no electricity in our house. He suggested we spend the night in a hotel.

Now that we had reached our destination, however, we were determined to move in straightaway. A drive through extensive grounds took us to a two-storey house. With some borrowed candles, we felt our way in. As best we could see, there was a tiled entrance hall opening out into sitting and dining rooms. The furniture consisted of one small rug, an old broken-down sofa and a couple of chairs, a dining-room table and beds.

Setting up camp, I got together a meal of bread and sardines accompanied by Ambo, the local mineral water. By the time we had eaten, it was after nine o'clock. Exhausted after our long day, we went to bed.

I was just dozing off when I heard a crash as something was knocked over on the verandah. I woke Reg. 'Quick, we're being robbed already.'

As Reg began to get up, there was a loud pounding on the front door. Fumbling around for matches, he struggled into a dressing gown and made his way by candlelight to the entrance.

'Good evening,' a cultured English voice greeted Reg. 'I'm Sylvia Pankhurst. I've come to see how you're settling in.'

Sylvia Pankhurst was the daughter of the famous English suffragette Emmeline Pankhurst. Like her mother and sister, Sylvia had been a controversial figure in Britain, and had been imprisoned numerous times for her campaigns for women's rights.

In 1930, while she was in Italy studying mosaics, the sight of the *squadristi* beating up their political opponents had given her an abiding dislike of Fascism. When Mussolini invaded Ethiopia in 1935 she became an ardent champion of the Resistance. She campaigned in the British press, speaking in Parliament, demanding sanctions against the Italians, and founded a pro-Ethiopia newspaper, *The New Times and Ethiopia News,* which she continued to publish for the next twenty years.

During the Occupation Miss Pankhurst had become friendly with the Emperor's youngest daughter, Princess Tsehai. In exile, the Princess was working in British hospitals during the German Blitz and she often spoke to Miss Pankhurst about her ambition to found a modern hospital and nursing school in her country, which would be a centre of excellence. She herself underwent training in London and returned to Ethiopia as the country's first qualified nurse, with the intention of setting up the hospital.

Sadly the Princess died in childbirth in 1942, a little over a year after Ethiopia's liberation from the Italians. After her death, Miss Pankhurst wrote to the Emperor, Haile Selassie, and his consort the Empress Menen, asking if they would become patrons of a hospital to be named after their daughter. They agreed, and in her typically energetic way, Miss Pankhurst set about raising money in Britain and there became the Honorary Secretary of the Princess Tsehai Memorial Hospital Fund.

By the summer of 1950 she had raised £748,000. The Ethiopians contributed land and the shell of a building which had been begun by the Italians. The hospital was opened in 1951.

Four years later Miss Pankhurst decided she had done as much as she could for Ethiopia in Britain so when the Emperor invited her to make her home in Addis Ababa she readily agreed. Such was his gratitude to her that he also gave her a 'grace and favour' house to live in. She continued to be involved with hospital matters, raising funds, organising equipment and maintaining contact with the directors and staff.

Sylvia Pankhurst was not the sort of woman to be put out by a mere power cut, or by our primitive circumstances. Ushering her cautiously through the dim hallway, Reg showed her to the broken-down sofa. All I could offer her was mineral water. She graciously accepted, then, as though we were having a polite conversation over tea in a proper drawing room, she proceeded to tell us all about the hospital and the Emperor.

There had been some opposition to Princess Tsehai's vision by people within the government who thought the country could not afford an elitist hospital. The Emperor had supported his daughter wholeheartedly and his will had prevailed. The school of midwifery, which we were to establish, was part of the Emperor's plan for this hospital. Miss Pankhurst told us she had good access to the Emperor, and if we had any problems we were to come to her.

By now we so tired that we were scarcely taking this all in. Eventually our visitor left, and we stumbled once more to bed.

The following night we went to dinner at a big hotel in the city with Professor Burrow and some of the other doctors. Amid the blur of memories the one which stands out most is our conversation with Margaret Fitzherbert, for it was then that Reg and I got our first inkling of the tremendous task which we faced.

Dr Fitzherbert warned us that we would see obstetric complications and suffering on a scale that could scarcely be imagined in a Western hospital.

She told us that Ethiopia was a land of high plateaux, towering mountains and deep ravines, large parts of which were only accessible on foot. Roads were scarce, and even if the peasants could get to them, the few country hospitals were chronically short of equipment and trained staff. Because of the lack of funds, for years she had regularly donated much of her salary to buy medicine and pay the hospital fees of poor patients, especially the fistula sufferers.

We had read in our textbooks about obstetric fistulae but we had never seen one. To us they were an academic rarity. If a woman in a developed country has obstructed labour, she simply goes to hospital, where she may have a forceps delivery or a caesarian section. By contrast, obstructed labour in some remote part of Ethiopia, far from medical help, places a woman in terrible trouble. She may squat on the floor of her hut or lie on a thin straw mattress, sometimes for days on end, straining to deliver her baby. An infant will not stand more than two days of being pressed upon by a uterus contracting every five minutes. After a time, the placenta starts to separate, the blood supply to the baby is cut off, and it dies. Once it is dead, maceration happens, where fluid from the baby is absorbed, and the skull bones get smaller and collapse. She is then, at last, able to expel her dead child.

By now the mother may have been in labour for five or six days, but her misery is only beginning. The pressure of the baby has cut off the blood supply to her bladder, and the tissue has died. The poor woman is left with a hole, or fistula, between the bladder and the vagina. In some cases there is also a hole in the rectum. The contents of bladder and bowel leak continuously through the vagina. Because of her offensiveness, she is usually deserted by her husband and ostracised by the village. She is condemned to a life of loneliness and shame.

Dr Fitzherbert had valiantly tried to repair some of these fistulas but was discouraged by poor results. Many times she was forced to reroute the ureters (the tubes which drain the kidneys into the bladder) into the lower bowel. This is an operation of last resort, as some women develop infection in the kidneys resulting often in death at an early age.

Reg and I listened with rapt attention as she described these tragic cases. At the time we had no idea how important they would become to us. We had been hired to practise the whole gamut of obstetrics and gynaecology. The fistulas seemed like a minor curiosity. But they would become much more than that. I shall remember forever her prophetic words, 'The fistula patients will break your heart.'

Chapter Two

I am sometimes asked how I have come to spend the greater part of my life in Ethiopia. The answer is simple. I believe that Reg and I were guided here by God. It is not inconceivable that the call was uttered long ago, before either of us were born. There is a verse in the Psalms which says, 'For you have heard my vows, O God; you have given me the heritage of those who fear your name.' Both Reg's family and mine have a tradition of missionary service dating back at least to the nineteenth century. It is quite possible that one or another of our ancestors might have prayed for their work to continue with future generations.

My great-grandfather, Henry Young, was born at Masulipatam (now better-known as Machilipatnam), India, in 1803. As a young man he worked for the Honourable East India Company. He was a keen scholar, so gifted that he rapidly gained promotion until he became the youngest judge in India.

Although he seemed set for a brilliant career, he heard a more compelling call. He gave it all up to travel with his wife, Catherine, to England to preach the gospel. Having resigned his post, he thought it would be wrong to accept the large pension to which he was entitled. His daughter, Florence, wrote in her autobiography *Pearls from the Pacific,* that she 'often heard him speak of the joy of this ministry and of the blessedness of entire dependence on God for the supply of daily needs'.

Despite these sentiments, in 1860 the necessity to support his family brought him to New Zealand, and he began farming near Invercargill in the South Island. The family struggled to make a living from the land. Rabbits were in plague proportions, and they had to wage a constant battle against weeds, thistles and other pests.

Catherine was by all accounts a frail woman, constantly beset by ill health. In the exceptionally cold winter of 1875 she and one of her sons, Horace, contracted pneumonia. At eight o'clock one evening the doctor was called. He informed the family that Catherine was too frail to fight the disease and would probably not live through the night. Two hours later she passed away. Horace, however, survived.

Horace was my grandfather.

Three years later Henry Young decided to sell up and move to Australia. He bought property near Bundaberg in Queensland, which he named Fairymead. Among the children who went with him were Horace and Florence. With the help of a labour force of Kanakas from the Solomon Islands and the New Hebrides, they commenced cultivating the land and building a mill for a sugar plantation. While this pioneering work was going on Horace married Ellen Thorne, whose family was originally from Tasmania. They were to have three sons and five daughters. One daughter, Elinor, was my mother.

When Florence, my great-aunt, got to know some of the Pacific Islanders, whom she described as 'Merry, warm-hearted and very responsive to kindness,' she was appalled that they had never heard of Jesus Christ. She decided to try to remedy the situation, beginning with a Sunday class in an old wooden humpy, attended by ten stalwart men and the housegirl. With the help of coloured pictures, she taught them about Creation and the death and resurrection of Jesus.

By the time the first harvest was in, in 1885, the classes had increased to 40 and by the following year there was an average attendance of 80 people on Sundays and 40 every evening. She must have had tremendous energy. By 1887 she had founded the Queensland Kanaka Mission, administering to 10,000 Islanders.

Florence writes that in 1890 she turned her attention to the 'unreached heathen' in China. Although the Chinese were reluctant to embrace Christianity, she persevered for ten years, rejoicing in the occasional convert, until the Boxer Rebellion forced her to quit the country and return to Brisbane.

Shortly after she came home, in October 1900, the Australian Government passed the Pacific Island Labourers Act, sending all Kanakas back to where they had come from. The thought of these people being cast adrift in a pagan land weighed heavily on Florence, and in March 1904 she and a companion, Mrs Fricke, and three male missionaries, left Sydney bound for the Solomon Islands. They found the Islanders split into two fiercely divided groups – the saltwater people, who lived on the coast, and the bush people, who lived deep in the almost impenetrable bush of the interior. The bush people were in a state of constant war with one another. Men, women and children were shot, speared or clubbed in endless vendettas. Missionaries and Islanders who had converted were regarded with suspicion and hatred.

Undaunted by these obstacles, Florence began spreading the gospel, journeying back and forth from Queensland to the Solomons for the next twenty years – often laid low by fever, encountering setbacks and hostility, but never giving up.

She lived to the age of 84. I cannot remember meeting her, but my two sisters, Sheila and Ailsa, have faint recollections of visiting a rather formidable old lady in retirement at Killara in Sydney, where she still occasionally taught Sunday school.

I do have clear memories of my grandmother, Ellen. When she and Horace retired, they left the heat of Queensland and built a grand house, Silvermere, at Wentworth Falls in the Blue Mountains near Sydney. They had been there only a year or so when Horace died. Granny kept the big house on. Our family used to visit her every Boxing Day with all her other grandchildren. We spent many happy holidays with her.

After rising early and starting the day with a cold bath, Granny would shepherd us together for prayers then accompany us on the harmonium while we sang hymns. The servants were expected to take part as well.

With an aunt like Florence and a mother like Ellen, it is little wonder that my mother, Elinor, had strict Christian values and a vibrant faith, which she passed on to all her children.

My father's father, James Nicholson, was born at Stirling in Scotland on 10 March 1863. He became a partner in the London engineering firm of Richard Waygood and Co. In 1891 he was sent to Australia to sort out some management problems in the Melbourne office and ended up taking over the branch in exchange for his London partnership.

After marrying my grandmother, Ethel Beath, Grandfather moved to Sydney. His company merged with another to become Standard-Waygood Ltd. They became renowned as lift manufacturers. Grandfather had a flair for business. He made a great deal of money and gave much of it away, living without ostentation. 'I try to lay up treasure in heaven,' he would say, 'rather than on earth.'

Most of his philanthropy was anonymous. He was deeply interested in missions and missionary work, and so was my grandmother. Three of her sisters were missionaries and three of their descendants also became missionaries.

Grandfather was a great supporter of the Sudan Interior Mission with which, coincidentally, I had dealings myself decades later. When the Italians invaded Ethiopia in 1935, the SIM in Addis Ababa decided they would either have to leave Africa altogether or re-establish in Khartoum. One of the missionaries, Mr Cain, wrote to my grandfather asking for funds to make the move. For weeks they waited without receiving a reply. After praying about this they resolved that if the money hadn't come in a fortnight's time, they would pull out and go back to Australia.

On the final day a parcel arrived. As they unwrapped it their spirits rose and then plummeted again as they saw what it contained. It was a week-old *Sydney Morning Herald*. Despondently, one of the missionaries opened the paper and out fell a cheque for the exact amount they required. Suspecting that it could have been opened at the post office and stolen, Grandfather had hidden the cheque inside the rolled-up newspaper.

Grandfather had four daughters and two sons. His daughters all remained single – because, it was jokingly said, their father didn't want them to marry unsuitable people. During the war Mary worked with the Sands homes for soldiers in Northern Ireland; these were recreation centres where soldiers on leave could relax and have contact with a Christian ministry. Elaine worked with the poor in the London slums. Constance went to China as a missionary, while Hope stayed at home and looked after her parents into their old age. Of the two sons, Jack, the younger, went onto the land in New South Wales. Theodore took over management of Grandfather's business.

Theo was my father.

The Youngs used to come to Sydney each year from Bundaberg to escape the heat of the Queensland summer. Through their mutual interest in Christianity they met the Nicholsons, and the two families became friendly. Naturally, Eleinor and Theo saw a lot of each other, but it wasn't until the families went on a skiing holiday together in Europe that their friendship began to develop into something deeper. The first hint of interest on my father's part came in Switzerland, when he asked Eleinor to sew a button onto his shirt. She thought it was an odd request when any one of his sisters could have done it.

My mother was seventeen and my father was nineteen on that holiday. Their friendship slowly blossomed into a romance. When Theo visited Eleinor he would always take her a bunch of violets, knowing that they were her favourite flower.

Theo proposed when Mother was 23; the pair were on a picnic together. She did not doubt that she was in love but there were complications. Inspired by her mother and her aunt,

Florence, she had long had the idea of doing something great for God. If she agreed to marry it would mean the end of those ambitions. She told my father that she would have to go away and pray for guidance. Theo patiently sat on a stump while Mother prayed. A verse from Jeremiah came into her mind, 'Should you then seek great things for yourself? Seek them not.' When she returned she told him she would be his wife.

In 1803, the same year that my great-grandfather, Henry Young, was born in India, George and Jean Hamlin, in a village in Somerset, England, gave birth to a son named James.

As a child of humble parents, James Hamlin received only such education as could be gained from attending Sunday school. He took up the occupation of flax dresser and weaver. Like Henry Young in India, he felt a deep need which could not be satisfied by his secular work. When he was about twenty he applied to join the Church Missionary Society.

With his limited education, James Hamlin might have been considered an unlikely prospect for a missionary, but the society was interested in establishing a flax industry in New Zealand and using it as a means of introducing Christianity to the Maoris. Probably James's skills in this area had a lot to do with his being accepted.

After training at the society's institution in London, he and his wife, Elizabeth, and another missionary couple embarked upon the sailing vessel, *Sir George Osborne.* Its cargo of stud sheep was bound for Sydney; next stop was New Zealand. On 26 March 1826, eight months after leaving England, the ship dropped anchor off Paihia, in the Bay of Islands. From there they made their way by canoe another 15 kilometres to the mission station at Kerikeri.

One month after arriving, Elizabeth gave birth to their first son, James. They lived in a crude hut, the walls of which were made of raupo, a kind of grassy weed. The Hamlins and their fellow missionaries conducted daily school lessons for Maori children. On Sunday mornings Maoris and Europeans attended divine services, and on Sunday afternoons the missionaries visited villages. The Hamlins were required to study the local language, and it was here that James began to show a natural flair for which he would later become renowned.

There were constant comings and goings of Maoris from other parts of the district. War parties would sometimes pass through on their way to do battle with rivals. On several occasions the missionaries had to intervene to prevent battles taking place on their doorstep. James, through his fluency in the local language, became skilled at negotiating peace by shuttling from one side to the other.

He was resolute in the face of danger. Once, when an angry Maori chief fired shots into a missionary's hut next door to theirs, James gave shelter to his neighbours then confronted the chief and calmed him down. On another occasion they were moving their children and belongings across the interior when the porters went on strike, demanding payment of tobacco in advance. Even when they fired shots over the missionaries' heads, James refused to give in. They continued the trek to their destination without further incident.

James's work as a lay catechist frequently took him away from Kerikeri, often for a month or more. Elizabeth would be the only adult European in the settlement. From daybreak to breakfast time and in the evenings, she taught at the mission school. For the rest of the time she instructed Maori girls in how to cook, launder and sew, as well as caring for her own family.

It was a hard and uncomfortable life, more so because they could never completely settle. No sooner would they become established then they would be ordered to move elsewhere.

In middle age the couple found themselves at Wairoa, on the east coast of the North Island, where, in April 1847, Elizabeth gave birth to their twelfth and last child. The following years were marked by continuing ill health for both James and Elizabeth. Elizabeth made frequent long visits to Auckland for medical treatment. James, too, was feeling the weight of his years of constant work but he still drove himself seven days a week, resting only when he was too unwell to carry on.

In 1856 Elizabeth made a trip from Wairoa to Auckland which was to be her last. The years of toil in primitive conditions were catching up. She was never strong enough to return to the mission and two years later, on 8 August 1858, she died.

James continued his work at Wairoa, beset by loneliness and failing health. In January 1865 he resigned and in November he died.

One of the Hamlins' sons, Francis, was conscripted into the Army at the age of sixteen and rose to the rank of major. After distinguishing himself in the Maori Wars, he later retired to take up farming and politics. He had six sons and three daughters. One of his sons, Reginald, became a builder and motor car dealer in Napier.

He was Reg's father.

Both of Reg's parents had passed away by the time I knew him. From what he told me I have the impression that his father was an austere, distant man, who found it hard to praise his son. Reg was in awe of him, perhaps even a little afraid.

One day when Reg was about twelve, his father came home from work limping and driving another car. The boy was bursting with curiosity to know why.

'Ask no questions and you'll be told no lies,' said his father.

In the Hamlin family, if you received a rebuke like that you didn't press the point. Next day Reg learned from a school friend that his father had been involved in a level-crossing accident and had been lucky to escape with his life. That was typical of him – he probably loved his son but he found it impossible to communicate.

If Reg's father was cold and unapproachable, his mother was the opposite, a kind, gentle woman. Bessie, as she was known, was born in the south of England, the eldest of a large family. At the age of nine her parents, Ted and Annie Banks, had emigrated to New Zealand on a sailing ship, taking six months for the journey and burying two small boys, James and John, at sea on the way.

They settled in Napier, where they found work, Ted as a cabinet-maker for the New Zealand Railways and Annie as a teacher. Reg's maternal grandparents played an important part in his early life. He received from them and his mother much of the affection that his father found himself incapable of showing. From his grandfather, Ted, he inherited a wonderful singing voice.

His singing brought him to the attention of Harry Brusey, the organist at the family's church. Mr Brusey was so impressed by Reg's voice that he took him under his wing and taught him how to sing properly. He used to take him around the district competing in choir competitions, and soon Reg began to accumulate prizes. When he was thirteen, thanks to Mr Brusey, he was offered an educational scholarship so he could join the celebrated Christchurch Cathedral Choir in the South Island.

Reg's father thought this was nonsense. He shouldn't have to go down there for his education; why couldn't he continue with high school in Napier?

Bessie took Reg's part, saying that it was a terrific opportunity, not to be missed, and with ill-grace his father gave in. Bessie paid for his fare on the train south and the ferry across Cook Strait out of money she had saved from her housekeeping allowance.

Mother and son travelled to Christchurch together and presented themselves before the choirmaster. He was somewhat dubious about Reg's prospects because of his age – choirboys usually start at around ten. He asked Reg what he could sing. Reg sang two pieces, and the choirmaster was immediately won over. 'You have a fantastic voice,' he said, 'and although you're really a bit old, I'm going to take you on.'

Reg's voice did not break until he was seventeen. He became the leading soprano chorister in the cathedral, enjoying life at Cathedral Grammar School and the acclaim which his talent brought him. He sang before governors, dignitaries and the leading citizens of Christchurch.

From an early age Reg wanted to be a doctor, but for some reason his father was not willing to pay his fees, although he could easily have afforded them. Reginald Senior believed his son should make his own way in life and carve out a career for himself. So instead of going to medical school, Reg first trained as a primary school teacher at Christchurch Teachers Training College. Later he was able to go to Canterbury University, where he earned a BA and an MA with second-class honours in history.

Although they were not what he had wanted to do, these studies stood him in good stead in later life. He never worked as a qualified school teacher but he became a gifted teacher of obstetrics and gynaecology to medical students and postgraduate students.

By the time Reg had graduated in arts his father had died and he could then do what he had wanted all along. He enrolled at the Otago Medical School in Dunedin, found digs and settled down to a long medical course, interrupted for a year when he was diagnosed with pulmonary tuberculosis. Old friends from that time remember that he was hard working and conscientious and went around with a worried look at times, as though he might fail. He needn't have been concerned though. He was one of the top students, and qualified in 1941 second in his year.

Reg had three sisters. Myra and Lucy were older and Iris was much younger – I think she was unplanned. Reg took a fatherly interest in her welfare. After their father died, Reg encouraged Iris to go into medicine. She went to Dunedin to study at the same time as Reg, although she was a few years behind him. He used to keep an eye on her and make sure that she was all right. She went on to become an eminent pathologist, working in a leading cancer hospital in London.

Reg's first job was house surgeon at Christchurch Hospital, but he was desperate to join the armed forces fighting in World War II. Although his tuberculosis had long been cured, the Army was reluctant to send him into active service. Instead they offered him a posting in New Zealand. He did not want to accept that so he applied for the Navy. When he went for his interview it turned out he knew the examiner and Reg managed to persuade him that he was perfectly fit. They assigned him to the cruiser HMNZS *Gambia*, as a surgeon-lieutenant.

Reg was proud to fight for his country and enjoyed his time in the Navy. He loved being at sea with the feel of a ship under him and the knowledge that he was part of a momentous time in history.

There were three doctors on board the *Gambia*; the senior, Derek Symes, was 'straight navy', and the other two, Reg and a friend from medical school, Pat Dunn, were 'wavy navy'.

Reg found some of the naval traditions hard to get used to. When he was newly commissioned, he once raised his hat to a rating who saluted him. Reg apparently didn't much look the part of a naval officer. In a book about HMNZS *Gambia* he is described thus: 'His cap always tended to be crooked and his limp salute seemed more like a scratch at an itchy eyebrow, but he could relate history, past, present or predictable.'

For a short time Reg experienced the British way of doing things at first hand. When one of the medical officers on the destroyer HMS *Argonaut* became ill Reg was transferred across by breeches buoy, along with his luggage. He found this exercise, as they steamed through the heaving Pacific, both exciting and terrifying. On board *Argonaut* the unbridgeable gap between the ratings and the officers made him think of Lord Nelson's days. And he felt that despite the British spit and polish, the hygiene left a great deal to be desired.

Reg was intensely patriotic. In 1945, as *Gambia* steamed north towards Japan, the alarm for action stations sounded and a squadron of fighters was seen approaching from the east. Pat Dunn and Reg were on deck. While most people were rushing about preparing for action, Reg's eyes were fixed on the white ensign fluttering on the mainmast flagstaff. 'Look at that, Pat,' he yelled. 'Wonderful, isn't it?'

For all the excitement of fighting a war at sea he was always happiest in the sick-bay. The doctor–patient relationship was even more personal than usual as Reg also had the job of censoring the crew's mail. He knew their hopes and dreams as well as the details of their love lives and family troubles. No doubt his ministrations were the better for it.

In August 1945 the *Gambia* was off the coast of Japan in company with the United States Third Fleet. Reg wrote some articles home to the *New Zealand Herald*. I found them again recently. Reading the faded pages I could sense his excitement as his ship joined in the bombardment of the Kamaishi steel mills, 550 kilometres north of Tokyo. '*Gambia* began the bombardment, firing the first shell, the New Zealand battle ensign was at the foremast and the White Ensign at the mainmast. I feel very proud to think that we from such a small country as ours were thus able to strike a really active blow for ourselves and for the general war effort.'

The United States had just dropped the atomic bombs on Hiroshima and Nagasaki, and the war against Japan was in its final throes. A few days later *Gambia* anchored in Tokyo Bay and began pounding the Japanese capital. Japan surrendered, and on 2 September Reg watched through binoculars from the deck of his ship as the Japanese representatives boarded the USS *Missouri* to sign the surrender.

With the war over, *Gambia* sailed to Auckland, where Reg was discharged. He was prepared to go back to work in New Zealand, but then fate took a hand. He was asked by the captain to join another naval vessel going to Sydney, as the governor's wife was on board and a doctor was required to accompany her. Steaming up the beautiful harbour and jumping ashore at the Man o' War Jetty, he decided to try to take up his Obstetrics and Gynaecology scholarship in Sydney. He applied for a job as senior resident at Crown Street Women's Hospital and was accepted. A year later he became the medical superintendent.

~

I was going to high school in Sydney while Reg was fighting the war in the Pacific. There were three boys and three girls in our family. We lived in a large house in Ryde called the Hermitage. Built in 1842 by John Blaxland, son of the explorer Gregory Blaxland, it was constructed partly of sandstone and partly of hand-made bricks. I think it must have been convict-built because in the cellar someone had written on the wall, 'I did not kill I did not steal I lived on yonder hill.' My father discovered a human skeleton there, but who it was and how he or she got there was a mystery.

When I was a child the house seemed huge, with endless rooms and a big attic in which we could crawl about and play with all the old junk that had accumulated over the years. There were eight bedrooms. The upstairs attic rooms were rather poky, but my father had gable windows put in and then we had a beautiful view all the way down to the Parramatta River. Downstairs, the rooms were wood-panelled, and there were wide verandahs in the front and back of the house. The garden was my mother's special interest and delight. It was beautiful and, to me, the most perfect garden I have ever been in.

Ryde is built up now, but during my childhood we were surrounded by orchards, market gardens and farms. The big grounds of the Hermitage were kept up by full-time gardeners. One of them, Mr Small, was about 60, with grey hair and a moustache. He was a sweet man, with a lovely sense of humour, who used to make up stories for us children. He lived in with his wife, who was the cook.

We had horses, cows, chickens and dogs and cats. One of Mr Small's jobs was to milk the three cows. I used to get up early to help him. We'd sit in the big, friendly kitchen having a cup of tea together before going out into the frosty morning to start milking. One of Mr Small's favourite tricks was to aim the teat right at our mouths so we would drink the warm milk straight from the cow. When I turned twelve and had to go away to boarding-school, I hatched an elaborate plan to elope with Mr Small, which in pretence he showed enthusiasm for. He was a nice person, always joking with us.

There was a housemaid, Bertha, and a succession of nursemaids when we were small. Bertha became a dear friend and companion to my mother and stayed with her right up to the day she died.

My mother, Elinor, was a beautiful woman of about medium height with fair skin, blue-grey eyes and straight brown hair which she wore pulled back in a bun. Being short-sighted, she always wore glasses. Father was also fair; he was tall and handsome with gentle blue eyes. He wore a moustache and, like everyone else in my early childhood days, he smoked but he gave it up later. He had a quick mind and if he wanted to say something he spoke rapidly, expressing himself clearly and succinctly.

My parents were loving but firm. They brought us up to know the difference between right and wrong, with strict rules on how to behave. Mother believed in corporal punishment. If we were naughty she would take us into the spare bedroom for a 'whipping'.

It sounds much worse than it really was. She would put us over her knee and use the back of a hairbrush or her hand. I remember lining up outside her door with Sheila, my eldest sister, and my brother Peter. My siblings soon learned that the best way to cut the punishment short was to cry from the outset. However, I had a stubborn streak and refused to do so. In fact I would often laugh instead, which of course only prolonged things.

When he was little, my youngest brother, Jock, tried a creative new tactic to escape punishment. He refused to close a door when my mother asked him to and was questioned as to why he was being so naughty. He replied, 'God told me not to.'

We had prayers every morning before breakfast, when usually the servants would be present, too. On Sunday morning we went as a family to an Anglican church where my uncle was the rector, returning to a sumptuous Sunday dinner.

We did not play much with the neighbouring children. Our social life revolved around our family, relatives and the Church. My father and mother, worried that there was no church nearby, had a hall built in the grounds of the Hermitage so that weekly Sunday school could be held there. Many local children came and were taught by volunteer teachers, including myself when I was older. In the same hall my mother started classes for the mothers. She often organised people to speak and would then put on a lavish afternoon tea.

I was the tomboy of the family, always riding horses and climbing trees. One of these had a tree-house in it from which, I am ashamed to say, we once dropped hot potatoes onto some cows trying to rest underneath. I was also keen on throwing mud pies from the rooftop onto our governess and pelting the next-door neighbours with manure. These exploits often earned an appointment with the hairbrush.

My father was mad on boats, and we always had a yacht or a motor boat moored somewhere on Sydney Harbour. In school holidays he would sail from Sydney to Broken Bay, a harbour about 40 kilometres up the coast, mooring in a bay named The Basin. A bunch of cousins and my family would camp ashore, using the boat for trips around Broken Bay and across to Goddard's boatshed on the other side, where there were shops to replenish our supplies. I loved the camping life and all the fun we had. The smell of cooking bacon still brings back memories of those childhood days.

Later on, my parents bought a block of land at Palm Beach. While my father went ahead in the car, my mother and we children would spend practically the whole day travelling from Ryde by horse and sulky. We would set up a tent and put the horses in a fenced paddock down by the beach. There were few houses there then, although now Palm Beach is full of holiday homes owned by wealthy people, and the smallest block of land is worth a fortune.

At the age of twelve I went with Sheila to Frensham, a girls' school in Mittagong, whose motto is, 'In love serve one another'. There were about 180 pupils, all boarders, divided into houses. Mine was Hartfield House. It had big, open verandahs where we slept and invariably froze in winter. It was so cold that we wore special knitted nose covers, to prevent frost-bite. Inside were cubicles with lockers where we kept our clothes and schoolbooks.

At 6.30 in the morning the bell would ring for us to get up. We had to have a shower every day. My memory of boarding-school is of always being cold, but we were luckier than the girls in some of the older accommodation. At least our showers were warm. They had to endure cold showers every morning, and the first ones in often had to bang the pipes to loosen the ice.

Every morning I would read my *Daily Light,* a little book of Bible verses for each day of the year. More than 60 years later, I still start the day in exactly the same way.

Frensham was an unusual school. They did not believe in academic competition. The school emblem was the iris, chosen for its beauty, strength and variety, and its ability to flourish in poor soil as well as good conditions. The presentation of an iris from the garden to a girl who had excelled was Frensham's only prize.

In my last year at school I decided I wanted to be a doctor. After I matriculated I lived at home and studied medicine at the University of Sydney.

When I was in my fifth year of university I had one of the most defining experiences of my life. I went to a big Presbyterian church in Sydney to hear a famous missionary speaker, Reverend Hugh Paton. He chose as his subject the passage towards the end of John's gospel where Jesus reinstates Peter in his love, despite being betrayed by him. At the time of Jesus's trial Peter had denied him three times. After he had been crucified and had risen, Jesus again met Peter and asked the question, 'Do you love me?' Three times Peter said that he did, and he was then commissioned by Jesus to feed his lambs and sheep.

Paton was a powerful speaker and as he preached this message of Jesus's love, his words touched me deeply. I went home and read the part of John's gospel which Paton had referred to. It describes the lakeside scene with a fire cooking fish for breakfast and Jesus calling the disciples to join him from their boat. I put myself in Peter's place and felt Jesus saying to me, 'Do you love me? Feed my lambs.'

Like Peter, I had been a self-centred Christian and had often denied Him. I knelt down and prayed, 'Jesus I'm going to give you my life. I really want to follow you and live for you.'

I had a powerful conviction then that some day I would become a missionary. Before that could happen I had first to complete university. In 1946, at the age of 22, I graduated with a medical degree. I still had a desire to go out into the undeveloped world but for the time being I had to settle for something a little more prosaic, working as an intern, first at St Joseph's Hospital, Auburn, and later The St George Hospital, Kogarah.

After these two years I heard that there was a resident's position available at Crown Street Women's Hospital. I was by no means sure which branch of medicine I wanted to specialise in, and was trying to decide between obstetrics and paediatrics. The chance to work at Crown Street, with its reputation of being one of the leading women's hospitals in Australia, was too good to miss. I applied for the job and made an appointment for an interview with the medical superintendent.

His name was Dr Reginald Hamlin.

Chapter Three

Being a Christian I never believe that circumstances simply happen at random. My husband's great-grandparents, James and Elizabeth Hamlin, were pioneering missionaries in New Zealand. My great-grandparents, Henry and Catherine Young, were also evangelical Christians. Of our other great-grandparents I know very little, but this I can say – these four unrelated family lines pursued separate destinies, their children married and had children of their own, who in turn married and produced their children. And in the middle of the twentieth century these wandering genealogical strands crossed at Crown Street Women's Hospital in Sydney, Australia.

Crown Street's excellent reputation was not reflected in its outward appearance. It was situated in Surry Hills, which in 1948 was one of the most unsavoury slums in Sydney – the sort of place where you would be afraid to walk in the streets at night. The hospital was an enormous complex of unprepossessing buildings which took up practically an entire city block.

My mother came with me on the day I went for my interview. While she waited outside, I was shown into a large, plain office by Dr Hamlin. He was of medium height with a good strong jaw, wavy brown hair, blue eyes and a Roman nose.

Right from the beginning, as he questioned me, I thought he was a warm and gentle man. Naively, perhaps, I told him of my ambivalence about specialising.

'That won't do,' he said. 'You'll have to make up your mind. There are a lot of people applying for this job.'

I hesitated for a moment and then nervously conceded that, yes, I supposed I would be happy with a career in women's medicine. He asked me if I was sure, as obstetrics was a difficult field and required total dedication.

We talked some more, then he said that before he could offer me a job I would have to be approved by the honoraries, as specialists in public hospitals were known. Following directions, I made my way through the corridors to the office of a Dr Stevenson. I knocked, and a voice asked me to enter. Dr Stevenson was busy at his desk. Without paying me too much attention he ordered me to hold out my arm. He finished with his papers then began to apply a blood pressure cuff. The procedure was well under way before I summoned up the courage to tell him that I hadn't come as a patient.

'My dear,' he said, 'every woman who walks through my door I consider pregnant until proved otherwise.'

I assured him that I definitely was not pregnant. 'I am applying for a job here and I need your approval.'

Laughing, he removed the cuff from my arm and proceeded to interview me instead. After such an awkward beginning I must have redeemed myself somehow because before long I was sent back to Dr Hamlin, who confirmed my appointment.

Rather than just send me on my way he took me on a tour of the hospital. The public wards were called Nightingale wards, having been set up on a similar pattern to those designed by Florence Nightingale. They were of great length with beds down each side and a sister's station at one end so that she could view all the beds from her desk. Dr Hamlin told me that in busy periods they would often put a row of stretchers down the middle of the wards. It was the only way they could accommodate everyone. On the first floor there were five obstetric wards, starting a little bit up from Albion Street and going right up to Fitzroy Street.

Dr Hamlin also showed me my living quarters – a tiny room up on the roof. It was a lot of trouble for him to do this, but as I got to know him better I learned that he was renowned for his painstaking attention to detail in everything he did, whether it was looking after his patients or a new resident.

After the tour he handed me back to my mother. As we said goodbye she said to him, 'Please take good care of my daughter, she's really very frail,' much to my embarrassment; it was quite untrue. Dr Hamlin laughed and assured her that I would be in safe hands.

As we discussed the eventful day on our way back home to Ryde we agreed that we liked Dr Hamlin very much. I thought to myself, I'm going to be happy here.

Crown Street was a wonderful training ground. Australia was in the midst of a postwar baby boom, and there was a shortage of hospitals. There were only four women's hospitals in Sydney then – the Royal Hospital for Women in Paddington, King George V, St Margaret's and Crown Street – so we saw abnormal obstetrics from all over New South Wales. At Crown Street there were about 5000 deliveries a year. The outpatients' department was packed every day. Everyone from nursing staff to doctors was frantically busy. As a junior resident I was on duty in the labour ward for a week at a time. I could call an honorary if I got into trouble, but basically it was up to me to keep the ward running smoothly. I soon found that this involved working practically non-stop. When I went on duty I used to fill my pockets with sweets because I knew I wouldn't have time to sit down and eat.

At night I was called out of bed to attend any abnormal deliveries, so if there were a lot of complications I got very little sleep. It was good to know that I could always call on the superintendent if I got into trouble and that he always came.

Although I worked hard, my hours were easy compared to Reg's. It was not unusual for him to put in twenty hours a day. He lived at the hospital and was on call at any time, day or night. If he was called out for an emergency he would always take the opportunity to do a round afterwards. Other doctors would come in at 8 am, feeling rather virtuous about such an early start, and find that the notes were already written up in beautiful copperplate and any complications sorted out. Reg would have done it all two or three hours earlier. On some days he spent so long standing on the hard floors that his ankles became swollen.

He would never go to bed without checking the labour ward. Last thing at night he would ring up and ask the sister to take him on a round on the telephone. If she missed a bed, he would instantly realise. He was driven by a tremendous concern for each and every patient. Most doctors develop a certain detachment from their patients, out of self-preservation. Not Reg. He would worry about them endlessly. He wanted to know every detail about what was going on, and if one of his patients had some misfortune he would be as upset about it as if they were his own family.

He was a creative thinker and wouldn't let rules stop him from doing what he believed was good for the hospital. Dr William McBride, who later became world-famous for discovering the relationship between birth defects and thalidomide, applied for a job shortly after the war. Because they were giving preference to ex-servicemen he was passed over. A little while later Reg offered him a two-week locum. On his last day McBride went to Reg's office without his white coat and dressed in his sports clothes, to say goodbye.

'What are you doing here dressed like that?' asked Reg.

Dr McBride explained that his time was up and he was leaving.

'Nonsense. You're here now so you might as well stay. No one will know.'

Reg was mad on cricket. Don Bradman was his hero, but he could never afford the time to sit through a Test match. When the Tests were being played in Sydney he would have a hired car standing by and keep track of play on the radio. When it was Bradman's turn to bat he would rush downstairs and dash off to the cricket ground. As he could never stay long, the car would have to wait for him so he could race back to the hospital again.

I was nervous of him at first. He seemed always in a hurry. Once, when we were in the communal staffroom, I asked him why he was eating so quickly. 'Because I know I'll probably be called out,' he replied. And sure enough, in the middle of the meal he had to drop everything and run up to the labour ward to attend to a patient.

Every morning he used to do a round in the antenatal ward. And like many things involving Reg, this was often attended by drama. One minute he would be listening with a foetal stethoscope to the baby's heart, then he'd have to rush out and take a phone call. One day when he was running backwards and forwards, he put the stethoscope on the woman's abdomen and said, 'Hamlin here.' The entire staff burst into laughter.

On another occasion an ambulance pulled up outside the hospital with siren wailing, carrying a pregnant woman suffering from eclampsia, a disease which causes fits. Unfortunately she had died just before arrival, but there was still a chance to save the baby if they acted quickly.

The woman was wheeled inside and the trolley parked in a hallway. 'Someone get me a knife,' shouted Reg. A student nurse ran into the kitchen and returned with a carving knife. Great confusion. Meanwhile, someone else had fetched some proper equipment and Reg performed a post-mortem caesar then and there.

Reg loved to teach and was marvellous at making up little ditties which helped people learn. In those days we applied chloroform as an anaesthetic. It was highly dangerous if you used it in the wrong way. You had to drip just a few drops onto the patient's mask. Reg would demonstrate the technique saying, 'Always use care, prayer and plenty of air.'

Young doctors often had trouble with the spelling of the

drug pethidine. Reg told them, 'Remember, the eyes are in the middle and the ears are outside.' When he lectured about abnormal deliveries, he would say, 'If there's a problem, it's either the passage or the passenger.'

Reg was an extremely good manipulative obstetrician. He had written a textbook on labour ward diagnosis and taught me to do all the difficult forceps deliveries and many other procedures which were tremendously useful later in Ethiopia, where there are so many abnormal deliveries. He took me on his rounds of the labour wards, encouraged me and made sure he was always present at any difficult deliveries I was nervous about.

The students used to regard him as a bit of an eccentric but they appreciated the fact that he was such a good communicator. The staff all loved him, and so did the patients. Once the students were grouped around a woman who was being internally examined. Reg bustled in and offered to demonstrate the correct technique. The patient's face was obscured by bedding. As he began his demonstration, she exclaimed, 'Oh, it's Dr Hamlin.' The students fell about the ward laughing.

There was something special about Crown Street. Everybody said so. Fellow staff members who left to work elsewhere would often come back and wistfully tell us that we didn't know how lucky we were. The special atmosphere was partly because of Reg's leadership and partly due to the matron, Edna Shaw.

Matron Shaw ran her hospital from an over-furnished room on the ground floor, with a mixture of iron will and compassion. She was a friend to all the waifs and strays. The unwed mothers, the victims of abortions gone wrong, the single girls who had to give up their babies for adoption – the sort of people who tended to be frowned upon by upright citizens – all had a friend in Matron Shaw.

She was tall and grey and had an odd, rolling gait. She spoke in a funny, quavery voice, which Reg could take off perfectly.

Many unmarried mothers came down from the country to have their babies at Crown Street. Matron Shaw kept a drawer full of wedding rings in her office. When they were admitted she would lend them one, telling them it was their choice whether they told the other patients about their circumstances.

She helped to arrange hundreds of adoptions. The prevailing school of thought was that the mothers should never see their babies. Matron Shaw disagreed strongly. She insisted that it was a baby's right to be cuddled and breastfed by its mother before being placed for adoption.

Like Reg, she worked incredibly long hours, and tried to visit every mother and baby daily. Often she would take a little rabbit in her pocket as she did the round and show it to the mothers whom she thought needed a bit of cheering up.

Many matrons adopted an aloof, authoritarian manner with the nursing sisters. While she maintained high standards, Matron Shaw was anything but aloof. Once one of the honoraries came to work to find her scrubbing the front steps. When he asked her why she was doing this she replied, 'Doctor, this is my home and I like to see it kept clean.'

If there was a shortage of staff, she didn't mind pitching in. On various occasions she was known to stoke the boilers and work the switchboard, and one New Year's Day, when the domestic staff failed to turn up after celebrating all night, she personally carried the breakfasts around the wards.

Usually she ensured things ran according to her wishes by a mixture of diplomacy and guile, although if pressed she could be simply rebellious. A new system was put in whereby she was able to talk to all the wards directly from her office, by telephone. For some reason Matron took a dislike to it and on the first morning had the whole thing torn out. That afternoon all the honoraries came round to find out how the marvellous new system was working. She told them flatly that she didn't like it and she wouldn't countenance its presence as long as she was in charge. Wisely, the honoraries accepted defeat.

Her years dealing with mothers and babies gave her a kind of sixth sense. One typically busy day, a number of mothers were sitting on a long bench outside her office. Telephones were ringing incessantly, and staff were coming and going; mothers were gossiping and babies were crying. Suddenly Matron noticed a cry that sounded different from the rest. She rushed out to find one of the mothers in great distress. No matter what she did she could not console her child. She had fed him and cuddled him, but to no avail. Matron took them into her office, put the baby on the desk and took his nappy off, and the source of the trouble was revealed. The mother had put the safety pin through his penis.

Hospitals in those days didn't have full-time public relations people as they do now. Because she was so approachable, Matron Shaw became the hospital's unofficial spokesperson. If ever a reporter wanted to know anything, they would go to her. Unlike today, doctors kept a low profile. Being identified in a newspaper story was considered to be seeking publicity and was strictly forbidden. Matron Shaw wasn't bound by the same rules and when there was some newsworthy occasion she would usually be the one who got her picture in the paper. I doubt if the most skilled public relations practitioner today could create the goodwill she generated.

Some things had to be kept quiet, though. She used to take in old down-and-outs from the street and let them sleep in her bedroom. And she was not averse to using hospital facilities for the treatment of their ailments. She asked one young doctor, who did not know about her mothering instincts, to sign an X-ray form.

'Who is it for?' he enquired.

'Just a destitute old woman who's been sleeping on my couch. She's been coughing very badly, and I want to make sure her chest's all right.'

She also had several old people living in the boiler room, which only became general knowledge after she died. Reg knew what was going on but turned a blind eye. They were on the same wavelength. They loved caring for people, no matter what their status. And they believed in treating them as human beings first rather than just as patients. Their approach was what made Crown Street a unique place.

Matron Shaw's compassion and humanity earned her a reputation far beyond the hospital. Towards the end of her career she was nominated for an OBE. The Governor-General presented it to her at a big ceremony in the gardens of Canonbury, the harbourside rest home annexe for Crown Street patients. After the reception was over she was riding back to the hospital on the tram when an old drunk noticed the medal pinned on her coat.

'What did you get that for?' he wanted to know.

'I got it for helping with mothers and babies.'

His rheumy old eyes lit up. 'You must be Matron Shaw.'

When I joined the staff of Crown Street I was the only woman among the residents, most of whom were older ex-servicemen returned from the war to pursue their careers. Being a woman among so many men, I was made a fuss of and enjoyed a lively social life. I received one proposal of marriage, which I did not consider seriously. Later more women joined the staff so I was not so special.

Reg was fifteen years older than me, but this did not enter into my thoughts. After I had been there about a year, an undeniable attraction began to develop, which I soon realised was mutual.

At first we were discreet. I would walk down Crown Street towards the city, and Reg would follow a few minutes later and pick me up in a taxi. We would sometimes have dinner at Ushers Hotel or go to a film. If we had a day off together on the weekend, we might go surfing at Cronulla or Manly.

As our courtship continued, Reg met my family. He went out on my father's boat and attended church a few times with us on Sundays. On Sunday evenings when we all gathered around the piano at home, we were terribly impressed with his beautiful singing voice, especially when he sang his favourites from Gilbert and Sullivan.

There was an intercom system in the hospital where the wards could communicate with Reg's living quarters without going through the switchboard. If I was on night duty we would sometimes use this to speak to each other. I remember fondly Reg sometimes lying in bed and calling me up to read me a psalm that he thought I might like. Once when I was expecting his call, I answered the phone, 'Hello, Darling.' It wasn't Reg but one of the medical staff enquiring about a patient. Despite our precautions it wasn't too long before everyone was aware of our courtship.

After we had been seeing each other for about six months, I went into his office one evening to discuss a patient. I was standing on the other side of the desk when he came round and put his arms around me. He kissed me and said he loved me. I was quite overcome and said that I loved him, too.

The timing was rather unfortunate because I had already made plans to leave Crown Street and go to England. The following day, a Saturday, we went to Manly for a picnic. There were hardly any houses there then. We walked out to the headland, spread our rug and ate our sandwiches looking out at a lovely view. When we had finished, Reg asked formally if I would marry him.

I wasn't going to be rushed and, besides, I was about to set sail for the other side of the world. I told him I'd need some time to make up my mind and I would write to him from England. A few days later Reg, rather crestfallen, saw me off.

The ship went south down the coast and then west across the Great Australian Bight to Perth. During that long sea crossing I had time to think about his kindness, decency and enthusiasm and all his endearing qualities which were so appealing, and I realised what my answer had to be.

I wrote to him from Perth. A few days later, while he was going up in the lift at the hospital, he opened the letter. There was only one other passenger with him, Sister Martin from the labour ward. Reg read what I had written, turned to her with a delighted look on his face and to her astonishment declared, 'Sister, she's said yes.'

He sent an engagement ring to me in England, and a year

later I returned for our wedding. I was 26 years old and Reg was 41.

We chose Trafalgar Day, October 21, for our wedding. This seemed appropriate with Reg's love of the sea and his naval background. We were married by my godfather, Archdeacon Begbie, a saintly old man whom I had known since childhood, in the old church of St Philip in Sydney.

The reception was to be held in the grounds of the Hermitage in a big marquee erected on the tennis court. Reg gave me a little red Morris Minor for a wedding present and in it we set off down to the south coast of New South Wales for a holiday, camping and staying in hotels.

After the honeymoon was over we returned to the hospital, where I had my old job back again, and we both moved into Reg's little penthouse up on the roof. When we had got engaged, the cleaner, Mrs Thomas, who used to do our rooms, had said to Reg, 'You're not marrying that Dr Nicholson, are you? Well, heaven help you because your room is untidy enough but hers is like a drunkard's dream of home.'

She was probably right, but it was because of the pace at which we were living. Being married changed nothing in that regard. We still worked as hard as ever, only now we were a team in more than just a professional sense.

Chapter Four

Eclampsia was a great danger to pregnant women. Sufferers gained excessive weight due to fluid retention, and developed high blood pressure and poor kidney function. If not treated, they could have epileptic-type convulsions, and in severe cases both mother and baby could die. Eclampsia affected about one in every 350 pregnant women.

The senior honorary was Dr Thomas Dixon-Hughes. In his large obstetric practice he had succeeded in confining over 5000 women without one suffering an eclamptic fit. He put down his success to a careful regimen of antenatal care. Excited by Dixon-Hughes's results, Reg agreed to supervise a controlled study in Crown Street over two years, using the methods he advocated.

Dixon-Hughes was a peppery Welshman. He was short and bald with a florid complexion that would turn bright red when he lost his temper, which he did often. While he was a brilliant obstetrician, he could not tolerate anyone making the slightest error. The staff at Crown Street lived in fear of his tantrums. One incident illustrates the point.

One of Dixon-Hughes's patients went into labour, and the baby's cord could be felt in front of its head. Reg rang him in his offices at Macquarie Street and asked him to come immediately and do a caesarian section. Dixon-Hughes asked Reg to get the woman to the theatre as quickly as possible and start the anaesthetic, he would be there in ten minutes. Until he could get there, he wanted someone to put their finger up the rectum and hold the baby's head off the cord so it could get oxygen. This task fell to one of the residents, a refugee from Central Europe named Ferry Gruntsite.

The woman was trundled out of the labour ward to the lift to take her down one floor level to the theatre. Accompanying her were a nursing sister with an oxygen cylinder and Ferry Gruntsite, running beside the trolley with his finger up the rectum. When the lift doors opened, they pushed everything in then realised there was not enough room for Ferry. 'Never mind,' he said. 'I'll run down to the next floor and meet you there.'

By this time, Dixon-Hughes had arrived at the hospital and pressed the lift button. Instead of stopping at the theatre the lift went directly to the ground floor. The doors opened and there was the patient on the trolley with the oxygen cylinder and the sister but no Ferry Gruntsite. In the confusion to get the lift going again someone pressed the wrong button. Up they went again. The doors opened and, without realising the mistake, the sister got out and wheeled the patient along – not to the operating theatre but to the nursery.

In the end the whole thing worked out well, and a live baby was delivered. But Ferry Gruntsite was mortified that he had failed to carry out Dixon-Hughes's orders to the letter. At a meeting at the end of the week there was an enquiry into the whole affair. One of the honoraries asked Ferry, 'When you had the finger up the rectum, what were you feeling?'

He answered, 'Well, sir, I couldn't feel anything at all.'

'Then why didn't you take it out?'

'I was frightened to.'

Dixon-Hughes might have been demanding but he could not have wished for a better man than Reg to supervise the clinical trial. Reg was as much a perfectionist as he was, if not more so. The trial involved careful monitoring of pregnant women over a number of weeks leading up to the birth, to check for a sudden rise in blood pressure or excessive weight gain. Those patients who required it were put on special diets and, if necessary, admitted to the hospital so they could be more closely supervised.

The participants were taken from the outpatient lists. For the study to be accurate the doctors had somehow to ensure the close attendance of some 14,000 women. Reg instituted a system where each woman was checked to make sure they attended the clinics they were supposed to. If they didn't turn up, the hospital would ring them, but as there were very few private telephones at that time they usually had to send a telegram. If the patient still didn't come, they would call the local police station and have an officer go round to the house with a message.

Making sure that the staff chased up the patients, ensuring that the antenatal regimen was followed to the letter and interpreting the test results was an enormous task. Reg threw himself into it with his usual enthusiasm and thoroughness. For two years it seemed as though he hardly ever slept.

While the study was going on, his close friends and colleagues – Dr Peter Crowe and the assistant medical superintendent, Bob MacBeth – both left to go to England and do their higher degrees, MRCOG, Member of the Royal College of Obstetricians and Gynaecologists. They had been of enormous support to Reg, and without them even he, with his capacity for hard work, began to find the job too demanding. He also decided it was time to change and tendered his resignation, to take place in early 1952. A letter he wrote to his sisters in November 1951 tells in his own words how he was feeling.

Dear Myra, Lucy and Iris,

I am writing you a joint letter with carbon copies because my life is always so hectic here. I just don't get the time to write letters separately as I want to. I have neglected my friends all over the world since I have been at this hospital. Since Peter Crowe and Bob MacBeth left at the end of last year I have been anchored down and really overwhelmed with work. I have never really been off duty as I have been the only one here (except Catherine) with a long experience of obstetrics and everything has had to be kept up without the help of those two stalwarts. I could not keep it all up forever, and so several months ago I resigned, giving six months notice.

I could not go on doing this job forever. It is for me like being the captain of a ship who is always on call day and night (continuously) and have to carry the heavy burden whenever the weather is really rough. I would die here if I went on much longer, although at the moment I feel of course extremely well and never was in better health. Catherine has been a brick this year. She has shouldered many of the burdens and is tireless. She is a most efficient and gentle obstetrician. Patients are always telling me how wonderful she is, but they do not need to tell me of course. I have always known that. It is better for me to resign now when the results speak for themselves. The board of directors made very flattering remarks when they received my resignation. I only tell you that so that you will know that I have evidently coped with the work here reasonably well. I suppose you should know that during my time here:

The maternal death rate for the hospital has fallen rather remarkably.

The baby death rate has fallen from 25 per 1000 to 16 per 1000.

The puerperal sepsis rate, the thrombosis rate and the postpartum haemorrhage rate have all been halved.

The eclamptic fit rate has fallen from 1 in 350 to 1 in 8000 confinements. This figure is undoubtedly equal to or better than the eclampsia rate anywhere else in the world.

In the year 1947 this hospital had 17 eclampsia cases among its booked patients and two mothers died of this disease. During the last 19 months there has been no case at all of eclampsia in booked cases (8000) patients and no mothers have died of eclampsia (booked patients) in the whole of my term of office.

I only tell you this to let you know that I am resigning when the results for this hospital are the best in all its history, because I have felt it better to resign at such a time than to wait until one feels physically incapable of maintaining such standards.

I shall write letters to each of you before I go, but please understand that the work here crowds in on me so much that I just have no time to write as I would of course like to do. It is all I can do to keep everything going here and eat and sleep. I hope you have understood this. Isn't it wonderful that Churchill is back?

Much love to you all
From Reg

The eclampsia study continued, and after two years the results were dramatic. The rate of eclampsia had dropped from one in 350 to none in 10,000.

Reg and Dixon-Hughes each interpreted the result differently. Dixon-Hughes's main theory was that eclampsia was due to a relative rise in blood pressure, while Reg placed emphasis on weight gain in the twenty-fifth to thirtieth week of pregnancy. Both wrote separate papers. Dixon-Hughes sent his to *The British Journal of Obstetrics and Gynaecology*. Nowadays the editors of such journals send articles out to two independent reviewers before they publish them, but in those days the editor, Professor Dougall Baird, ran the journal according to his own judgment. If he liked an article, he'd publish it; if he disagreed with it, he wouldn't. Baird rejected the article because he disagreed with Dixon-Hughes's claim, that eclampsia was a preventable disease. He thought if you said eclampsia was preventable people could sue.

Reg, meanwhile, had sent his paper to *The Lancet*. He did not go so far as to say eclampsia was preventable, and the article was accepted. When it came out it created quite a stir in international medical circles. Interestingly, it is thought now that the reason they got such good results was not so much due to diet or blood pressure but because of the careful antenatal supervision.

Reg's *Lancet* article, 'The Prevention of Eclampsia and Pre-eclampsia', appeared in January 1953. In his summary Reg acknowledged his colleagues in these words: 'In writing this account I have set down only my personal opinions. The successful results described, however, support the views held for many years by the chairman of the honorary medical staff, Dr Dixon-Hughes, and all other members of the honorary medical staff . . .'

Dixon-Hughes's article eventually appeared in the *Australian Medical Journal*. He was absolutely furious at being pre-empted, and the whole affair became a cause célèbre in the Sydney medical community.

Reg and I had left the hospital by then and sailed for England. But later the row would have consequences which were to change the course of our lives.

Chapter Five

Reg got a job as ship's surgeon on the cargo ship, *English Star*. When we arrived in Britain we bought an old grocer's van, fitted it out for camping with two bunks and set off to tour the Continent. We had a lovely few weeks in Europe living like gypsies in the van then returned and drove around Britain, staying in camping grounds and visiting all the cathedral cities. After a while neither of us could stand another cathedral so we were quite glad to come back to London and start work.

Reg took up a position in the Samaritan Hospital for Women. I was doing a course at Great Ormond Street, the famous children's hospital. We hadn't been in England long when two important events occurred. I got pregnant and almost at the same time I was diagnosed with a blood disease that could be fatal.

The first sign that something was wrong was ulceration of the throat and a sore mouth. The GP sent me at once to hospital for a white blood cell count. After doing some bone marrow punctures they told me that I had a disease called agranulocytosis, where the white cells, which combat infection, disappear. Usually you get it from taking an overdose of drugs such as aspirin, but I hadn't taken anything so I never knew what caused it. I knew enough about the disease, though, to know that it was serious.

For the next two months I stayed in hospital having doses of penicillin night and day. All the time the baby was steadily growing. Reg tried to keep my spirits up by bringing in bunches of wattle to remind me of home.

One day after I had left hospital, as I was crossing the street on my way back to our flat I was knocked over by a bus. I was unconscious for a while and when I woke up I was lying on the pavement. The baby was due in three weeks, and the first thing I did was feel to see if it was still there. Then I felt for my teeth. Both seemed to be all right.

I was rushed to St Mary's Hospital, and a policeman went round to the Samaritan Hospital to tell Reg what had happened. He was in the operating theatre when he was given the news that his wife had been knocked down and was in hospital. The policeman did not say whether I was alive or dead but told him he had better come. Reg had nearly finished the operation so he left the resident to sew up and rushed over as quickly as he could. By the time he arrived I was awake and feeling quite all right.

Three weeks later our child was born. Despite all of my professional expertise I was still unprepared for my own experience of childbirth. I should really have had a caesarian section, but because of the blood disorder this was not possible, the risk of infection beeing too great. So I had a difficult forceps delivery instead. The baby was big – 9 pounds (4 kilograms) – and when he was born he had prominent forceps marks on his cheeks. The obstetrician, quite shaken, came out and told Reg that I had had a difficult delivery and the baby wasn't breathing.

'Never mind the baby,' said Reg. 'How's my wife?'

Being still under the anaesthetic I was unaware of what was happening. The baby didn't breathe properly for half an hour, but all was well in the end.

He was a lovely boy, and we named him Richard.

~

The Samaritan was a specialist gynaecological hospital, where Reg met many distinguished surgeons. Among them was a famous gynaecologist, Leslie Williams, who had attended one of the Queen's deliveries. While there Reg received his MRCOG. We could have stayed and made careers for ourselves but somehow neither of us felt suited to a life of predictable comfort in England. We needed something more challenging. After fifteen months we set sail for Hong Kong, where Reg had been offered a post in the Queen Elizabeth Hospital.

I worked in a mission clinic on the Kowloon side run by a Mrs Donnythorn, whose husband was an Anglican archdeacon. It looked after the impoverished Chinese who lived nearby, crowded into teeming, high-rise tenements. I used to cross to Kowloon every morning and work in the outpatients' clinic, attending to anything from boils to malnutrition.

We lived in a flat called Branson Towers on The Peak. Your position on The Peak was an indication of your status. Rich people lived at the top. We were about halfway up. It was here that Richard took his first steps. Reg and I were fortunate to be together when, at the age of about eighteen months, Richard took ten staggering paces across the polished timber floor unaided.

After nine months in Hong Kong I began to get warning signs of a low white cell count again. It started off with infected sandfly bites all over my legs. Because my level of neutrophils, the cells which fight germs, was very low, the bites became infected. I then got a bad skin condition and became ill with high fever. The enervating heat of Hong Kong was only making things worse, so again we decided it was time to move on.

On our way home to Australia Reg did a one-month obstetric locum for a doctor in New Zealand. During that time I received word that my dear father had suffered a massive heart attack while mowing the lawn. He was hospitalised but quickly suffered a second attack from which he did not recover. It happened so fast that I did not have time to go home to see him.

I was shattered by my father's death at the age of only 59. He had been a wonderful, loving parent and very dear to me.

In 1956 we returned to Sydney, where Reg intended to go into private practice and become an honorary at Crown Street. Having been the medical superintendent, his appointment onto the honorary staff should have been a mere formality, but when he applied he found that the unfortunate business with Dr Dixon-Hughes had come back to haunt him. Dixon-Hughes was chairman of the hospital board. He told Reg flatly that as long as he had influence he would make sure he would never be accepted.

It was a devastating blow, which left Reg dismayed and depressed. He had had a brilliant career and was popular with all the staff at Crown Street. To be thwarted like this was most unjust. He dealt with it in the best way he knew, by throwing himself into his work. He got onto the staff of three or four different hospitals as an obstetrician and gynaecologist. They were as far removed from each other as Hornsby in the north, Burwood in the west and Kogarah in the south. It was stressful work, involving a lot of travel. Reg was used to being able to deal with emergencies immediately. Now he found himself sitting in traffic jams worrying while a patient was haemorrhaging in a hospital half an hour away.

After a few months he was becoming more and more nervous and depressed. He knew he could not go on with this sort of life but he could see no clear alternative. We were living with my sister Sheila and her husband, John Knox, who was a successful gynaecologist. He advised Reg to get into private practice. 'Everyone has to do things they don't like. You've got to make your money,' he counselled.

We searched around, looking at houses in different suburbs. I said, 'I can't settle down in one of these horrible little boxes, Reg. I'd never enjoy that sort of life.'

Reg didn't like the idea any more than I did. Just when it was needed, a solution arrived. He was appointed medical superintendent of the Queen Victoria Hospital in Adelaide, and I was accepted at the Adelaide Children's Hospital.

In Adelaide we lived in a nice house attached to the hospital.

We enjoyed our work and made plenty of friends. But gradually, as before in London, we started to feel that we were unfulfilled. It took two years, but there came a time when we both said we could not spend the rest of our lives living in a suburban house in Adelaide when we had so much to offer people in a less privileged part of the world.

For a while we thought of going to Papua New Guinea. But with my blood condition, we were worried that I might not be able to stand the heat. We scanned all our medical journals for possible jobs – and one day saw the advertisement in *The Lancet.* It seemed ideal, and would fulfil Reg's two great interests – midwifery and teaching.

The hospital was run by a board of trustees in England. Reg applied to them, but the three-year job was given to someone else. At the last minute he could not take it up, so they wrote to Reg asking if he was still interested. He replied that he was, as long as there was a position for his wife, Dr Nicholson, to practise gynaecology. They quickly agreed.

I was very keen on going to Ethiopia, but having accepted the job, Reg began to have doubts, especially about the wisdom of taking six-year-old Richard to an undeveloped country. We wanted to find out more about Ethiopia, but there were very few people in Australia who knew anything.

Reg got a phone number for the mother of a missionary who was working there. I was listening to his side of the conversation as she gave him her views about the country, and the more she spoke the more despondent Reg's responses became. According to her it was a dreadful country – there were flies on the children's eyes; very few people lived beyond the age of 40; the Emperor was old and senile. Every time her son went back there she had to give him a sherry to get him on the plane. When Reg hung up he was crestfallen, but I told him not to worry, she was obviously a rather silly old woman.

When I told my mother that Reg and I were going to Ethiopia she was appalled. 'No,' she said. 'Oh, I always knew Reg would take you to some such place.'

We did get one positive report from another missionary, who knew the hospital and even had slides of it. But as the time for departure approached, Reg was still not sure if we were doing the right thing for Richard.

One morning, after taking him to school, Reg went for a long drive by himself in the country to think things over. Uncharacteristically, in mid-morning he stopped at a pub. He was drinking a beer when the barman said, 'What's up, mate? You look as though you've got something on your mind.'

Reg told him he was agonising over whether to take his little boy to Ethiopia. The man next to him, also quietly sipping a beer, said, 'I've just come from there. It's a marvellous place. I've been there for three years with a mapping mission and I love it. There's a good English school. My boy went and had no trouble getting into a good school when he got back to Adelaide. He'll love it. Just go.'

Reg came home very excited. All his doubts had been resolved. Later we looked back on that meeting as guidance from God. I knew Ethiopia was where we were meant to be.

Chapter Six

Our relationship with the Ethiopian Ministry of Health, which was to pay our salaries, did not begin well. After we arrived and moved into the house at the Princess Tsehai Hospital, we waited day after day for a contract. Some old hands had warned us not to start work before we had signed, otherwise we might never see one. While we cooled our heels the hospital was asking us to see patients. Reg went up and spoke to the staff and the medical director but insisted that we would not start until the contracts were signed.

Matters came to a head when we informed the Ministry that if the contracts had not arrived by the end of the week we would go home. On Friday night they were poked under the door and on Monday we started work.

We had seen our fair share of abnormal obstetrics at Crown Street but nothing like on the scale which we now encountered. We were dealing with women who had dreadful complications because of lack of medical care; often on the verge of death. This was due to the chronic shortage of skilled doctors. Many gynaecological patients arrived with horrendous pathology, such as tumours, which we had not previously encountered in Australia.

One of the chief difficulties at first was not being able to talk with the patients. The main language in Ethiopia is Amharic. It bears no relationship to European languages and is hard for English speakers to learn. Reg picked it up more quickly than I did and within a week or so he was trying out basic words on the staff and patients, often reducing them to fits of laughter in the process. However, we never lacked excellent interpreters among the nurses and doctors, so we were always able to obtain a good medical history.

We learned very early that blood was scarcer than gold. The idea of taking blood was rare in Ethiopia and the peasants, especially, were completely uneducated about anything medical. So naturally they were frightened. Consequently there was often no more than a pint or so of any one type in the refrigerator. In those early days there was no blood bank.

One woman due for an operation had a rare type. When I asked her husband if I could test him to see if he matched, he flatly refused.

'But your wife might die,' I told him.

'Better she should die than I give blood.'

'What if *you* were sick? She would give blood for you, wouldn't she?'

'No, she wouldn't. She'd wait until I died then quickly marry someone else.'

In desperation Reg rang the British Embassy and went and collected car-loads of possible donors. We found one – a wispy little English girl who happily agreed to donate. Her friend, a far more robust young lady, stayed while we took her blood and promptly fainted. Thanks to that lovely English blood we successfully removed an enormous ovarian cyst.

It was nerve-racking to have a haemorrhage in the middle of an operation knowing that there wasn't an adequate supply of blood to deal with it. Once a patient haemorrhaged suddenly after giving birth. She just bled and bled, and we only had two pints of her blood type. If we had had a similar situation in Crown Street, we might have used up to 30. We battled for many hours to keep her alive and by about 3 am she was sitting up in bed thanking us for saving her life. Exhausted, we went to bed. Suddenly at 7 am she died.

It was depressing to lose a patient, but knowing we probably could have saved her for want of a proper blood bank was even more upsetting.

The hospital employed a full-time laboratory technician who was very able and willing, but at night-time and on weekends he was not available. On these occasions we ourselves took blood from many patients' relatives or friends who were willing to donate. We had learned at Crown Street how to type and cross-match blood, and this often stood us in good stead.

One time we were entertaining a teacher and his wife from the French school to dinner, when in the middle of the meal we were called up to the hospital. An important member of the royal family had gone into labour. After a difficult delivery she gave birth to twins and then proceeded to haemorrhage. There was no blood available, and Reg immediately called for all the nurses and doctors. There were pitifully few on duty, but we managed to get enough blood to save her. Mother and babies did well. While all this was going on Richard manfully kept up a conversation with our guests.

These dramas must have made a deep impression on Richard. He wrote a composition at school on the subject of being a doctor: 'I am the sooprintent of Tsehai Hospital. I got a sist out of a woman and it was the wate of a baby. I got another lump of puss and I asked the gardener to bury it in the garden. The next day I had to do an oprashen on a woman bleeding to death. I have to send for blood every day.'

The teacher gave him six out of ten.

In another tragic case a woman began bleeding heavily after delivery, and we had only one pint of her blood type in the bank. Her uterus just would not contract. In desperation we removed the uterus and stayed up with her all night, but she died at four o'clock in the morning. Poor woman – she already had nine children, and this last one was healthy.

The lack of a first-class blood bank created other problems – we could not be completely certain that the blood was compatible. We lost one patient who had undergone a routine hysterectomy. She hadn't really needed blood, but the anaesthetist gave her some anyway. It contained a rare antibody which was undetected during routine testing and cross-matching in the laboratory. The kidneys always fail after the wrong blood is given, and it happened in this case. We struggled with her all weekend, giving her medication. We managed to get the woman's blood pressure up, and the kidneys had started to secrete urine again, which was an encouraging sign, then she died. It was especially upsetting because she hadn't needed the transfusion in the first place.

After this we realised the risk of giving blood even if it was available, so Reg wrote to an old friend who ran the Red Cross Blood Bank in Sydney, asking if he would be willing to send us dried plasma. An arrangement was soon in place for a supply to be flown over periodically. They generously did not charge us for it and also paid the air freight. We greatly treasured this life-saving product, which we kept for desperate emergencies. The precious Australian plasma saved many lives.

We developed some unusual ways to save lives, one of which you won't find in the medical textbooks. In an ectopic pregnancy, where the foetus develops in the Fallopian tube outside the uterus, a patient can quickly lose a lot of blood into the abdominal cavity. This warm, fresh blood we would literally bale out with a soup ladle which Reg bought in the market. The blood was strained through gauze into a funnel and from there inserted via a tube into the patient's arm. We saved many women by putting their own blood back into them, thus avoiding any risk of incompatibility.

Some of the most dire emergencies were patients with a ruptured uterus. Usually the woman would have had previous babies. Although the muscle of the uterus is the strongest muscle in the body and seldom ruptures during the first pregnancy, it weakens after repeated child-bearing. If obstruction to the birth occurs due to an abnormal position of the foetus, the uterus can burst like a paper bag. The baby is then expelled into the abdominal cavity where, because the placenta has separated and there is no more blood supply, it quickly dies. If left there for a time, the decomposing baby grows germs which form gas. This causes septicemia, followed inevitably by the mother's death.

We were able to treat many of these desperately ill, shocked women. Reg imported a blood pump with which we could rapidly pump blood or other intravenous fluids into the patient. Mostly it was necessary to remove the torn uterus. Then, using all the available antibiotics during the post-operative period, we could often save the patient. But such patients frequently came to us too late, and there were many we did not save.

One woman who was carried down from the country on a stretcher by her relatives, had been to about six hospitals, all of which had rejected her. She died as she came through the front door. Reg asked the men carrying her why they had taken so long to get her here. They told him they'd spent twelve hours trying to get her admitted, and staff at every hospital had said there were no beds. Obviously no doctor had looked at her because they would have seen she was in urgent need of care. Quite possibly a guard at the gate or a porter had turned her away.

This sort of thing was extremely distressing. We had a good team of nurses who could help us resuscitate these shocked women. We couldn't always get blood quickly, but if it was available we would put in three or four intravenous drips, cutting down on their ankles, finding the veins and pumping the blood into them, or plasma if we could get it. As soon as their blood pressure came up we would be able to operate then give powerful antibiotics.

We began to get a reputation for saving lives. Reg could use his skill at manipulative obstetrics to correct most abnormal presentations, enabling the women to deliver normally.

From time to time we hosted visiting gynaecologists from other countries. One I remember, from America, came on a

WHO scholarship. He was in the labour ward when we were dealing with a patient in obstructed labour. The baby had died and was lying transversely in the uterus with its arm protruding. He was amazed when we were able to deliver the girl by turning the baby round under a deep ether anaesthetic. This can only be done when the uterus is soft and relaxed with ether. You gently put your hand in, feel for a leg and pull on it, thus turning the baby around slowly so it can be delivered as a breech.

Our visitor's reaction on seeing this patient was to say that he would have taken her to the theatre for a caesarian section. Had we done so in this condition, however, sepsis would certainly have followed the operation – making it a dangerous procedure and possibly a fatal one.

Although many of these abnormal and difficult deliveries were far more serious than anything we had seen in Sydney, our Crown Street training enabled us to cope with them.

On the mornings when we were not operating we had huge clinics of over 200 people, and often there would be some gravely ill woman there whom we had to get to the theatre in a hurry.

Infertility was a problem with many of the outpatients. One day a Muslim girl of about seventeen turned up complaining of sterility. When I had finished examining her – which I did with great difficulty as she was so modest – I asked to have a word with her husband. I was shocked when I saw him walk in. He was at least 80 years old, with a lined, leathery face and piercing black eyes. I immediately thought, no wonder this girl isn't having a baby, but I had to revise that opinion when he produced a toddler from under his robe. He informed me it was from his third wife. My patient was his fourth.

Another woman Reg examined presented with the same complaint. She said she had had eighteen husbands and had never had a baby. I think we were fairly safe in assuming that she was the one who was sterile and also that she had been exaggerating.

Once Reg was joking with one of the patients about her mother-in-law. 'Which one?' she said. 'I've had fifteen.'

She was another Muslim. She was literally skin and bones when we admitted her, with gross anaemia as well. We managed to get her six pints of blood, all from Americans, but when we asked her own friends, they deserted her. We found it hard to get her to eat anything as most strict Muslims wouldn't eat meat prepared by Christians. This presented a problem as she was going to be with us for months. She had severe osteomyelitis, or infection in the bones, of both legs following sepsis after childbirth, and needed to eat plenty of meat for her health. After she refused several meals, Reg gave her some fish. She asked suspiciously who had caught it. He assured her it had been caught by a Muslim, and she ate ravenously.

Living in the hospital compound, we were on call night and day. Getting up at night was exhausting, and we soon began to get very tired. At first we went up to the hospital together, but it became obvious that neither of us would ever get any sleep if we continued, so we took it in turns and slept in separate rooms so at least one person got some rest.

There was a good nursing school run by tutor–sisters from England so the Ethiopian nurses were well trained. The nurses loved Reg. He used to tease them and give them nicknames. They would go to no end of trouble to assist him. He taught them many things which only doctors may do in Australia – how to position the woman in the bed, deliver the baby and give intravenous drips.

If we had to resuscitate a woman who had been haemorrhaging and was in danger of dying, everyone moved quickly to help. Once, when one of these shocked patients arrived, Reg asked a nurse to get him a drip set. As she sauntered away slowly, Reg called after her, 'Run, nurse, run.'

She replied, 'Doctor, it's not in my nature to run,' but all the same she did manage to hurry.

Sometimes when we were operating there would be a power

failure. We had no generator in the hospital. If it was daytime we could finish by pulling the table over to the window. At night it was awkward. There were battery-powered emergency lights which were adequate when they worked, but often the batteries were flat, so we finished quite a few operations by torchlight.

There was never much time to eat, especially on busy clinic days. When we had the chance we would eat local food made in the hospital kitchen. The staple Ethiopian meal is *injera* and *wat*. *Injera* is a flat, rubbery bread which is made from *tef*, a fine grain related to millet. It contains all the amino acids, minerals and vitamins necessary for growth. First it is fermented then the liquid mixture is put onto a hotplate which is covered with a lid, and cooked quickly so that the vitamins are not destroyed. *Wat* is a sort of hot spicy stew, usually of vegetables or lentils, although on special occasions chicken, lamb or beef is used. The *injera* is spread on a plate and little mounds of *wat* placed on top. You eat it by tearing off pieces of *injera* with your fingers and using it to scoop up the *wat*, always using the right hand. The Ethiopians eat this twice a day, day in and day out, and never get tired of it. It is good, healthy food, and I developed quite a taste for it, especially if I was hungry, although Reg never really enjoyed Ethiopian food.

We had been at Princess Tsehai Hospital for only a week or so when we saw our first fistula case. She was a young woman of seventeen. The poor little thing had been in labour somewhere out in the country for five days and eventually gave birth to a stillborn child. She had suffered a complete breakdown of the bladder, and urine was just pouring out uncontrollably. Her husband of course had left her. Her father brought her in and told us she was his only child and he would spend every cent he had if we could only make her better.

Neither Reg nor I had ever had to deal with injuries like this, and the thought of trying to operate was too daunting. We sent her to a German gynaecologist at another hospital who had some experience of fistula repairs.

What shocked us most was the realisation that if this girl had had access to a trained midwife early in labour, or better still, a doctor, they would have recognised something was wrong and sent her to the nearest hospital. There should have been trained midwives available all over the country but there were none. These poor women were left without any skilled help while they laboured for days in agony.

Although we were not due to begin our school of midwifery for another five months, Reg resolved to start some informal training right away for any of the sisters who wanted to come. He also sent off dozens of letters to newspapers in Australia and New Zealand and to private individuals, trying to raise money for the school.

Fistula injuries only occur in Western countries when a surgeon makes a slip of the scalpel or else through cancer. A gynaecologist in Australia might see one fistula every couple of years. Until about the late 1800s, before the advent of modern obstetrics, they had been as common in Europe and America as they are in developing countries now. There was some literature on the subject. We sent away for as much as we could find.

While the peasant women bore their illnesses with great stoicism, we found our private patients were more demanding. They all wanted to be looked after personally, so even if a woman was having a perfectly normal delivery she wanted Reg or me to be there.

Rich patients would sometimes bring their own carpets, furniture and servants. One woman had a little servant girl who slept under her bed. If she wanted a glass of water she would clap her hands and the girl would emerge and scurry away to do her bidding.

And then there was the aristocracy. Ethiopia was a feudal society. The Emperor was head of state, and scattered throughout the provinces were dukes and nobles, rather like mediaeval

England. Some of them were fabulously rich and they were used to privilege. If they considered we were not being attentive enough they would complain to the palace and we would receive a query from the Ministry of Health asking why we were neglecting these important patients. In truth it was often because we had a poor woman in far greater need than the private one.

My sister Sheila had been at school in England with two of the Emperor's grand-daughters. This was while the Emperor had been in exile during the Italian occupation. Because of this connection we became friendly and delivered some of their children.

The royal deliveries were always attended by one of the family members, who watched everything closely to make sure the baby didn't get mixed up with someone else's. It could be nerve-racking if it was a difficult delivery. The first time this happened was with Princess Mary Abeba, a beautiful girl who had been born in England while the Emperor was in exile. She had been brought up there and graduated in law from London University.

Her older sister, Princess Sybil, came with her and sat in an armchair in the room for the last few hours of the labour. The baby was stuck in an abnormal position and its heart was giving us a lot of anxiety. Reg decided to do a forceps delivery and I administered an open ether anaesthetic. Ether is a difficult anaesthetic to induce, especially if someone is a smoker, like the Princess, because they can spasm and the airway becomes obstructed. Sure enough she started to cough and choke, and her sister began to look particularly worried. I am sure she thought I was killing her.

After a bit of trouble we got her under nicely. Reg rotated the baby's head into the correct position and she was delivered of a beautiful 7 pounds 2 ounce (3 kilogram) boy.

Most of the royal family had been away in another part of the country when Mary was admitted. Once they heard the news, a steady stream began arriving, and we had to put aside a private room as a sitting room for them.

Princess Mary's background was typical of the diplomatic

intricacies that ruled the private lives of the aristocracy. She was the offspring of the Emperor's daughter, Princess Tenagnework. While in exile in England with the Emperor during the Italian occupation, Princess Tenagnework, whose husband had been killed by the Italians, had fallen in love with a man called Abeba Retta. They wanted to marry but the Emperor did not consider this a suitable marriage. And so Mary was born out of wedlock. She was brought up in an English coastal town by a nanny, was educated and got a degree in international law. She was then summoned home to Ethiopia, where the Emperor had arranged for her to marry. Her husband was Seyoum Haregot, the son of the Mayor of Asmara, who was knighted by the Queen on her visit to Eritrea.

We went to their wedding, a lavish occasion, a mixture of Ethiopian and Western customs on a grand scale. We liked Seyoum immensely and always thought him to be a kind and gentle person, with the natural dignity and perfect manners of so many Ethiopains. In spite of this, though, Mary found it hard to adapt to such a different style of life, and often when I visited her she would pour out her heart to me, and we would talk and often pray together. I feel the fundamental reason for her unhappiness was that she was not really in love with Seyoum.

Mostly she was bright and attractive and a great favourite of the Emperor. He gave her the title of Princess and welcomed her into the royal family. Even so, she never felt that she was completely accepted, and this preyed on her mind, as we saw later with tragic results.

We delivered another two babies for Mary. She ended up with three sons, Jonathan, Thomas and Abbai. She and I became good friends. We were both mad on gardening and whenever we visited one another socially we would come away laden with cuttings.

Princess Sybil and Princess Ruth, who had been at school in England with Sheila, were also my friends. Sybil had a long, oval-shaped face, and wore her hair pulled back in an attractive way on either side of her face. With quite fair skin, she was striking to look at, although not beautiful in the conventional sense. She was married to Lij Kassa, the President of the University of Addis Ababa, previously a Governor of one of the Provinces.

Ruth was softer in appearance and wore her hair attractively around her face. As a girl, she had been in love with an Englishman, but the Emperor would not allow her to marry him. Instead her marriage was arranged with a general in the Emperor's army, General Negga. It was sad that Ruth never had a baby. She came to me about this, but I could find nothing the matter.

Another princess who was most popular and very charming was Princess Edjigayehu. She was the Crown Prince's daughter by his first wife, and always known as Mainite, so she was a cousin of the others I knew. The Princess had six children.

The royal family was greatly loved by the people, and we all thought then that they would endure forever. While they gave us some stressful moments in the hospital, these were not as bad as the experience of our head of surgery, Dr Asrat Woldeyes. He had to remove the Emperor's grandson's appendix – a routine operation, except that the Emperor insisted on being in the theatre and wanting to know every detail of the procedure as it was happening.

There was another hazard in Ethiopia not encountered in Australian hospitals. A few months after our arrival, a woman was admitted who had been bitten by a rabid dog. Unfortunately her relatives didn't inform me. I examined her carefully and concluded that she had some sort of mental condition or was perhaps suffering from hysteria. She had not drunk for four days. As soon as we offered her water she went completely mad, and while I was trying to examine her throat she bit me. It was only then that the relatives told me her full history, and of course I realised straightaway what her real ailment was.

There was no doubt that she was going to die. Meanwhile

I had to have injections in case I had caught the disease, too. They were rather horrible. Over a period of ten days I had to have ten injections of 10 cc each, usually given into the abdominal wall. Reg was sqeamish about giving these, so I decided to give them to myself. Each one was painful, and caused much bruising. Nowadays there are better vaccines.

Rabies was a common problem. We would sometimes see mad dogs while we were out riding and went to great lengths to avoid them. The Ethiopians were terrified of the disease. If they thought a dog was rabid they usually stoned it to death.

So far I have had to go through three anti-rabies courses. There was that time I was bitten by a patient. Once one of our horses diagnosed with rabies bit me and died three days later. The third time I pricked myself giving our dogs the injections to immunise them. The firm in Paris that made the vaccine advised me to have the course of injections just in case a live virus was lurking in the vaccine. I felt the last course probably was not necessary, but with this fatal disease you did not take chances.

Chapter Seven

We had hardly settled into our new home when the invitations started coming in. There was a busy social scene in Addis Ababa, and if we had wanted to we could have gone out every night of the week. Ethiopia was not like other African countries. It had never been colonised, therefore expatriates were treated well, with the respect of honoured guests. We had many Ethiopian friends as well as expatriates. We were invited to royal weddings and aristocratic parties and to the christenings of babies we'd delivered. There were gymkhanas at the British Embassy, children's Christmas parties and pantomimes, while the dramatic society put on plays and Gilbert and Sullivan operas.

The oldest British residents were Brigadier and Mrs Sandford. In 1913, while on secondment from the British Army to the Sudan Political Service, Dan Sandford had been sent to Ethiopia as a liaison officer between the British Legation and the Sudanese. He left to fight in World War I but returned again with his wife, Christine, in 1919. This time he was working for a British company, The Abyssinian Corporation, with plans to explore the possibilities of trade. He hadn't been there long when head office in London decided that there wasn't much future in Ethiopia and closed down the business.

Without a job, but very much in love with the country, Dan began looking round for some way to make a living. He had become friendly with the Regent, Ras Tafari Makonen, who later became the Emperor. Together they went into partnership, buying some farmland about 70 kilometres out of Addis on the edge of a beautiful gorge, looking across glorious country towards the Blue Nile in the far distance. They called it Mulu Farm.

The Sandfords built a house in Ethiopian style. The walls were of sticks, tied together and filled with a mixture of mud and *tef* stalks. There was a thatched roof and earthen floors. This attractive dwelling was set in an extensive and beautiful garden, with Australian wattle, bottlebrush, agapanthus, roses, periwinkle, masses of annuals, loganberry, native juniper, and cedar and pine trees.

The Sandfords were always experimenting with ways to make a living. For a while they ran a dairy, then they went into pigs and produced their own bacon and pork, which they sold in the capital. Neither of these endeavours lasted. They had some success with strawberries, while other crops including maize, wheat, barley, oats and linseed brought them varying fortunes. Money was always short, but the Sandfords were of indomitable British stock and they never thought of giving up.

It took the Italian invasion in 1935 to force them out of Ethiopia and back to England, where they were destitute but undaunted. Chris got a job as a teacher, and the Brigadier worked as a fundraiser for Guildford Cathedral.

The British and their fellow members of the League of Nations were reluctant to do anything about Italy – that is until the Italians entered World War II on the side of Germany. When that happened Britain suddenly became interested and decided to invade Ethiopia to dislodge them. The invading force, under General Orde Wingate, was named Mission 101. Brigadier Sandford was sent in to secretly make contact with the Rases in northern Ethiopia and assess the climate for an invasion. He spent five months organising the patriot forces to harass the Italians. After Addis was recaptured and Haile Selassie returned in triumph, the Brigadier served as his principal military and political adviser.

As soon as Brigadier Sandford was back at Mulu Farm he sent for Chris and their children to join him. They journeyed by ship to Kenya, and then bought an old Ford van. Against all advice from the authorities, Chris drove with two of their children across Kenya and through southern Ethiopia to Addis, an amazing journey through some of the most lawless country in Africa.

Finding that there was no one to teach her children, she started teaching them herself on the dining-room table in their town house in Addis Ababa. Soon four Ethiopian boys joined the lessons, and before long there were so many pupils that they had to move to rooms provided by the British Council. By the time we arrived the English School had expanded to become a proper school with purpose-built classrooms and playing fields. There were several hundred students of many different nationalities. The teachers were a mixture of locals and Europeans. When Richard came home after his first day there he told me he had an Arab on one side and an Israeli on the other. 'Well, it's just as well you're in between them,' I said. His four closest school friends were Indian, Armenian, Ethiopian and English.

The Sandfords were also involved in founding the Anglican Church in Addis Ababa. Originally the English Anglican Church services were held in the Sandfords' town house. The first attempt to found a church was in 1926 when the British Embassy arranged for the Rev. John Ethelston Cheese to come out through the auspices of the Society for the Propagation of the Gospel. Disembarking at Aden to begin his journey to Ethiopia, Rev. Cheese met some Somali people, a meeting which influenced the rest of his life. Instead of settling down in Addis Ababa to minister to the spiritual needs of the British community he felt God's call to go to Somalia. For the next two years he made frequent safaris from Addis Ababa into that country before giving up his settled job completely and disappearing into the wilds. For the next 40 years he wandered all over Somalia as an itinerant missionary, devoting his life to the nomads. He died on the ship on his way back to England.

In 1928 when Rev. Cheese left, the Sandfords invited a friend, Canon Austin Matthew, to come out from England and take his place. For many years services continued to be held at their town house and occasionally out at Mulu Farm – Canon Matthew would ride out on horseback. Later, when the congregation became too large, the services were held in a big rented building in the main street of town.

Things went on in this way until they were disrupted during the Italian occupation, and it was not until some years after the Emperor's return from exile that the need for a proper church building arose. Canon Matthew, like the Sandfords, had left the country during the occupation. When they returned fundraising began, and on 10 October 1953 the foundation stone was laid. In April 1955 the church building was completed and St Matthew's Anglican Church was consecrated. Mrs Sandford would play the organ there. This was the church that Reg and I attended and looked upon as our spiritual home. I taught Sunday school and have worshipped there throughout my time in Ethiopia.

The Sandfords were one of the leading lights of Ethiopian society. They loved going out, attending all the plays at the English School and the Gilbert and Sullivan musicals, where Mrs Sandford often played the complete score. She owned the first piano in Ethiopia and was an accomplished pianist. The Sandfords were frequent guests at embassy lunches and dinners. Mulu Farm constantly had visitors, and we went out there many times to take tea on the lawn or to hike down into the gorge for picnics.

The Brigadier had a rugged, weather-beaten face, full of character. He was a typical old British soldier, unfailingly polite, and he always got to his feet when a lady approached. Mrs Sandford would greet you on the lawn at Mulu Farm wearing a big straw hat, as she always did when outdoors, a simple print dress with usually a few inches of petticoat hanging below the hem, and sandshoes.

Her welcome was unfailingly warm and sincere. You always felt you were her special guest, even though there may have been many others taking tea on a sunny afternoon on her lawn. As more and more people arrived, a servant would replenish the teapot with boiling water, although not necessarily with more tea. Reg, who hated weak tea, soon learned that it was best to arrive early.

The Sandfords were so renowned for their hospitality that people often used to turn up uninvited. This became too much, so the family put a notice at the gate, saying 'Private Property'.

We became firm friends, but because of our hospital duties Reg and I could rarely visit together. Sometimes, if I had a day off by myself, I would stay the night at Mulu. The 70-kilometre journey from Addis was mostly on dirt road. In the early days you had to ford several rivers and during the wet season you had to travel the last 10 kilometres on horseback.

The house was spartan. Bathing took place in a big wooden tub by candlelight. In the spare bedroom the basin was not connected to a drain. There was a curtain round it and when you pulled the plug the water would run into a kerosene tin underneath.

There was always good conversation at the Sandfords. They ate late – about nine o'clock – then guests might play cards until well after midnight. On Sunday nights Mrs Sandford would accompany us on the piano while we sang hymns.

The Sandfords were very friendly with the royal family. The Emperor said to Mrs Sandford one day, 'I want you to come to the palace for dinner. And by the way, bring your piano.' At least that's how she told the story; I expect His Majesty would not have said it quite like that. She had to put the instrument onto a platform and transport it a couple of kilometres from their house in town on the backs of a pair of donkeys, running down the road beside it all the way, hanging on to make sure it didn't fall off.

The piano was placed in a huge banqueting hall, the floor

of which was covered in green rushes. The Sandfords sat at a big feasting table and ate with the Emperor. After the meal had finished Mrs Sandford gave a recital which received loud applause from the Monarch and his audience.

There was an endless round of embassy functions. It seemed as though the British Embassy had to entertain everyone from Britain and the colonies in turn. Our invitation came only a few weeks after we had arrived.

The embassy compound was surrounded by a high fence with a thick bank of shrubs behind. After we were cleared by the guards, an imposing gate swung aside and we drove up a long driveway through what seemed like another country. The chancery building was the original British Legation, built in 1900. It consisted of an attractive collection of whitewashed *tukul*-style buildings with thatched roofs, surrounded by beautifully groomed lawns and tall trees. At the far end of the compound, nestling into the base of the Entoto Hills, were stone stables with a walled courtyard. The whole compound was immaculately landscaped with acres of lawn and exotic trees.

The residence was a grey stone building with an imposing flight of steps leading to the front portico. The front walls were covered in bougainvillea which seemed to flower all year round. We went through the front door into an entrance framed by stone columns bearing the gold-embossed names of past ambassadors.

The guests were a diverse lot. Two of the princesses were there, the Egyptian consul, a famous Ethiopian artist, a retired professor of English who was an authority on the Amharic language, an Ethiopian businessman and a Polish professor of economics.

Dress was black tie. I was seated next to the English professor, Mr Wright. He had clearly put on a lot of weight since the last time he wore his evening clothes. His waistcoat was so tight he could hardly breathe. When a champagne bottle was opened with a pop he clutched his waist in alarm and cried, 'Oh, my buttons.'

The seating arrangements at these functions, we found, were always a question of luck. Sometimes you met most interesting people but at other times you might get stuck with a bore. Being next to Professor Wright, I expected to hear something interesting about the Amharic language, but we spent the entire meal discussing cats. He was mad on them and could talk of nothing else.

It took us a while to get to know our way around the city. By day it was difficult enough as the roads wound about like a labyrinth with no apparent plan, but at night the difficulty was compounded as there was very little lighting and no street names or direction signs of any sort. It was awfully easy to get lost.

Shortly after our arrival in Ethiopia we received an invitation to dinner at the home of the head of the British Council. We were invited for 8 pm and left with about twenty minutes to get there. We soon became quite lost and for an hour drove around winding, potholed streets, dodging people and carts and livestock in the dark and stopping now and then to ask if anyone spoke English.

Eventually we found a man who was a pilot with Ethiopian Airlines, who kindly offered to lead the way in his car. We pulled up somewhere on the edge of the city, with hyenas making their distinctive 'whooping' cries all around, well over an hour late. A white-coated servant opened the gate but unfortunately did not point out a ditch. I fell headlong into it, grazing my hand and splattering myself with mud and blood.

As soon as we were inside I headed for the bathroom to clean myself up. I was too flustered to listen to any of the names of the other guests we were introduced to. I spent most of the evening talking to a retired English colonel who was in Ethiopia growing begonias for a living. Not surprisingly, we were never asked again.

On another disastrous social occasion I invited a rather important English couple to dinner then forgot all about it. I was in the kitchen wearing old clothes with an apron and Reg was in his study working when there was a knock on the door. There they were, wearing evening dress.

It was useless to pretend so I apologised profusely and ushered them in. I then hurried in to Reg and told him to get some presentable clothes on.

All we had was a small, very tough roast of beef, which was to have been our evening meal, some baked beans and a few potatoes. This I served up, and we sat down to dinner. We were ploughing our way through this dreadful meal, making conversation, when I got a piece of meat stuck in my throat. Excusing myself, I went outside, and, coughing as hard as I could, tried to dislodge it. At one stage I really I thought I was going to have to get Reg to do a tracheotomy with a carving knife, but eventually out it came and I could breathe again.

Funnily enough, we never saw that couple again, either.

At night we would hear hyenas all around the compound. They were unattractive animals who preyed on anything weaker than themselves. They played an important role as rubbish collectors for the market and the city. Everything that was thrown out disappeared completely overnight.

In the mornings an Ethiopian girl, Workinesh, came in to do housework and look after Richard if he was not at school. They spent hours together on the verandah plaiting long whips and mats out of grass. Reg gave Richard strict instructions that he was to behave himself with Workinesh. Making sure Richard was watching, Reg ceremoniously gave her a length of rubber tubing to whip him with. Richard promptly took it and cut it into small pieces. I suspect he misbehaved with her, although she always said he was perfectly good. Workinesh was not very efficient at her work but she had a lovely nature and a good sense of humour, which made up for her shortcomings.

Richard had attended kindergarten in Adelaide for a year or so. His new life could not have been more different, but he had no trouble adjusting. In Addis Ababa he was making lots of friends and spending his afternoons after school roaming over the hospital compound with children of many different nationalities. It was wonderful to see the boy fitting into this exotic environment so well. He and Reg were very close. We still had that broken old sofa with a bit of iron sticking out of it, which had come with the house. I would wind the iron bit around and pretend it was the handle of an organ grinder while Richard and Reg pranced about dancing to Gilbert and Sullivan.

Richard subscribed to an English children's magazine called *The Eagle*. He loved it and would wait impatiently for every new edition to arrive. *The Eagle* was full of information about other parts of the world. It had stories about detectives and space flight, and Richard would see special offers for things that you simply didn't find in Ethiopia. He realised that he was apart from mainstream culture but it didn't bother him at all. He considered Ethiopia home.

Reg and I could rarely go away together on weekends as someone had to be available in case there was an emergency. Some of the other doctors said, 'Just go; that's what we do.' But we could never do this knowing that some woman might come in needing urgent help. Emergencies are far more common in our specialty than in any other branch of medicine.

Nevertheless a couple of months after our arrival we managed a weekend off together and decided to explore some of the country. In our second-hand Volkswagen Beetle, we drove 400 kilometres to Lake Awasa, in the Great Rift Valley. The journey took us through country quite different from that around Addis Ababa. We went through dry grassland dotted with native thorn trees then, as we neared the lake, through rainforest alive with brilliantly coloured birds.

Lake Awasa was set among lovely green hills covered with

trees draped in vines. The forest was full of monkeys shrieking and swinging about as well as flocks of birds. Once we saw a baby panther, which quickly slunk out of sight. There were only two houses at the lake plus an old hotel run by Italians. We had a big room which opened out onto a verandah overlooking the water. Inside were three camp beds and a few bits of furniture. It was spartan but clean, and the food was good – mostly fish from the lake and spaghetti.

The Italians had built a little jetty where there were a few small boats that we could use. Lake Awasa was popular with expatriates from Addis Ababa who used to swim and fish. Ethiopians preferred to sit around and play cards.

Driving around the lake we saw small children swimming naked, full of laughter and glee. These were Oromos, different in appearance from the people around the capital. The girls wore brightly coloured beads around their necks. Their hair was done up in dozens of tiny plaits close against the skull, with numerous tiny partings. When they saw us coming they darted into the bushes, the girls especially – so graceful, like frightened gazelles, teeth and beads flashing in the sun.

Reg and I both missed Australia now and then. Things like the swimming and being able to shop for whatever you needed. In Addis you couldn't just go to town and buy clothes so I used to make a lot of them myself on an old-fashioned sewing machine which worked by turning a handle.

In the market there was a street called Mattress Lane which was full of tailors. Reg would order material from England and take it to be made up by an old tailor who was almost blind. The only ties available were flamboyant Italian ones, which were not his style at all, so I would write to Sheila in Australia, enclosing a bit of the suit material, and get her to buy something that matched.

Our grocer was a Greek man named Bambi. His real name was Mr Tsimas, but everyone called him Bambi. He had a traditional grocer's shop when we first knew him, and he would sit behind the counter wearing a white apron, speaking fluently to his customers in six or seven different languages. Bambi was a marvellous businessman. You could ask him for all sorts of things and he would go to the back of the shop and find them.

We became good friends. Reg, whenever he went shopping, would have long conversations with him about the state of the world. One day when I was shopping, Bambi announced that he was going to find a wife.

I asked, 'Why do you suddenly want to get married, Bambi?'

'Because I want to leave my business to my son.'

'Oh, but how will you find a wife quickly?'

He said, 'I'm going to Greece where my family will help me.'

He set off and when I saw him next he looked a bit downhearted because he had been unable to find anyone he liked. But it turned out well in the end because later he met a Greek woman, Helene, who was living in Ethiopia, and married her.

In due time Helene became pregnant, and we looked after her. She had a quick, normal delivery, but it was not the son Bambi had hoped for. It was a lovely, healthy baby girl.

When I saw Bambi outside the delivery room I said, 'Never mind you'll get a boy next time.'

Eighteen months later Helene had a second child – another girl. Bambi was a bit disappointed but still hopeful. Then she gave birth to a third daughter. His face really fell this time. I said, 'Don't worry, Bambi, perhaps the fourth will be a boy.' The fourth child was also a girl. They gave up after that.

As the years went by Bambi became prosperous and bought a big supermarket and a new house but his life, like so many lives in this troubled country, did not always go smoothly.

There were two other people in those early days who would become important to us. Yeshi was a quiet young woman of about twenty who came to work for us for half a day a week. She learned English quickly, and we were so impressed with her intelligence and kind nature that soon she was working with us full time as our housekeeper.

Yeshi was married to Daniel, a driver for the Princess Tsehai Hospital. They had one son, Yohannes, who was about the same age as Richard. Before we had anyone living in the house we used to take Richard up to the labour ward and sit him in the office with the nurses. He often said, 'Daddy, I wish you weren't an obstetrician.' After Yeshi started working for us Richard was able to stay at home. She would lie down on a mat on the floor beside his bed while he slept. At first I tried to stop her because I didn't think it was good for Richard to have someone acting like a slave. But she wouldn't sleep anywhere else. She looked after him as if he were her own. Sometimes she would bring Yohannes with her, and he and Richard would play together.

One night during the rainy season we had a big operation which was going to take two or three hours. Reg went to pick up Yeshi. He had a rough idea where she lived but had never actually been to her house. Unfortunately, he forgot to take a torch. In the teeming rain he was staggering about calling out, '*Ye Yeshi bête yēt now*?' Where is Yeshi's house? There happened to be a man there who spoke English. He said, 'I know where Yeshi lives,' and led Reg up a muddy lane to her house.

Yeshi got out of bed and came, without hesitation. Reg was wearing his white coat. On the way back down the lane, they ran into a herd of cattle coming up the other way. While they pushed and jostled to get past, one of them trod on his foot. It was so painful he couldn't walk and fell down into the mud. When he finally got back to the hospital his foot was quite badly injured.

Birru was about eighteen when he came to us as a part-time gardener. At first he also worked for half a day a week, then a full day. When we employed him full-time we sent him to night school to be educated. He had been brought up in the country out near Mulu. The big influence in his life was his grandfather. He loved him and was always quoting him. I think it must have been his grandfather who helped to mould his good and trustworthy character.

He came to me once very upset about something. 'What is the matter?' I asked.

He replied, 'When I was a little boy I used to raid birds' nests and take their eggs and I feel guilty for taking the eggs out of the nest of the poor mother bird.'

Even as a young man he had a soft heart.

Yeshi and Birru's stories became part of our story. They would stay with Reg and me for the rest of our lives, sharing in our disappointments and triumphs.

Chapter Eight

One of the people to whom Reg wrote in his search for information about fistulas was an eminent Egyptian obstetrician and gynaecologist, Pasha Naguib Mahfouz. He was one of only three or four living surgeons who had wide experience dealing with these injuries. He wrote many papers on urinary and recto-vaginal fistulae in women during his lifetime. The first of these, published in 1929, gave details of some 234 operations he had performed between 1907 and 1928. He had succeeded in 86.5 per cent of cases.

Mahfouz sent us books and articles on the subject. We also corresponded with Professor Chassar Moir, the Nuffield Professor of Obstetrics and Gynaecology at Oxford, England, who had written several papers and was about to publish a book, *Vesico-Vaginal Fistula*, which would become the standard text on the subject at that time. And from Germany, Heinrich Martius contributed valuable refinements. As the information began to arrive, Reg and I spent numerous evenings reading the literature and discussing the techniques.

The first-known written reference to fistulas was a papyrus scroll, discovered between the knees of a mummy at Thebes, dating back to about 1550 BC. It contained a fragmentary reference to a 'prescription for a woman whose urine is in an irksome place: if the urine keeps coming and she distinguishes it, she will be like this forever.'

The Persian physician, Avicenna, who died in AD 1037, was probably the first person to recognise the link between urinary incontinence and difficult labour. His textbook, *Al-Kanoun*, one of the most famous medical books ever written, was used in medical schools for more than five centuries. In a chapter on preventing pregnancy he warned, 'In cases in which women are married too young, and in patients who have weak bladders, the physician should instruct the patient in ways of preventing pregnancy. In these patients the bulk of the foetus may cause a tear in the bladder which results in incontinence of urine. The condition is incurable and remains so until death.'

In the sixteenth century, Felix Platter of Basle, Switzerland described a 'ruptura' in a young country girl. 'As a sequence of a first labour, [the girl] had the opening of the bladder rent to such a degree that there was a long gaping furrow in its place, and the open bladder could be seen. I have twice inspected it and discovered that it was so by using a probe. On account of this injury there is a constant involuntary discharge of urine and the surrounding parts become excoriated and inflamed.'

At about the same time Luis de Mercado, a Spanish physician, wrote, 'What an empty and tragic life is led by the affected victims and how great are their embarrassments – uncontrolled urine runs from the fistula with ease.'

In 1935 Professor D.E. Derry at the Cairo School of Medicine examined the mummified remains of an Egyptian Queen, Queen Henhenit, who had lived around 2050 BC. When the abdominal cavity was opened Derry discovered an opening between the bladder and vagina. Queen Henhenit's pelvis was an abnormal shape and Derry postulated that it would have been difficult for a fetal head to pass. The severe damage he found probably occurred at the time of childbirth, resulting in Henhenit's death. The hole in the bladder, he thought, may have been caused by the abnormally narrow pelvis through which the child had to be dragged by force. Poor Queen Henhenit had the dubious honour of having had the earliest known vesico-vaginal fistula.

In 1663 the Dutch physician, Hendrick van Roonhuyze, proposed a method of repair whereby the vagina was held open with an instrument called a speculum. The edges of the fistula were first denuded with scissors, then held together by sharpened swan's quills. Following closure, a healing salve was applied, consisting of two or three large flat wicks moistened with warm balsam oil, and the vagina filled with surgical sponges which swelled and exerted some pressure. There were at least two successes recorded using this technique, although with large defects. Van Roonhuyze believed surgical cure was impossible.

From what we now know, van Roonhuyze was on the right track, but his technique does not seem to have been developed further. Any thought that repair might be possible faded away. A century later surgeons were still wary of tackling fistulas. Instead, they were attempting various methods to manage incontinence. One advocated inserting a wooden pessary into the vagina while others favoured using catheters, tampons and urinary receptacles of various kinds.

With the beginning of the nineteenth century, surgeons again became interested in the problem; there are instances of experimentation, resulting mostly in failure. Some of the patients in those days before anaesthetics must have had tremendous endurance. In the mid 1800s Wutzer of Bonn cured eleven of 35 cases. One of these, Lucy Stitch, underwent 33 operations until he was successful. Wutzer laid the patient on her stomach and held open the vulva with lateral retractors. He then denuded the borders of the fistula and sutured it together using insect pins held in place by twisted sutures. He kept the patient lying down with a catheter to drain her bladder until she was healed. One can only imagine the pain poor Lucy must have endured.

In 1834 a British surgeon, Montague Gosset, wrote a letter

to *The Lancet* describing the successful use of gold wire for sutures, instead of the normal silk or goose quill. The advantage, he found, was that there was little ulceration or irritation yet a great ability to keep the edges of the wound together for an indefinite time.

At roughly that time a brilliant American surgeon, John Peter Mettauer of Virginia, operated successfully on at least half a dozen cases, using wire sutures twisted together. The cut ends projected just beyond the vulval verge and were sheathed in oiled silk to help stop irritation. They were re-tightened at regular intervals. While the patient was healing, Mettauer used a silver catheter to drain the bladder.

Another American surgeon, George Hayward, had one or two successes but pointed out the enormous obstacles to be overcome. They included the narrow space in which the operation was to be performed, the disposition of urine to pass between the lips of the wound and the proximity of the ureters. He commended, 'These are all factors likely to defect any operation no matter how well it may be done.'

Little by little the principles were being discovered. The use of various instruments to aid working in a confined space, catheters to drain the bladder during convalescence, and suture material of non-reactive metal were all important. The problem was that no one was yet able to produce consistent results. It needed someone with a special genius to pull these facets together. That man was an American, Dr James Marion Sims.

Sims was born in 1813 in Lancaster County, South Carolina. After gaining an MD from Jefferson Medical College, he set up practice in Lancaster. His first two patients, both infants, died, leaving him so discouraged that he decided to start again in a new state. He moved to Mt Meigs, Alabama, where his first patient was a woman suffering from puerperal sepsis after giving birth to a baby daughter. Unfortunately, this patient also died, but from then on things went well and he soon began to achieve a reputation as a clever surgeon.

Sims had been in practice for ten years when he saw his first fistula case, a seventeen-year-old slave named Anarcha. How familiar her plight sounds today. When Sims saw her, Anarcha had been in labour for three days and her baby was already dead. He pulled out the little corpse with forceps and the girl seemed to be making a recovery. Then, after five days, there was a sudden loss of control of both bladder and rectum. Sims told Anarcha's employer that her condition was hopelessly incurable and that he should take care of her for as long as she lived.

Within two months, two more slaves, Betsy and Lucy, had come to him with fistulas, but after examining them he concluded that these, too, were hopeless. He sent Betsy back to her master and gave Lucy a bed in a little hospital attached to his house while she waited for the next train to take her home.

Then an apparently random event occurred which would change the course of medical history. While Lucy waited, downhearted at the wretched future that awaited her, Sims was called to an emergency at the home of a Mrs Merrill who had been thrown from her pony when it was scared by a pig.

On examination he found that there was a retroversion of the uterus. Placing the woman on her knees on the edge of the bed, he introduced his middle and index fingers into the vagina and began trying to push the uterus back. 'I turned my hand with the palm upward, and then downward, and pushing with all my might, when all at once I could not feel the womb or the walls of the vagina. I could touch nothing at all. It was as if I had put my two fingers into a hat and worked them around without touching the substance of it. While I was wondering what it all meant, Mrs Merrill said, "Why doctor, I am relieved." My mission was ended but what had brought relief I could not understand.'

Sims told his patient to lie down on her side. As she did so there was an explosion as though there had been an escape of air from the bowel. Mortified, she began to apologise but Sims told her, 'That is not from the bowel it is from the vagina and it has explained now what I did not understand before.'

Sims concluded that when he dilated the vagina the air

pressure rushing in had restored the retroverted uterus to its proper place. He was gripped by excitement. 'I said to myself, if I can place a patient in that position and distend the vagina by pressure of air so as to produce such a wonderful result as this, why can I not take the incurable case of vesico-vaginal fistula and put the girl in this position and see exactly what are the relations of the surrounding tissues?'

Fired with this idea he forgot that he had twenty house calls to make that day and jumped into his buggy to drive home. On the way he stopped at a shop and bought a pewter spoon. When he arrived he ordered two medical students who were working with him to follow him to the hospital.

Telling Lucy to kneel with her head in her hands he instructed the students to part the nates and introduced the bent spoon handle into the vagina. 'I saw everything as no man had ever seen before. The fistula was as plain as the nose on a man's face. The edges were clear and well defined and distinct . . . I said at once, "Why can not these things be cured?"'

Sims immediately began designing instruments for the operation. The bent spoon was refined to become the Sims speculum, an instrument still used in modified form today. He wrote to the owners of Anarcha and Betsy and asked them to send them back, and scoured the country for other cases.

When he was ready he operated on Lucy. Knowing he had to drain the urine away while she convalesced, he inserted a sponge with a silk string running through it into the neck of the bladder to act as a capillary tube. But after five days she had a fever and blood poisoning; her urethra and bladder were inflamed. The problem was that her body had begun to grow around the sponge. There was no way to remove it other than by force. Brave Lucy suffered terrible agony when it was done and for a while it looked as though she might die.

Next it was Betsy's turn. Realising his mistake, Sims used a different catheter. All seemed well. When the sutures were removed the hole had partly healed but there were still three little openings. This operation also was a failure.

Anarcha was his next case. She had the very worst type of fistula – in both bladder and rectum. She was constantly dripping onto her clothes and bedding. As Sims described it, 'Her person was not only loathsome to herself but to every one who came near her.'

Anarcha's operation also failed. Sims had thought he was on the verge of a great breakthrough but for the next four years he continued to operate on the women in his hospital without ever achieving a permanent success. His colleagues, who had been so supportive to begin with, deserted him, and he was advised by friends to give up this mad obsession which he was funding entirely out of his own pocket.

In spite of all this opposition he continued to persevere with his long-suffering and ever-hopeful patients. Gradually, he eliminated one technical problem after another but still he kept failing. One obstacle remained – he needed some way of tying sutures high up in the body where he could not reach. At three o'clock one morning, lying sleepless in bed, he hit upon the idea of using perforated lead shot, which he would slide up the suture and compress with forceps when drawn tight.

In great excitement he performed the operation on Lucy. He waited a week to see the result. When he examined her it was, as usual, a complete failure.

Sims would not admit defeat. He had improved his operation until it was as near perfect as he could make it, yet still there was something wrong. He wondered if it could be the silk thread he used for sutures. He had heard of earlier surgeons using metal and had tried a leaden suture himself without success. Musing on the problem as he was walking from his house to his office, he picked up a little piece of fine brass wire in the yard, which had probably been used as a spring for suspenders. It was as fine as horsehair. He took it to his jeweller and asked him to make some silver wire of the same diameter.

Anarcha was chosen for the experiment. It was the thirtieth time he had operated on her. Stoically she mounted the operating table and prepared to endure once more the probing and cutting without anaesthetic. Sims brought the fistula together with four of his fine silver wires and fixed them with lead shot, and as she had done so many times before, Anarcha went to bed to allow the healing process to take place. He waited out the next week in a fever of impatience then, with a palpitating heart he turned Anarcha on her side, introduced the speculum, 'and there lay the suture apparatus exactly as I had placed it. There was no inflammation, nothing unnatural, and a very perfect union of the fistula.'

Over the next few weeks Lucy and Betsy and all the other patients were cured. Sims was in no doubt about the importance of what he had done. He wrote, 'I realised the fact that, at last, my efforts had been blessed with success, and that I had made, perhaps, one of the most important discoveries of the age for the relief of suffering humanity.'

In 1853 Sims sold his medical practice and moved to New York. Again he had a radical vision – he wanted to open a hospital devoted entirely to the diseases of women. It seems a perfectly reasonable idea today, when specialist women's hospitals abound, but back then many leading medical people dismissed it as fanciful. There was nothing that ailed women which required any special treatment, they insisted, and there would never be enough patients to fill such a hospital.

After many disappointments Sims enlisted the support of a group of wealthy New York women who were already involved in helping poor women. A suitable four-storey building was found in Madison Avenue, and one of the women, Mrs Doremus, guaranteed the rent for three years. Even then, some of the leading medical men of the day lobbied the founders, saying that the hospital was unnecessary and that any operations needed by women could easily be done at the present New York Hospital.

These arguments only hardened their resolve, and on 4 May 1855 the Women's Hospital opened with 30 beds. Sims immediately began performing fistula operations with such success that the hospital was soon inundated with patients.

He went on to demonstrate his techniques all over the world. He has become known as the father of modern gynaecology.

Marion Sims wrote about all of this in his autobiography, *The Story of My Life*. Reg and I got a copy from England and sat up late at night avidly reading about his efforts to start the world's first fistula hospital. We had no inkling that before many years passed we would build the second.

After absorbing all the information we could find, we felt able to tackle our first fistula. Many of the techniques had improved since Sims' day. For instance, with modern sutures it was no longer necessary to use wire, and instruments were more sophisticated. We chose a relatively easy case – a girl from the provinces with a small hole in her bladder. Reg performed the operation and I assisted. We put her to bed to convalesce and, just as Sims must have so often done, waited anxiously as the days dragged by. She was a brave little soul, trusting and calm. She had no idea that her case was such a landmark for us. After about fourteen days we took the catheter out, and she was passing urine normally. She went home completely cured. We were so excited that we took her outside the ward and had a photograph taken of her with Reg. I will never forget her gratitude as she kissed our hands and thanked us and set off to her village to begin a new life. We immediately treated two more fistula patients and they were also cured.

Chapter Nine

Our normal work continued at the same pace as before, but as word of our success spread we began to see more and more women suffering from fistulas. What a tragic sight they were. Offensive to smell, dressed in rags, often completely destitute, they would sometimes walk for two or three hundred kilometres to get to Addis Ababa. One girl turned up with her mother after walking for fifteen days. They had no money and nowhere to stay, so we paid for the girl's admission ourselves and allowed her mother to sleep on the floor beside her bed.

Another young woman arrived after walking for 450 kilometres. She, too, was in rags and had no money. She was a difficult case, with two big holes in her bladder, through which part of the bladder had prolapsed, making it painful for her sit down. She had endured this for ten years. Reg operated on her and after two weeks she was dry. It was an amazing transformation. Before she had been downcast and miserable; now she was reborn as a beautiful, smiling woman, with a look of joy in her eyes. We bought her a new dress to go home in, and she kept holding it up for everyone to see. When it was time for her to leave, we took her to the bus station and gave her the fare. She tried to kiss our feet and said, 'God will reward you for all you have done for me.'

Another girl had heard about the hospital in a faraway province where they spoke a different language. Someone had written a sign asking for her to be directed to the hospital and hung it around her neck, and she eventually found her way to us.

At first Reg did the operations and I assisted him. After we had done 22 with only one failure, I felt ready to do my first. Two cousins arrived in outpatients, both dripping urine everywhere under the bench where they sat. Reg did the more difficult one, and I did the other. They recuperated lying in adjacent beds and after three weeks they were both cured.

After the success of these first cases we felt encouraged to do more. Soon the number of arrivals began to place a strain on the hospital facilities. Being desperately poor, the fistula patients were usually unable to pay for their admission. The hospital provided half a dozen free beds, but these were always full, so often we paid their fees out of our own salaries.

Even when they were admitted we would often have to cancel their operations if an emergency case came in needing urgent surgery. Accommodation became a problem, and we found that some women were being turned away by the hospital guards or the porters, who would tell them there were no beds.

They would wait anyway and sometimes sleep in the hospital grounds. Reg started getting up early and searching the compound for any who had been turned away. He would tell them to sit under a certain big spreading tree near the outpatients and to wait for him there. After examining them he would gather the sad little collection and take them to the kitchen for something to eat. The hospital cooks cooperated wholeheartedly with this routine.

Reg was terribly touched by the plight of these poor women. He called them 'the fistula pilgrims', on account of the tremendous journeys they undertook to get to the capital. He would hear how they had suffered and been rejected, and of their struggle to get to the hospital, how they perhaps had to sell an animal or beg to raise the money, and often, as he listened to their stories, he would have tears in his eyes.

If fistula sufferers turned up at outpatients, the other women would push them to the end of the line because they were so offensive to be near. Reg would go to them and put his arms around them and say, 'You're the most important patient to me today. I'm going to see you first.'

If there were no beds, he would sometimes put them in storerooms or other places that were out of sight, where there was a bit of space. Once the medical director, Dr Asrat, came to us and said, 'The private patients are complaining about the smell of urine coming up the stairwell because you've got a collection of patients sleeping under the stairs to the private wing.' But he was sympathetic and tried to find room when he could.

These girls and women had suffered more than any woman should be called upon to endure. To meet only one was to be profoundly moved and called forth the utmost compassion that the human heart was capable of feeling. One girl, after making her way to us, arrived so late at night that there was no one to see her. In despair, early next morning she tried to hang herself outside the hospital gates. The guards found her in time and cut her down, and she was subsequently cured.

When they started to come in big numbers, Reg was called to the Ministry of Health to explain this new epidemic of fistulas that had struck Addis Ababa. He explained, 'This is not an epidemic, Your Excellency, this has been going on since the beginning of time. We just happen to have done something about it.'

The Ministry was not particularly interested in the plight of the fistula pilgrims. They had so many other problems to contend with that they told us, 'They are your problem. You can use the hospital facilities, but we can't afford to pay their hospital fees.'

If we were only able to raise some money we knew we could help many more. Reg wrote to a reporter friend on *The Advertiser* back in South Australia to try to generate some interest in a fund. In Addis Ababa the Rotary Club agreed to pay for one bed a month. A committee of local American women, The American Women's Club, pledged us US$60 a month to pay for patients' travel expenses and also agreed to supply ten dresses every month for them. It was a start.

Despite the fact that Reg was 51 when we came to Ethiopia, an age when many people would be starting to think about retirement, he was tireless in his enthusiasm. In all of our wanderings about the world he had been looking for something upon which to focus his tremendous energy and compassion. Even working as a medical superintendent in Adelaide had not been enough to satisfy him. He was driven by a need to create something. When Richard was old enough to discuss such things, Reg told him, 'Women have a built-in advantage. They're creating something that's visible, whereas men can't create something that's tangible like that.'

With the fistula pilgrims he found the great cause he had been seeking. He was drawn to them because he loved them. We found that looking after them was never a hardship and never once did we feel we wanted to do something else. We both knew that this was work that God wanted us to do and we were thankful that we so enjoyed doing it.

At the end of the first year in Addis Ababa the three of us went to Kenya for four weeks leave. We had to go to twelve different government departments and prove that we had paid our electricity and water bills, had no overdraft at the bank, did not owe anyone anything, and were not wanted by the police and so on, before they would give us our exit visas.

It was exciting boarding the plane for our first holiday. We booked into the Fairview Hotel in Nairobi, a famous old-fashioned family hotel favoured by British expatriates from Kenya and Rhodesia. These colonials were quite different from the expatriates we were used to in Addis Ababa. They were much more of a rowdy, hard-drinking type who would gather in the bar every evening.

One of the big attractions for us was a café at the New Stanley Hotel called the Thorn Tree Café, built beside the street with a big tree growing through the middle of it. We drank milk-shakes and ate sausage rolls, which we couldn't get in Addis, and watched an exotic populace of Africans, Europeans and Arabs walking past. Nairobi also gave us the chance to go to the cinema for the first time since leaving Australia. I remember seeing Alec Guiness in *Genevieve*, a hilarious British comedy about a lot of misadventures with a vintage car. In Addis Ababa we had not felt particularly starved of these Western luxuries, but when we were able to indulge ourselves we realised how much we had missed them.

Our journey from Nairobi to Mombasa was by train, far more enjoyable than a plane trip. We booked a double coupé sleeper so that the three of us could spread out. We hung out of the windows and watched the colourful crowd on the platform, waving to their departing friends, as we slowly gathered speed. Richard, especially, enjoyed the exotic sights – as we passed through Nairobi Game Park with twilight fading, we occasionally saw game. Soon the African night was around us, and we rushed forwards through blackness.

After a gong was sounded we proceeded through swinging carriages to the dining car, where each table was spread with a spotless white starched tablecloth, napkins, silver-plated cutlery and sparkling glasses. The waiters hovered about in white uniforms with red cummerbunds. There was a carnation in a small bracketed vase at one end of the table.

We made many stops during the twelve-hour journey, for the train had to fill up with water. As we lay in our bunks we could hear the shouting and the shunting and occasionally the cry of an animal in the African night.

When we woke the scenery was transformed. Now we could see the hills covered with lush, tropical vegetation. At Mombasa, an old coastal town with a strong Arab flavour, there was an old fort built by the Portuguese, Fort Jesus, and lovely tree-lined streets. We hired a car and drove to the Cosy Café where we ate a hearty breakfast, then we set off up the coast for Malindi. When we arrived we drove to a point overlooking the ocean and drank in the view of the sea which we loved so much and missed in Ethiopia.

Our hotel, Lawford's, was one of the oldest in Kenya. Built by a retired sea captain and named after him, it had bungalows right on the beachfront. Richard was wild with joy when he saw the surf. While we unpacked he raced down towards the water (with strict instructions not to go in) and promptly got lost. We could see no sign of him on the beach and naturally were greatly alarmed. Reg exclaimed, 'I've brought him all this way to drown him.'

It wasn't long before he turned up, although it seemed an eternity to us. He had been searching for us among the beach bungalows, but they all looked the same.

With two or three families we would sail out on an Arab *dhow* to a place called the Coral Gardens, several kilometres out to sea. It took an hour and a half to get there. We would put on face masks, jump into the water and goggle over the reef. We loved looking at the wonderful coral and shoals of brightly coloured fish, wheeling and flashing like shimmering jewels through the blue light. The first time we went we spent about two hours floating face down, just mesmerised. Richard kept saying, 'Heaven cannot be more beautiful.' We all got terribly sunburned.

When we were saturated with all this beauty we would collect shells. The hotel kitchen boiled out the little creatures inside, although not with complete success. So we arrived back in Addis Ababa with our luggage reeking of rotting fish.

Every Saturday there was a fishing competition with prizes for the heaviest fish. But the biggest attraction from Reg's point of view was the surf. We all loved surfing. Reg and Richard would spend hours in the water catching terrific shoots to the beach. Reg, being a strong swimmer, would also go out beyond the waves, do long lengths up and down the beach, then come surfing into shore on a big wave.

This first trip to Kenya and the events I have described became almost a yearly ritual, and we never tired of this routine. We would go to Kenya for our annual holiday for three or four weeks and often met the same people at Lawford's year in and year out. One old bachelor from up-country in Kenya somewhere said he came to birdwatch. He used to sit on his bungalow verandah with his binoculars, but I think he was really looking at the women. Later, when package tours were beginning, he became an even more avid birdwatcher!

In March of our second year we were able to take a short holiday in Eritrea. We decided to visit Asmara, the capital, then Massawa on the Red Sea coast. March was the cool season for Massawa, which was normally unbearably hot.

Asmara was very like an Italian town – houses with flat roofs and gardens full of poinsettias and jacarandas, palm-lined boulevards, shops full of expensive Italian goods. The streets were free of the beggars that were so common in Addis Ababa.

This feeling of Italy continued at our hotel, the Albergo Italia, where we enjoyed wonderful Italian soup and Red Sea fish. Next day we hired a car and started a spectacular journey down to the coast, winding our way at first down a frightening pass with many hairpin bends, through a landscape of barren mountains and ravines. On many corners crosses had been erected in memory of someone who had fallen over the side.

Towards the bottom of the pass there was a sudden change of scenery. It was now green and lush, with gentler slopes, crops growing on the hillsides and spreading trees in profusion. This was due to the moist breeze blowing off the Red Sea and dropping rain as it hit the mountains.

In the little town of Geda, we visited a well-run mission hospital. The doctors told us that they saw quite a few fistulas but were at a loss to know what to do with them. Later they would send many patients to us.

We continued our descent and, quite suddenly, were at sea-level, where flat desert stretched away into the hazy distance. As we drove along we counted seven bridges over dried up rivers. Evidently they contain water for the few weeks of the Eritrean rainy season, but we saw no sign of even a puddle in any of them.

We were relieved to be out of the mountains as we had been warned of *shiftas,* or highwaymen. We did not see any but perhaps that was because we were travelling in daylight. We would never travel there at night.

We reached Massawa in late afternoon and found our hotel – an old, Italian-owned wooden building right on the harbour's edge. It looked over to Massawa Island, where the old Arab town of Massawa is situated. The island is now joined to the mainland by a causeway. On the mainland side stood one of the Emperor's palaces – a glistening white building. After an easy stroll across the causeway, one plunged into the crowded port area, where many fine Arab buildings were scattered among the more modern Italian ones.

We visited the island port every day and here, as at Malindi, we soon found our favourite spots. There was one special café with the tables on the pavement, opposite an evangelical bookshop that had a brothel on one side and a crowded grocery on the other. Our order was always the same – grilled fish with fresh lemon juice followed by Italian creme caramella, Richard's favourite. Poor child – he was seldom allowed a second helping as we were a bit limited for cash. While we ate we watched the exotic scene before us – Arabs in long robes, Italian businessmen, donkeys and street vendors all mingling together amid the harbourside smells.

At the port men were loading into a ship sheep and goats bound for Jedda, Saudi Arabia, for slaughter, as a Muslim will not eat meat that has been handled by a Christian. To the delight of the Muslim stevedores, Richard helped them herd the animals onto cargo nets. Suddenly the net would tighten, and they would lift clear, heads, horns and legs hanging out of the mesh, bleating with fear as they were swung over and lowered into the hold. The head Muslim seemed impressed with Richard despite his religion.

One day we drove 12 kilometres over desert to a sandy beach on the Red Sea, Gorgoson Beach. Along the way we stopped at a well where people were drawing water. As usual Richard plunged into the throng of people, camels and donkeys to help. He loved being part of these exotic goings-on. We stayed a week at Massawa, doing little except swimming and eating, before returning home to Addis.

This also became our holiday routine. In those days there were vague murmurings about Eritrean independence, but no hint of the terrible war that would later erupt with Ethiopia. We would spend a week at Massawa in March and in the rainy season, August and September, we would go to Kenya for the long holidays. Every three years we had return tickets home to Australia and New Zealand.

At the end of our second year in Addis we went down to Malindi as usual. For three weeks we surfed, snorkelled on the reefs and relaxed in the sun. When we returned it seemed as though nearly all the hospital staff were waiting at the airport to meet us. They were amazed at how brown we were. Laughing about our changed colour, they kept saying we were no longer foreigners, and comparing the skin of their arms against ours.

Yeshi and Birru were waiting at home. Although they were both excited to welcome us, they greeted Reg and me in their dignified Ethiopian manner, extending one hand while holding the wrist with the other, and giving a slight bow. They were more relaxed with Richard. It was *Meskel* time, the ceremony of the finding of the true cross, when the countryside is ablaze with a bright yellow *meskel* daisy. Yeshi had filled our house with them and had coffee prepared.

The welcome from our eleven fistula patients was touching. As we gave each a small present, their faces lit up with spontaneous joy and, despite our protests, they kissed our hands. Yeshi cooked a big serving of *injera* and chicken *wat*, which we all shared. It was deeply touching and it was good to be home.

~

During the long lazy days on holiday, Reg and I had read the lives of Sylvia Pankhurst and her mother, Emmeline, and marvelled at what fighters for the poor women of England they and Sylvia's sister had been. Emmeline of course was best known for her tireless battle to obtain the vote for women. She had also started the first antenatal clinics and welfare clinics for women in the East End of London after World War I. The Pankhursts had suffered humiliating treatment at the hands of the authorities for their political activities – solitary confinement and even hard labour. We felt privileged to have Sylvia as a friend.

Two days after we got back Reg and I received an urgent call from Sylvia's maid, saying that her mistress had become ill. As it was our weekend on duty we went to her home at once. We found her in great pain and quickly realised she was suffering a coronary. We fought to save her, giving her morphia and oxygen, which we had brought from the hospital right next door. Knowing what a great friend of the Emperor she was, we rang the palace straightaway. Two of the princesses came immediately. Her son and daughter-in-law unfortunately were away on a camping trip. We did all we could with our limited ability in such a serious situation. Soon she lapsed into unconsciousness. As I sat beside her, now and then she squeezed my hand until, after about two hours, she died.

The Emperor, Haile Selassie, gave her a state funeral at the Ethiopian Orthodox Holy Trinity Cathedral. Normally only royalty are given that honour, and no foreigner had ever before had their funeral service there. The service was taken in Ge'ez – a language only used for religious occasions, so most people could not understand it. It was attended by every important person in the country. The Emperor himself stood at attention for two hours, without moving, during the service. She was buried in a royal grave just outside the church.

Despite the honours given to her by Ethiopia, Miss Pankhurst had never been decorated by her own country, which I thought was disgraceful.

~

Next day we were back at work and as busy as ever. We mostly operated together, not only on the fistulas but with other surgery as well. Sometimes I would operate and Reg would assist or vice versa. Even after a busy day Reg usually did an evening round of the labour ward and saw the post-operative patients. I helped Richard with any homework he might have, which was little in the early days, put him to bed with a story and heard his prayers. We had time to sit, perhaps around the fire when the nights were cold, discuss the day's activities and wonder what the future held. One thing was obvious, the hospital simply did not have the room to cope with the demand we were creating. We wondered – what if we could raise the money to build a special hostel just for the fistula patients, so that they would have somewhere to live while waiting for a bed in the hospital? We knew nothing at all about fundraising on a large scale, but the more we thought about it the more attractive the idea became.

Chapter Ten

We had met the Emperor, Haile Selassie, once or twice when he was visiting the hospital. We did not know him as well then as we would later but we admired him greatly. He had done a lot for his country. After defeating the Italians he had united Ethiopia and Eritrea as one country. He had secured Ethiopia's entry into the League of Nations, abolished slavery, set up an efficient civil service, introduced modern hospitals, schools and a university.

Haile Selassie was a man of great dignity. Although short of stature and slightly built, he had a commanding presence befitting his impressive titles, Haile Selassie, Elect of God, King of Kings, the Conquering Lion of the Tribe of Judah.

In 1960, while he was out of the country visiting Brazil, the head of the imperial bodyguard, a man who had been the Emperor's protégé and a trusted friend, staged a revolt. I was in the labour ward delivering a baby. The patient was lying in the left lateral position with a nurse kneeling, holding up the leg. I was about to use forceps to pull the baby out when there was the sound of gunfire, and a volley of bullets flew past the window. The nurse just dropped the leg and fled, along with the rest of her colleagues, leaving me alone with the patient under anaesthetic and undelivered. I thought I was going to get a failed forceps, which in obstetrics is the most disgraceful thing that can happen, as it means you are not competent. I shouted out for help, and after a while the nurses came back and we continued working. In the end we delivered the baby safely.

Reg had collected Richard from school early, as we knew something was amiss. He could not have thought it was very serious, however, as he drove to the American Embassy to collect a rabbit for Richard. Finding the gate was firmly locked and guarded by soldiers they instead started for home. Driving down Churchill Avenue, a main street in the city, they ran into gunfire.

'Daddy, guns are going off,' said Richard.

They certainly were. They were being fired from the Ministry of Defence at the bottom of the street up towards the centre of the town.

Reg swerved the car through the first gate he could find, which happened to be the Ministry of Commerce building. Inside they both took shelter under a big conference table.

'Daddy, I never thought this could happen to us,' said Richard. 'Let us pray that God will get us safely home.'

This seemed to Reg an excellent idea. Richard then knelt and prayed as only a child with perfect faith can. 'Now we shall be safe.' So saying, he proceeded to eat from a bag of roasted pumpkin seeds, quite happy to sit out the afternoon where they were.

Their prayers were answered. A man joined them and said he knew a back way to the hospital, avoiding the gunfire. He guided them, and soon they were safely home.

Meanwhile, back at the hospital one of the English nurses, Sister Garrett, was frantic to get home as she was worried that her Ethiopian housegirl would have run off to her own place leaving her baby alone. I ran with Sister Garrett to our house to try to borrow a car from Mr Barry, the Professor of Surgery, who lived next door. He wouldn't hear of us leaving and insisted we stay with him.

The whole hospital complex, including Mr Barry's house

and ours, was in a sort of no-man's-land between the airport and the telecommunications building, one held by the army loyal to the Emperor and the other in the hands of the rebels. For about fifteen minutes we huddled together in the hall while bullets flew around, some lodging in the walls of our house. Then Sister Garrett could stand it no longer. She was so frantic to get home that I walked with her to the hospital gate, ducking low now and then as bullets flew past. One split a fence post right beside us.

We met Reg and Richard driving home with their guide. Reg immediately turned round and took Sister Garrett back to her house, which was quite nearby. She found her baby safe and well.

The best thing to do seemed to be to go into the house and lie low. All the lights were off, and the telephone was not working. Using candlelight, we put together a meal which we had just finished when a terrific thunder of bullets hit the house. A window shattered, and one bullet shot through the curtains into the wall just above the dining-room table where we were sitting.

We hurriedly moved to a passage with thick walls. Suddenly there was a pounding on the front door. Reg opened it, and there stood Birru. Soldiers across the road were firing at him, thinking that he was a looter, and he was jumping from one foot to the other to avoid the bullets.

'You idiot, what are you doing?' shouted Reg.

'I've just come to see if you are all right,' said Birru. It was typical of him that he would risk his life to check on us. He was such a soft-hearted, loyal young man. Reg felt upset then that he had shouted at him. He pulled him inside, we all crouched down together.

The next time there was a lull we all beat a retreat up to the hospital. The doctors and nurses were there, too frightened to leave. We spread blankets and mattresses on the floor and tried to sleep as the firing went on all night.

The next day the hospital was inundated with casualties. There were people with multiple shrapnel wounds, others with limbs blown off. It was carnage. Reg and I took turns doing the smaller cases, resuscitating people, administering intravenous fluids, removing bullets and shrapnel, sewing up wounds and so on. Poor Mr Barry did the major surgery and had no rest for three days. We did what we could to help him.

The wards were a mass of casualties – soldiers, old people and crying children spread all over the floors on mattresses and stretchers. Richard, who was seven by now, was completely calm the whole time. During the first night at the hospital he said to me, 'Don't worry, Mummy, we shall be perfectly all right as I have prayed.' He never doubted for a moment that his prayers would be answered.

At one stage the Emperor's son, Crown Prince Asfa Wossen, came on the radio. We crowded around with other doctors and nurses and listened in silence as he solemnly began to speak. The Crown Prince said that he was going to take over from his father and that there would be a more democratic rule. He recited this in a flat monotone, not at all like his normal way of speaking. Others agreed that he did not sound as though he had been speaking from his heart. We heard later that his family had been lined up ready to be shot if he did not read the speech. He was criticised by some for giving in to the rebels, but I think I would have read it, too, if my family was about to be shot in front of me.

The fighting began on a Thursday. By Sunday night we were completely exhausted. At the end of one awful night, when we and the theatre staff were almost dead on our feet, we had to do an emergency caesarean. Right after that a woman with a ruptured uterus came in, although fortunately not a very bad one.

Things then quietened down enough for the staff from the British Embassy to come and give blood. It was quiet again on Monday and Tuesday, so we went back home. But abruptly on Wednesday night just after dinner, all the lights went out, and tremendous firing started again with bullets flying across the hospital compound. The wall of the house next door was full of holes where they struck.

In the end the army got the upper hand. The Emperor returned home in triumph but it was sad for him, too – the rebels had lured eleven of his cabinet ministers to the palace with a message that the Crown Prince wanted to talk to them, and then shot them. One escaped by jumping from a window and later told us the story of this carnage.

The three leaders of the revolt were publicly hanged, two in the main square and one right outside the hospital gates. They were left there for a few days, and every time Richard went to and from school he had to pass the bodies turning slowly in the breeze. This gruesome scene did not unduly disturb him.

Chapter Eleven

After the excitement of the attempted coup, life returned to normal. Normal, that is, for Ethiopia. The expatriate doctors and nurses led busy lives, but it was not the same for their spouses. They often found that there was not enough to do to fill in the days. Embassy wives weren't allowed to work and even if they could, it was difficult to find suitable employment for European women. Servants attended to all the household chores, and you could not just go into town for shopping or coffee as you would in a Western capital. Some people found the poverty in the streets of the capital hard to get used to – the beggars, the lepers, the cripples and destitute children – letting it prey on their minds so much that in the end they had to leave the country. Others just could not adjust to the lack of conveniences which we take for granted in the West.

One of those who found expatriate life difficult was the wife of our medical director, Professor Burrow. The Burrows lived next door, but their big garden meant they were well away from our house. I did not see much of Mrs Burrow but knew that they did not get on, because when we did meet she would regale me with stories, invariably critical, about 'the Professor', as she called him. She was his second wife, and we heard that she had previously been his housekeeper.

Some incident occurred, and the matron, Miss Hailwood, warned me that the Professor would be sleeping in the flat above our house for a couple of nights as Mrs Burrow had threatened to kill him. Two nights later Reg was up at the hospital and I was relaxing in a nice hot bath when I heard a fearful banging above, as though furniture was being thrown around. Mrs Burrow was calling out in the most fearful language and accusing Professor Burrow of terrible deeds with various women, including Miss Hailwood. This was a little hard to believe as Miss Hailwood was a former missionary, and a more upright woman you could not hope to meet.

I telephoned Reg in the hospital and told him, 'Come quickly, Mrs Burrow is killing Professor Burrow.'

He came down, ran upstairs and called through the door, 'Are you all right, Professor Burrow?'

'Oh, yes, I'm quite all right,' he replied. 'My wife is just disturbed.'

So Reg said, 'If you want any help, we're downstairs.'

We were expecting a noisy night, but all quietened down, and they soon left to go to their own house. Professor Burrow remained indoors behind closed shutters for two days before he finally emerged and went back to work.

There were other incidents like this. We never became friends with Professor Burrow. He had an ungracious and critical manner and didn't seem to like anyone. The year after the attempted coup Mr Barry was awarded an OBE for his heroic work looking after victims of the fighting. When he heard the news Professor Burrow quipped, 'That was quick payment for a haemorrhoidectomy.' In his sarcastic way, he was referring to an operation Mr Barry had done on the British Ambassador.

We were a close little community in the hospital and we all had to try hard to get on with each other. Still, everyone felt relieved when the Professor's tour of duty ended and he and his wife returned to England.

~

As a rule Ethiopians are gracious and polite, both to us and to each other. They are a unique race of people in the Horn of Africa with an ancient history and culture. We in the West can certainly learn a lot from their way of life and behaviour. Even the poorest peasant is dignified and impressive, for all his poverty and ragged appearance. I was always amazed at the old-world manners of the fathers who would come with their daughters to outpatients.

It is the custom, when meeting, to greet another with a bow if it is an older person or one of high rank. Otherwise when they see each other, friends will kiss three times or bow three times.

In our early days in Ethiopia these manners were strongly evident and impressed us enormously. But of course in any society, and more so in the cities, poverty and crime often go together and breed violence. We were shocked when one tragedy occurred in our midst.

Our matron, Miss Hailwood, became unpopular as a result of her critical approach when dealing with the local staff. She herself had high standards but was intolerant to an unreasonable degree towards anyone who failed to meet them. Often she would publicly criticise staff in front of others, something that Ethiopians, who are usually tolerant, do not bear easily. The cleaners, particularly, were singled out by her, and soon animosity built up between them.

One day Reg went into the sluice room beside the labour ward and found some of the cleaners trying to push Miss Hailwood out through the window. He was able to rescue her by grabbing her legs and pulling her in. If she had fallen to the concrete below, she would have been seriously injured or even killed.

A year or so later, while we were away on holiday in Kenya, we were shocked to read in a newspaper that Miss Hailwood had been murdered. Her two gardener boys organised a gang, broke into her house, raped and killed her. They were all caught and publicly hanged for the crime.

We were burgled once or twice but only lost a few things from the garden or verandah, or some clothes off the line. After Miss Hailwood's death Reg bought a revolver, which we never had to use. Rather as a joke, I kept an Ethiopian spear beside the bed and a pot of red pepper. But our best guards were our two bull terriers, a better deterrent than any weapon. Rangi was Richard's beloved pet, named after the Maori word for chieftan. He was Richard's constant companion for many years. Later we ordered another bull terrier from the same kennels in Kenya and called her Juno.

Although we never thought of Ethiopia as being dangerous and were never afraid, we were aware that sometimes *ferenjis* were unpopular. Once, when we were out riding, an old lady suddenly stepped right in front of Richard's horse. She was knocked down but uninjured. A large crowd quickly gathered, and some boys threw several rocks. Fortunately, before anything serious developed, an old man intervened and calmed everyone down. In the end we all apologised and bowed to each other and went on our way.

But the bad experiences were rare and were far outweighed by the good. On our first outing into the countryside, to visit some hot springs at a place called Wolliso, we had a puncture. While Reg was changing the wheel a car drew up and a well-dressed Ethiopian gentleman offered to help. This he did, getting his hands very dirty assisting total strangers. We thanked him and then found that he was the governor of a province on his way to a reception at the palace.

We set off again and as we neared our destination Richard was upset as he suddenly remembered he had left his toy kookaburra beside the road. We had our picnic and a swim, and just on the off-chance, we stopped at the spot where we had changed the tyre. Some women came rushing down the hill from the village with the kookaburra. They had been looking out for our return.

Such kindness was common, and we experienced it on many occasions, especially in the countryside. In the city, though, a different system operates. There was a well-tried system for recovering stolen goods, more reliable and less trouble than going to the police. One would drive to an area known as the Somali Terra, explain to the men what you were looking for, and quickly the missing goods would be handed over, after an exorbitant payment was made. We retrieved our car's hubcaps this way once or twice and on one occasion, my petrol cap.

Different nationalities react differently to sickness. The Ethiopian peasant women have an incredible ability to endure pain. We saw this again and again during our early days at the Princess Tsehai Hospital. A vivid picture comes to my mind which demonstrates not only the endurance of a patient but the kindness and concern of an Australian missionary nurse.

Her name was Mrs Fishwick, and she worked in a distant southern province from where she would frequently bring us patients. Once, when she had a woman in obstructed labour, she set out with her on the bus for Addis Ababa, intending to bring her to us. The description Mrs Fishwick gave us later of their journey is one I shall never forget.

Every time the poor patient cried out with pain the bus driver turned up the blaring music. This went on for hours bumping over terrible roads until the driver decided to stop for refreshments in a village. Mrs Fishwick took the woman into a chemist's shop where she attempted to deliver the baby in a small room on a makeshift couch.

Being a midwife, she knew what to do. She attempted an episiotomy (that is, making a small incision to allow the baby's head to be born) but her efforts were to no avail and once again she and patient boarded the bus to continue this nightmare journey.

Hours later patient and missionary arrived, the patient to be taken straight to the labour ward and Mrs Fishwick to our house to be resuscitated from a state of near collapse with cups of tea and buttered toast.

We were to offer Mrs Fishwick this remedy many times as she regularly brought patients from her far-off mission station. She travelled everywhere by public transport with these women.

We had great fun when staff had to point out one of her patients in the ward. They could never quite get their tongue around the words, 'Mrs Fishwick's fistula.'

She belonged to the SIM, or Sudan Interior Mission – a Protestant mission which ran clinics, hospitals, schools and various training centres and Bible colleges.

Catholic missions, too, were ardent in their work for the poor and the sick. Scattered throughout Ethiopia, their nuns worked with dedication simply for the love of Jesus, unsung by the rest of the world but known to God. But there was one who became well known and honoured. This was Sister Gabriel, whom I can best describe with the word 'radiant'.

She was an Englishwoman from a titled family and had worked first in China, until forced to leave when the Maoist revolution engulfed that country. She then came to Ethiopia with the Medical Missionaries of Mary and stayed until her death in 1993, at the age of 90.

Tall and regal, with striking features and a pure English accent, she was a distinctive figure in the streets of Addis Ababa. In a dark blue habit, which suited her beautiful blue eyes, she would search out the poor and destitute – never difficult to find. Often she visited churchyards and cemeteries where many sheltered among the tombs. She built shelters for the people she cared for and would personally take them to hospital if they were ill and provide for their basic needs. We frequently found her standing in the outpatients with her little group of pathetic figures, fistula patients among them. Her smile and her sense of humour endeared her to all she met.

Sister Gabriel was awarded a humanitarian prize by the Emperor. We were invited to the ceremony and were both almost reduced to tears to see her standing straight and tall in her simple habit receiving the award. She made a moving speech in which she quoted the verse from St Matthew's Gospel, 'Whatever you did for one of the least of these brothers of mine, you did for me.'

Sister Gabriel spent the last years of her life in Tigray Province in the north, where her order had a mission. From there she sent many patients to us.

Another missionary friend, Dr Don McClure, was in his sixties when we met him. Later, when he was older, Reg asked him once what was the secret of his long and vigorous life. He told this story. 'When we got married, my wife and I were very happy. As we came out of the church we said, "Let's stay like this forever. We're sure to have some tiffs, so if we ever feel angry with each other I'll go out into the garden and dig and you go into the kitchen and start cooking."

'That's the secret,' he said. 'I've been in the open air ever since!'

Dr McClure literally gave his life for Ethiopia. He was working down in the Ogaden near the Somali border – a primitive area that is mostly desert. He was doing general medicine in a clinic and used to send us patients now and then. Others worked in a school and an orphanage. Trouble with the Somalis was frequent, with sporadic raids and robberies, so that eventually working there became too risky. Arrangements were made for a plane from the Missionary Aviation Fellowship to fly down and evacuate the staff.

The day before it was due raiders from over the border arrived, in big numbers this time, with obviously more serious intent. They separated the women and children, locking them in one room, then lined up the men and threatened to shoot them.

Dr McClure pleaded with them, 'Take anything you like but do not kill us.' His plea went unheeded, and the Somalis opened fire. Dr McClure's son was visiting from America at the time and told us this story later. His father fell down dead beside him, and the blast from the gun so stunned him that he too fell, but was unharmed. He lay as if dead and after the Somalis left he crawled away and hid. Next day the plane arrived, and he, with the women and children, was safely evacuated.

Margaret Fitzherbert, whom we had so warmed to on that first night of our arrival in Ethiopia, was another who was entirely selfless. She had been the gynaecologist at Princess Tsehai Hospital, but when we met her she was working with lepers. She herself eventually became infected with the disease and needed treatment. She literally gave away her whole salary every month to the poor and when she died had only a few dollars in her bank account. I know that when she was working as a gynaecologist she paid for the fistula women to be admitted and treated. These were the patients she told us would break our hearts.

We were encouraged and inspired by such wonderful people around us and spurred on to greater efforts to help the increasing number of fistula patients who were arriving.

Even though the Ministry of Health allowed us a month's holiday every year and a ticket home every three years, we could not just walk away for a month leaving patients without a doctor. It was relatively easy to get volunteers to do a few weeks work in Ethiopia who were even willing to pay their fares out, but more difficult to get the Ministry to agree to this arrangement. When they realised that it was for the sake of the patients that we sought their cooperation, they agreed, as long as the doctors replacing us could prove that they were fully qualified.

We knew Professor Hugh McLaren of Birmingham through his articles outlining his stand against abortion on demand, but mainly through his pioneering work on the early detection of cervical cancer using the pap smear method. Because we were seeing many women with this terrible malignant condition, Reg wrote often to Hugh, arranging eventually to send an Ethiopian to his research unit to learn the pap smear technique.

Hugh and his wife, Lois, agreed to do a locum for us while we went to Kenya for our second Malindi holiday. I was concerned that we would not recognise him, so asked how we would distinguish him at the airport, which was becoming quite a busy one. He replied, 'I shall be wearing a tweed jacket and a tam o' shanter and I have a nose that looks like a boxer's.'

We had no difficulty spotting him, and of course as soon as he spoke with his marvellous Scottish accent there was no doubt that he was the right man.

We had a few days together before we left for our holiday. Mealtimes were hilarious, with his fund of Scottish stories enhanced by his accent. It was a tonic to be with him. Lois was a charming foil to his boisterous nature, pretending to look down on Hugh because he was a lowlander and she a proud highlander. Although long widowed, Lois even now still sends money every Christmas to Yeshi and Birru, whom she met on that first visit 40 years ago.

Hugh was deeply affected when he saw our fistula patients. He experienced for himself the crowded ward and the shortage of accommodation. We often discussed with him our desire to build a hostel to house patients while they waited for surgery, and after he left us Hugh did not forget.

One night, after Hugh had returned home, the American evangelist Billy Graham staged one of his meetings in Birmingham. Hugh went along to the meeting and noticed sitting in front of him a man he knew named Harry Paine. Mr Paine had made a fortune out of shoe repair shops on railway stations. Hugh tapped him on the shoulder and said, 'I've just come back from Ethiopia, where I've met a couple of doctors who are trying to raise money to build some hostels for women who come from the country.'

Paine said, 'I'll talk to you after the meeting.'

As a result of that conversation Harry Paine provided the funds to build our first hostel. Reg then went to the medical director and the administrator and told them he had the money, all he needed was permission to build a hostel in the hospital grounds. They readily agreed. The hospital would feed the patients, but we would be responsible for their fees when they were admitted for surgery.

We chose a nice piece of level ground among some eucalyptus trees, and an architect from the Ministry of Health drew up a plan for a ward with ten beds, with a shower and bathroom. When the builders started work, Reg and I used to walk over to the site each evening and watch with excitement as the foundations were laid and the walls slowly rose. It was a simple structure made of concrete blocks but it was a palace to us.

We opened the hostel in 1962. A local committee of American women gave us the beds, and the British Embassy supplied the bedding. We needed a lot as the sheets had to be changed two or three times a day. The patients had their own washing area and they would wash their own sheets and hang them out. In the rainy season a covered area constructed of tin and held up by eucalyptus poles was used for drying.

The hostel made a great difference, but so many patients were arriving that almost immediately we found we were still short of accommodation. With no place available for these poor women, they sought refuge at churches, at bus stops or in the streets, often surviving by begging until we could take them in. One woman arrived after being carried by her husband for three days, and we had no bed for her. We found her a spot on the floor of a storeroom, and her husband slept there with her until we could get her into the hostel.

The new matron was not at all happy about allowing some women to sleep in the outpatients' department, so Reg often smuggled them in after dark, bedding them down with a blanket and plastic sheeting. They were leaking urine, so of course this caused a smell, and their presence could not be hidden for long.

The fistula patients were so grateful. One morning when I opened outpatients, a young woman jumped up and kissed me on both cheeks. Another I remember in particular was literally in rags, with gaping holes in her dress. She was just eighteen, with a lovely face and black hair in plaits. She had come over 900 kilometres from Eritrea and was cold and wet, and her little feet were caked with mud. I had an angry argument with Matron about her and told her, 'You may be happy to throw them out into the street, but I cannot.' After some grumbling she gave in.

We were always scrounging for money to keep everything going. Friends in Australia sent us donations, including AUS£100 which arrived out of the blue from one of our old Crown Street colleagues, Sister Faye Kennedy. If we were still short we would put in money from our salaries.

It soon became obvious that we would have to expand. We extended the hostel by another ten beds and then built a separate wing, bringing the total up to about 30. It still wasn't enough, and we often had 60 women sleeping two to a bed. We began to use some of the girls to help in the outpatients, bringing in patients and cleaning the examining couches.

On some mornings Reg used to drive our old VW down to the bus station, where he would ask if there was anyone there leaking urine. It was not difficult to find a fistula patient. She would usually be standing alone, in the distinctive clothes of the country women, her *gabi,* or big shawl, usually impregnated with butter to keep out the cold. Then he would go to the market to a broken-down old hotel called the Gojam Verandah, which was the only place in the city that would allow the fistula pilgrims to camp outside. He'd pile them in the car, all jammed together and take them back to the hostel. Richard once enquired, 'Daddy, why do we have to have the car smelling of urine all the time?'

One evening we were having a big dinner party at home to introduce Hugh McLaren to some friends. He had come out to do another locum for us while we went on holiday. Princess Mary and her husband, Seyoum, were there plus a lot of other friends and some of the hospital staff. At about 10 pm we received a message from the palace that the Emperor was coming at nine next morning to see our fistula patients.

We stayed up most of the night preparing for the visit. I was cutting flowers for the ward when I sliced the top of my thumb off with the secateurs and fainted in the kitchen as Hugh was binding it up. My last job was to make a small posy for one of the girls to present to His Majesty, then we had a few hours sleep.

We were up at 5 am and Reg went up to the hostel to inspect a new water heater with a charcoal burner that we had just installed. He roused the girls and by six they were cleaning and wiping the floor with disinfectant; our favourite was one smelling strongly of eucalyptus.

Punctually at nine the Emperor arrived, wearing a military uniform covered in medals and his customary gabardine cloak. He was accompanied by an entourage including the Minister of Health, a couple of generals and several armed guards. We were standing waiting in our white coats and bowed low as we were introduced. The previous evening Princess Mary had advised us to include Richard in the party as the Emperor loved children. He hovered around in the background until a soldier pushed him forwards. He bowed and shook the Emperor's hand.

'Can you speak Amharic?'

Richard replied, 'A little, Your Majesty,' and they exchanged a few words. Then Reg asked the Emperor what he would like to see.

'You lead the way, and I'll follow.'

He toured the hostel and then went to the hospital and saw some of our patients who were recovering from surgery. There was one there whom we had repaired two years previously. She was nine months pregnant and waiting to have her baby. Reg told the Emperor, 'This is how we like them to come back.'

Later in the tour the Emperor said to Reg, 'Why do my women get fistulas?'

'It's not your women, Your Majesty, it's your country, because you haven't got enough roads and hospitals for these women to get help when they need it.'

The Emperor responded, 'I'm so glad it's not my women. I thank you from my heart for your generous services to my beloved people.'

Reg replied, 'It's an honour to serve Your Majesty and your people.'

I had asked one of our patients, a shy girl named Amina, to present to the Emperor the posy I'd made, but in all the rush I forgot to give it to her. Anxious to do the right thing, she came forward holding a milk bottle containing a few drooping flowers. She handed it to him and he gravely accepted.

As he left, the Emperor put his hand in his pocket and handed Reg US$500, saying, 'May your work for my people long continue.'

Chapter Twelve

It seemed that no time at all had passed before our three-year term was over and we were making plans to return to Australia for six weeks leave. As usual we had to start well in advance, traipsing around all the government departments to reassure them that we didn't owe anyone anything. Towards the end of the preparations all the hard work of the last three years really caught up with us. We realised that we were both close to exhaustion. At the airport, where we had to board an Ethiopian Airlines flight to Nairobi, then on via Mauritius to Perth and, finally, Sydney, the airline official checking our passports said to Reg, 'You're not leaving are you, doctor?'

'No,' replied Reg, 'but if I don't have a holiday, I will die.'

'If you don't come back, many will die,' was his reply.

There was never any question about not coming back. It was wonderful to visit friends and family and to enjoy luxuries like ice-creams and milkshakes, but while we were on holiday our thoughts often turned to Ethiopia and the fistula pilgrims whom we knew would be waiting for our return. We felt we had at least ten years work ahead of us before the Ethiopians would be able to take over their care. Although we still had strong ties to Australia and New Zealand, now we also had a stake in Ethiopia.

In three years we had made a home for ourselves. Richard was extremely happy at the English School, although they, perhaps, were not quite so happy with him. His reports often said things like, 'Richard is an intelligent boy but unfortunately does not try hard enough and does not know how to behave.' He was caned several times, once for talking in class. He'd remarked to the boy next to him, 'Isn't Mr so-and-so an old stinker?'

In an attempt to help him learn French, we enrolled him in a special course at the French school for part of the academic holidays. The Sudanese Ambassador's daughter went there too, so every morning Richard was picked up in a limousine and shared a ride.

He didn't impress the teachers there much, either. One day he had to write out a hundred times, *'Je suis un garçon insupportable.'*

As far as Reg and I were concerned, these misdemeanours merely showed that Richard was a normal young boy. He certainly had a normal child's love of pets. On one trip into the country we bought a little black lamb from a shepherd, which Richard named Ink Pot. In addition to the lamb, we had the lovable bull terrier, Rangi, whom I mentioned before. Although he was a pedigreed dog, Rangi had only one eye, this was why he was sold cheaply! But this did not cramp his style in the least. Both Rangi and the lamb adored Richard and followed him everywhere.

The Emperor was a frequent visitor to the hospital to see family members or friends. It was his habit to get out of his car at the gates and walk with his two little chihuahuas up the long drive. This was a constant worry if I happened to be riding, as Rangi always came with me and would certainly have killed the miniature dogs. So Birru and I went through a routine. He would hold Rangi while I rode to the gate. Then, if no Emperor was in sight, I would raise my hand and Birru would release him. The dog would then streak across the compound to join me.

I had one or two near disasters when the Emperor arrived unexpectedly, and on these occasions the only thing to do was to turn tail and tear back to the house, hoping that Rangi was following and that I had not been seen, as the correct thing would have been to dismount and bow.

We had a collection of pets over the years – rabbits, a huge tortoise which was attached to a long string so it could wander about the garden, and later horses. They gave us all tremendous pleasure and filled Richard's childhood days with interest.

Not long after we arrived we noticed many vultures sitting in the trees which surrounded our house – ugly birds. When a baby one fell from its nest Richard nursed it and put it in a cage hoping it would survive. I found him in his bedroom one afternoon praying. He told me he was praying for his baby vulture.

His prayers were answered, for the bird began to put on weight at a great rate. It was so fierce that Richard had to feed it raw meat from a fork. Eventually it grew so big that it had to be released.

Horses were my weakness, so I particularly wanted Richard to learn to ride and have a pony. Also, there were other children living in the compound and at the English School who rode and owned ponies. Our first pony was a gift from a Swedish family, obviously wanting to get rid of it as he was unreliable and blind in one eye as well – our second animal with only one eye! He did not last long as he was not suitable for someone learning to ride.

We then bought a pretty little palomino and called him Amber. We kept him in a little *tukul*-like building in the garden which had been used as a toolshed. Richard was delighted with him and soon learned to ride.

I then heard about another horse, which was being sold by someone from the British Embassy who was returning home. He was a lovely dark bay gelding called Sahara, quite big enough for me, beautifully trained and a most comfortable ride. The day I bought him I rode home 15 kilometres through the traffic from the Embassy, and he behaved perfectly.

We built bigger stables, unfortunately too near Professor Burrow's fence, and soon there was a complaint from Mrs Burrow about the smell of the horses. So eventually this was used as our garage and another site selected as far away as possible. All was then peaceful again and remained so until the Burrows left and Mr Barry, the surgeon, moved in next door with his wife and three children. They all owned ponies and were, like Richard, enthusiastic riders.

Now that we had two horses and the Barry children as neighbours, we often rode together. In those early days we were near the country, with few houses around us, so it was easy to be in beautiful riding country soon after leaving the hospital gates. There were no fences anywhere, just open land, lovely hills, wooded valleys and streams. I have vivid memories of the beauty and peace of this countryside – the scent of wild jasmine and dog rose, the fields of shimmering *tef,* haystacks, wide open plains spread like a cloth of gold when the *maskal* daisies were flowering, and clear mountain streams.

The scattered villages were a peaceful sight – one of the small, round mud *tukuls* with thatched roofs clustered together, would often be issuing a column of smoke through the roof into a clear blue sky. At harvest time we would see men and boys cutting grain, or treading it out with their oxen and winnowing it by tossing the stalks into the air with pitchforks.

Near the bigger villages there was often a church – usually a round building, perched on a small hill and surrounded by a grove of trees. In the late, still afternoons or early mornings, the sound of chanting might be heard wafting over the hills.

I remember the sound particularly after one night out, sleeping on a haystack. We used our sleeping bags as saddle cloths, took two Ethiopian grooms with us, enough food for tea and breakfast and set off for the hills. The local farmers built a fire, and one insisted on staying with us all night to protect us. He could not be persuaded to go home, saying we were his guests. The children in our party enjoyed this expedition, but I do not recall sleeping much.

Riding was my greatest relaxation. Richard and I loved it, but it was not something Reg enjoyed. He did not join us on these trips but he liked hearing about them and was pleased that Richard had become a good horseman.

Some of our picnics were quite grand affairs, particularly if organised by riders from an embassy. The Italians, British and

Swiss, especially, were known for their horses and fine stables, so there were many riders amongst their staff. They would arrange for the food to be brought by Land Rover to a meeting point. We would unsaddle the horses and water them, then sit under the trees enjoying a lavish lunch.

Gymkhanas and amateur races were also popular. We all competed in these events, and Richard and I won quite a few ribbons and cups. The gymkhanas were usually held at the British Embassy paddock or at the English School. Our horses would be taken by Kass, our *syce,* or groom, to the other side of town where most of the embassies and the English School were.

Keeping horses was easy for us, with men to catch and saddle them when we wanted to ride, and to groom, rug and stable them at night. We were really quite spoilt. Originally I tried to encourage Richard to care for his own pony, but it was an uphill battle with so many people willing and anxious to do the work.

Dick and Anne Sandford were prominent personalities in the riding fraternity. Dick, the youngest son of Brigadier and Mrs Sandford, had been born in Ethiopia. One time when we wanted to buy new horses, he suggested we join him on a trip to a horse market about 100 kilometres north-east of the city. This was Galla country, known for its horses and horsemen.

We arrived at a grassy plain where a great collection of horses were gathered; their owners were all anxious to display their animals and show off their paces. It was a chaotic mob, and quite dangerous, with horses stamping and pulling nervously, and shouting men importuning us to buy. We were able to select and try out likely animals and had an exciting time as we galloped to and fro over the open plain.

I eventually chose a dark brown horse with the thickest mane and tail I had ever seen. This, I discovered on closer inspection, was because he was a stallion, but he turned out well and was easy to ride. The one Dick selected was more difficult, immediately bucking and rearing so much that it threw him off. In typical Sandford style, Dick regarded this as a challenge and bought it. He could only mount it if he first put a sack over its head, but even with this precaution and with training, the horse remained wild and unmanageable, so it finally had to be sold.

Our most exciting and longest rides were out to Mulu Farm, where Brigadier and Mrs Sandford lived. Richard and I went on these treks, usually with eight or ten others. We gathered at a spot out of the city over the Entoto Hills, then rode 40 kilometres across beautiful countryside to Mulu. The trip took most of the day, as we had frequent rests and some mishaps crossing streams when the horses tried to roll. We usually got a bit lost as there were no roads, and our guides were often as confused as we were. When we eventually arrived, we always had a warm welcome from the Sandfords and drank numerous cups of tea to revive us.

If we managed to get a weekend off we could trek down 900 metres into the Mugga River Gorge below Mulu Farm. With porters carrying our equipment, we descended a precipitous, winding track to the bottom, setting up tents or sleeping in small *tukuls* built by some of our friends who had more time to spend on weekends and wanted something more permanent for their camp.

The gorge was alive with baboons, bushbuck and colobus monkeys, while many birds soared overhead, including an especially rare species of vulture, the lammergeyers, which are only found in the highlands of Ethiopia. It was wonderful to watch them floating on the wind currents on motionless wings.

An icy river ran through the gorge with pools deep enough for swimming in, and if we walked to the head of the valley there was a spectacular waterfall. It was a steep, hard climb up, which I took carefully, but Richard and his young friends always rushed ahead trying to break the record, which stood at a little over an hour. They invariably had a long wait while the stragglers caught up.

We loved Ethiopia and felt no desire to be anywhere else. We kept in touch with the outside world through newspapers ordered from England. Although sometimes they were well out of date and four or five would arrive in one day, we at least knew what was happening beyond our isolated little world.

Reading the papers I was shocked at the moral degeneration that was taking place in Britain. This was the 1960s when everyone was talking about free love, and disregarding the sanctity of marriage and even the necessity of it. I knew Richard would most likely have to complete his schooling in England and I was worried about the sort of place we would be sending him to. I knew the English regarded themselves as civilised, but it seemed to me that in many ways Ethiopia was a far more civilised place.

At the same time there were things about Britain that I thought were good and worth preserving. The monarchy was a wonderful institution that Reg and I both supported wholeheartedly, admiring the Queen for her selfless devotion to duty.

We were both shocked and upset when an Australian ambassador we were entertaining for dinner suggested that Australia needed to break away from England and the Queen, change the national anthem and become a republic. This was when Mr Whitlam was Prime Minister. Reg and I strongly disapproved of his views and told him so. Reg said afterwards that he was going to start a loyalist society, and I wrote to the *Sydney Morning Herald*, saying we must hang on to English traditions at all costs. But of course it was not published, and Reg never started his society.

I still feel that way and wonder why we need to change from a form of government that works perfectly well and is part of our heritage. Possibly, looking back, these views have been strengthened by the upheavals we later lived through in Ethiopia when a stable government was disturbed, a monarchy overthrown and a communist regime introduced, with devastating results. But I am getting ahead of my story.

Chapter Thirteen

The Emperor, Haile Selassie, was famous for his love of lions. He had no fear of them, and I am sure they knew this. Once or twice we saw him drive by in his magnificent car with a lion draped across the back seat. There was another, or perhaps the same one, wandering free in the palace grounds. We were on quite good terms with the English governess who used to tutor His Majesty's grandchildren. She told us how nervous she was walking through the palace gardens to her schoolroom. When it became too much for her she spoke up. 'Your Majesty, I cannot be responsible for the safety of these children if the lion is loose in the gardens.'

The Emperor told her that for her peace of mind he would make sure no lions were loose when she came.

Another story about lions comes to mind. One of our English nursing sisters, who was in charge of the operating theatre, was being married, and we were invited to the wedding. The reception was held in the home of an American, Colonel Garry. He lived in a big house which had an upstairs verandah opening off the drawing room. The reception was in progress when Reg walked in and said, 'I've just been patting a lion, but he seems more than a cub so you had better not go out there, as it might be savage.'

I was too curious to heed his advice so I went out to the verandah and saw a beautiful lion who padded up to me and seemed friendly. As I patted him he scratched my arm, possibly playfully, but I was not sure, so I hurriedly retreated to the safety of the drawing room.

He had been with Colonel Garry since he was a tiny cub but was now almost fully grown. Jumbo, as he was called, loved the Colonel. He rolled on his back for him and would rub his head against his master's belly like an affectionate cat. As he got older he took to following Mrs Garry about the garden and suddenly jumping onto her back. She became frightened, and finally they had to give him to the Emperor for his zoo.

We had heard that the Emperor had a lion in the hall of the palace where he held receptions and met dignitaries. We did not think this could really be true until one day we went to the palace ourselves for an audience. There was indeed a lion, sitting in the hall outside the reception room.

We had arranged the audience at the request of two visitors from Australia, Suzanne Woolcott and Sul Stuart-Fraser. Sul was a well-off woman who owned nursing homes in Sydney. She was a great personality, flamboyant, garrulous and kind. She was taller than average, wore heavy lipstick, and used to dress in bright clothes with lots of beads hanging low like armour. She had a habit of talking out of the side of her mouth as if imparting a great secret.

Her friend, Suzanne, was also a great traveller, and Sul had asked her to accompany her. Sul was most anxious, indeed determined, to meet the Emperor. They must have thought this possible because they had already bought presents in Sydney to give him. We had enormous difficulty arranging for the audience, but finally, with the help of influential friends, it was granted.

Dressed in our best clothes, we drove up to the palace and were ushered into an antechamber beside the reception room. After about a half hour wait we were shown in. The Emperor was sitting on his throne flanked by his Minister of the Court, who interpreted for him. Although he could speak English well he preferred to speak Amharic.

We bowed low as we entered, and were formally presented. Sul was nervous. I could see her hands shaking as she tried to undo the box containing her present – silver coffee spoons inlaid with opals in the handles. I think her gloves may have been the problem. Leaning forward, his Majesty said, 'Let me try,' and clicked open the catch with ease. I noticed a distinct twinkle in his eye as he did this.

As we were leaving we passed the lion in the hall, fortunately chained. Both our guests stopped and with an official standing by, patted the beast. It lay quietly as if it was used to such affection.

Sul and Suzanne visited the hospital and were both deeply affected by the tragic cases they saw. Sul told me later that there and then she had made a vow before God that she would raise money for these women when she returned to Sydney.

When they finally did return, Sul and Suzanne gathered some other friends together and formed a committee. They dreamed up all sorts of ways to raise money. They would invite well-off friends to morning teas and ask them for donations. Suzanne lived in a fine house, Claremont, on Sydney's north shore. She opened it and her garden for inspection, charging people admission, and got the local nursery to come and sell plants, with 10 per cent of the profit going to the committee. Another time they hired a cinema and showed a popular film of the day, *Love Story*. They charged $10 a ticket, which was a lot of money then.

As good as her word, Sul and her friends faithfully helped us for many years.

On 5 May 1966 Ethiopia celebrated the twenty-fifth anniversary of the overthrow of the Italians. A national holiday was declared, and is still an annual holiday known as 'Patriots Victory Day'. On the morning of the big day Richard, Reg and I joined thousands of people going into the city to watch the celebrations. The

Emperor sat on a throne on a huge stand, flanked by his military commanders. Brigadier Sandford was there and received a special liberation medal.

We found a seat on a grassy bank outside the walls of the old Gibi, the Emperor Menelik's original palace, which stood in a commanding site on one of the many hills in the city. From there we had a good view of the procession passing along the street below.

First there was a march-past of Army, Navy and Air Force personnel, then came ranks of old patriots wearing monkey and lion headdresses, carrying ancient weapons and shields. Looking warlike, fierce and proud, they brought vividly to mind the many stories we had read and heard about their endurance and bravery when facing Mussolini's far better equipped army.

The Galla horsemen were an awe-inspiring sight, with their monkey skin headdresses and their mounts draped in colourful blankets falling to their hocks. As they trotted past they brought cries of admiration from the crowd. The men were followed by a group of women patriots. When I met one of them afterwards, she proudly told me she had personally killed five Italians.

Overhead, Air Force fighters flew past with red, yellow and green smoke (the colours of the Ethiopian flag) pouring out behind them, then they drew a big 25 in the sky with the smoke.

Following the Ethiopians came British soldiers who had played such a decisive part in the war against Italy. The Emperor had personally invited them to be his guests, paying their fares and hotel expenses.

One of the old soldiers was now our Professor of Surgery, appointed to this chair at the recently established Medical School of Addis Ababa University. As a young man, Eric Goulston had been seconded from the Australian Army as a surgeon with the Ethiopians fighting the Italians. He was present in the last great battle of the war to liberate Gondar in the north and was known as 'Goulston of Gondar'.

As part of the celebrations the Emperor planned a huge banquet. At about 6 pm on the night it was due to take place I was at the hospital. I called at the reception desk to see if there was any mail for me and found an envelope with the royal seal on it addressed to Eric Goulston. I knew he was out with his daughter and, suspecting that it might have something to do with the celebrations, I opened it. Eric was commanded to attend a reception at the palace at eight o'clock that night.

I drove quickly to his house, which was not far away. Eric was still out, but his servant knew where he kept his dinner suit. It was unfortunately locked away in a shed and the only keys were in the pocket of another servant who had the day off. With the help of some tools we broke the door open and got the tails out. While the servant was ironing them I called the palace to try to find out if the invitation included Eric's wife, Nancy. Phoning was always fraught with delay, especially on this night of all nights. It was after 7 pm by the time I finally learned that Mrs Goulston was expected too.

Nancy found a long dress, and just as the servant started to iron it, in walked Eric. I left him searching for his studs. They got there in time and had a wonderful night.

A day later Reg and I attended a dinner given by the Crown Prince, Merid Azmatch Asfa Wossen. Unlike the Goulstons, we had plenty of notice, and I was able to hurriedly have a long black velvet skirt made. I bought a pale blue Italian blouse with a pattern of silver threads in it. With this outfit and an evening bag I felt reasonably presentable. The men only had to wear dinner suits, so Reg was all right.

When we arrived at their magnificent house, we were greeted by the Crown Prince and his wife, Princess Medferashwork. The last time I had been there had been to examine the Crown Princess when she was ill. I hoped she would not remember. They greeted us warmly, and we walked up a long flight of stairs past rows of servants and uniformed guards. The guests were being shuffled off into various reception rooms, I think according to their social status. I fear we were in a rather low room.

As we mingled for a while with the other guests, I could not help noticing how elegant were the Ethiopian women, compared to the Europeans. The young ones, especially, were slim and graceful with fine features and beautiful eyes. After drinks we all moved into a huge, silk-lined tent in the garden, bigger than any circus tent I had ever seen, and carpeted with exotic rugs. There we served ourselves dinner from a lavish buffet.

The Emperor sat on a low stage surrounded by his grandchildren. His throne was so big it almost seemed to swallow him up. He watched the proceedings with a benign look on his face and slipped away early as the dancing began. He was 74 at this time. I saw Princess Mary a few days later and asked her if he was finding the days of celebrations tiring. She said not at all. He was full of energy and revelling in every moment.

One of the former British soldiers looked a typical old Colonel Blimp with a red face and a big white moustache. He got the Prime Minister's wife, a Frenchwoman, and whirled her round and round the dance floor with terrific gusto. Then he seized the British Ambassador's wife, Lady Russel, and nearly killed her with his enthusiasm. He was a fit old man, well into his seventies, having the time of his life.

If our social life was rather unreal at times the work at the hospital always brought us back to earth. Nearly every day we would see young women arriving with injuries so shocking and damage so great to the vagina that we felt hopeless about our ability to cure them.

The worst patients were those who formed keloid, or scar, tissue, sometimes completely occluding the vagina and thus distorting the normal anatomy beyond recognition. Others were a challenge because of the size of the actual fistula, with such loss of bladder tissue that there was difficulty closing the gap.

A technique that was of enormous value to us was one pioneered by a German gynaecologist, Heinrich Martius. The Martius fat pad graft, as it was called, had been used by him successfully in the few fistula cases he had encountered. They had possibly been caused by a surgical mistake or radiation burns after treatment for cancer and only very rarely by obstructed labour. This latter cause is almost unknown in the Western world.

The technique involves dissecting out a pedicle of fat from the side of the vagina, leaving one end attached to preserve the blood supply, then threading the free pedicle of fat through a short tunnel into the vagina. There it lies over the repaired bladder, acting as a reinforcement to the repair and bringing in a new blood supply. It is also a safeguard if another baby is born vaginally.

You really make the patient better than before, because there's a nice big pad in between the bladder muscle and the skin of the vagina, or the mucosa.

After we had been using this operation for many months with a high success rate, we had a visit from an English gynaecologist working in northern Nigeria, Dr Una Lister. Comparing our high success rate of 90 per cent to hers of 70 per cent, she could not believe our results. She worked with us for a few months and on her return home wrote back excitedly saying that her success rate was now 90 per cent since she, too, was using the Martius graft.

When we wrote to Heinrich Martius and told him of the success we were having, he replied, 'I'm glad you're curing these women with my operation, I've only done 26.'

We had a visit from another fistula surgeon, a highly celebrated one, and author of a textbook on the subject. He was Professor Chassar Moir from England. We had written to him when we first encountered our fistula patients, seeking his advice, so on his way to India he called in to see us. He was very upset when he saw our cases. He'd never seen such injuries and considered some of them inoperable. He confided, 'I don't know how you're tackling these because they're so much more difficult than the ones I'm seeing.'

He was anxious to operate with us, and we, of course, were keen to see him perform with his knowledge and skill. He was a meticulous surgeon and tackled the first cases beautifully.

When we confronted him with a difficult one he seemed nonplussed. After about half an hour he said to Reg, 'I think this is beyond me; you take over.'

Reg diffidently gave him some advice, telling him to tackle it more radically because of the scar tissue. This he courageously did and was successful in closing the fistula.

I recall his remark as he watched Reg operating, 'You do excavate, don't you?'

He returned to Ethiopia a few years later to operate with us and then he also excavated.

Seeing the tragic plight of the fistula pilgrims only made us more keen to make the school of midwifery a success. This was what we originally came to do. Reg corresponded with a famous tutor–midwife who was the author of the best book for nurses on the subject. She was Maggie Myles of Scotland. Miss Myles agreed to come out, and so our first girls were honoured to have the best teacher in the world.

Although she did not stay for the whole year, she was able, during her time with us, to set up the curriculum, teach the pupils and work with the tutor–sister in the government nursing school at the Princess Tsehai Hospital. She also donated many of her own textbooks to the library.

We had endless trouble with customs trying to import these books duty-free. Miss Myles became extremely irate when told she had to pay duty. 'But I'm giving these books to Ethiopia,' she railed.

Perhaps the customs official could not follow her Scottish accent, I had difficulty myself, but he was obstinate and would not give in.

The flat above us happened to be empty during her visit so she was able to stay there. At the end of her first day, as we said good night at the bottom of the outside staircase she enquired if hyenas could jump. She was very frightened of them.

With this excellent tuition our first six nurse–midwives

graduated and all went on to teaching jobs themselves. We felt proud but we got no further with our school as the Ministry of Health decided it would be too expensive to pay nurses the extra money for being midwives. They thought, in any case, that ordinary nurses should be able to look after women in labour just as well.

There could have been no greater proof of the need for midwives than the fistula patients who were arriving at the hospital each day. What was required was a network of trained midwives throughout the country and an education program to persuade women to see them. There are schools in Ethiopia now, but there are still pitifully few midwives out in the country, where they are needed.

Poor obstetric care was not the only reason for the fistulas. The other big problem was, and still is, that of child marriage. It is practised in three northern provinces, Gondar, Gojam and Tigray. Most rural marriages are arranged by the parents, and often the first time bride and groom meet is on their wedding day. Girls may be betrothed at the age of eight and can be married as young as twelve. On her wedding day the frightened girl meets her husband. She sits, scared and bewildered, through a noisy ceremony with music and feasting and then she is taken away to live with her husband's parents.

The husband promises not to sleep with his bride until she is old enough, but of course the promise is not always kept. It is hard for a girl to resist the sexual advances of a healthy young boy. They are just little girls. They are not mature enough, emotionally or physically, to cope with a sexual relationship. It is rape, really – condoned by their parents.

They are often pregnant with their first baby at the age of thirteen or fourteen. Many girls in their early teens are not sufficiently developed to deliver a baby. These are the ones who get into difficulty, often labouring for four, five or six days trying to push the baby out. Sometimes the *wogesha* or village doctor might be called in to help. But all he can do is administer a local potion made from herbs, and tell her to push.

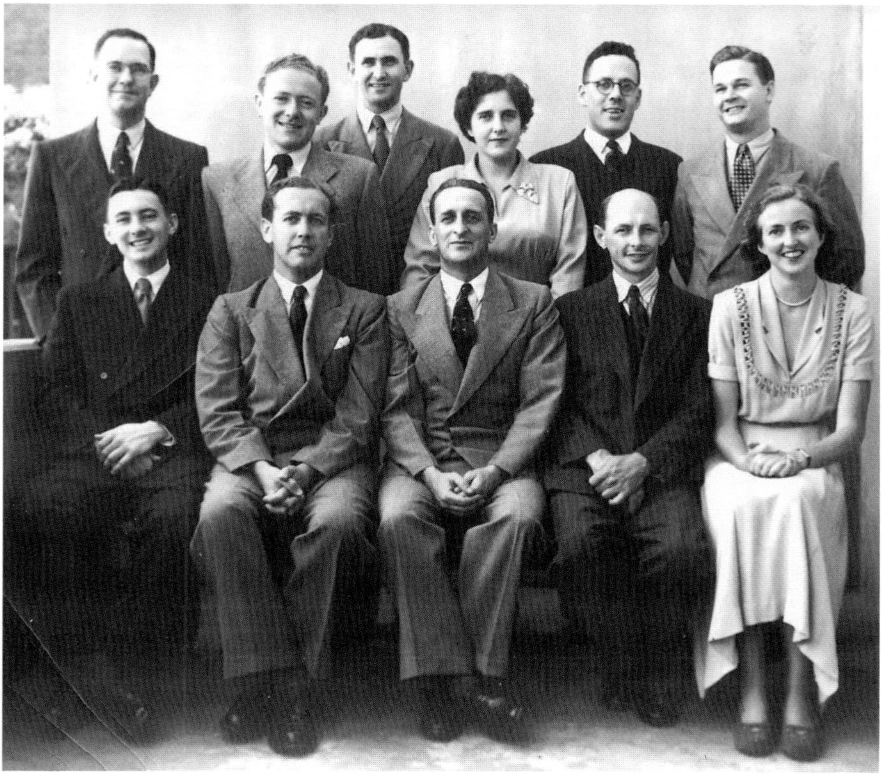

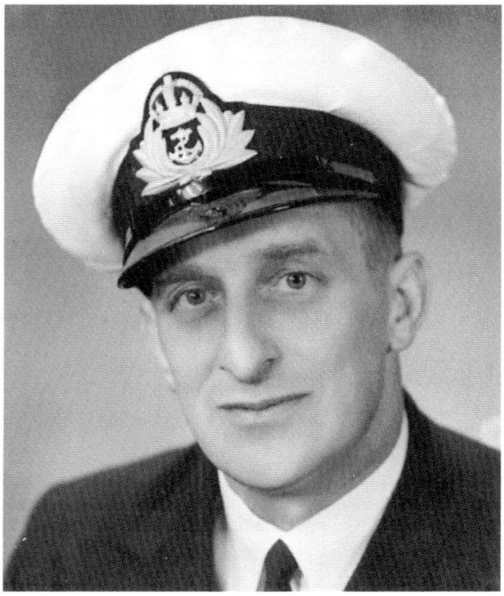

Reg (centre) and me (front right) with the honorary staff of Crown Street Women's Hospital in about 1948.

Reg served in the New Zealand Navy during World War II, first on the HMNZS *Gambia* as a surgeon-lieutenant.

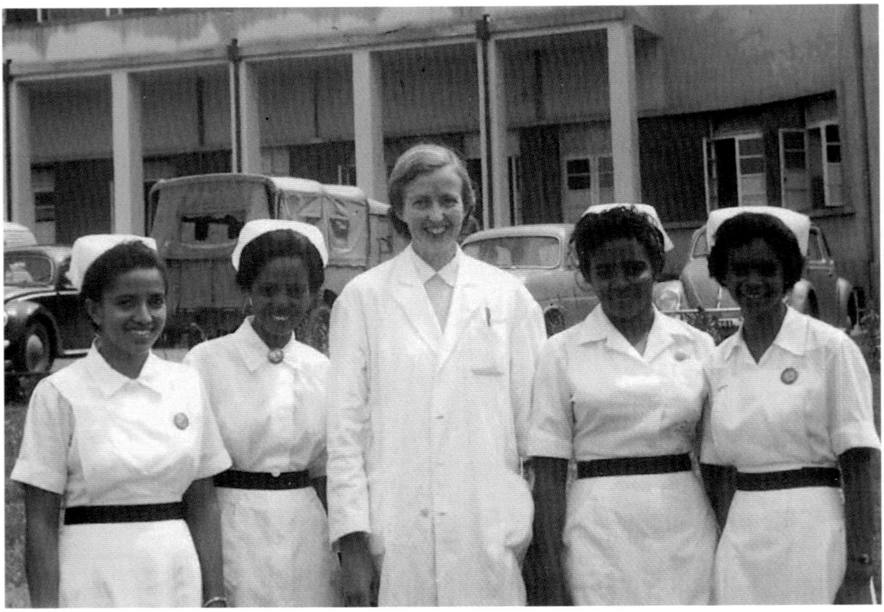

I am standing with four of our midwifery graduates outside the Princess Tsehai Memorial Hospital.

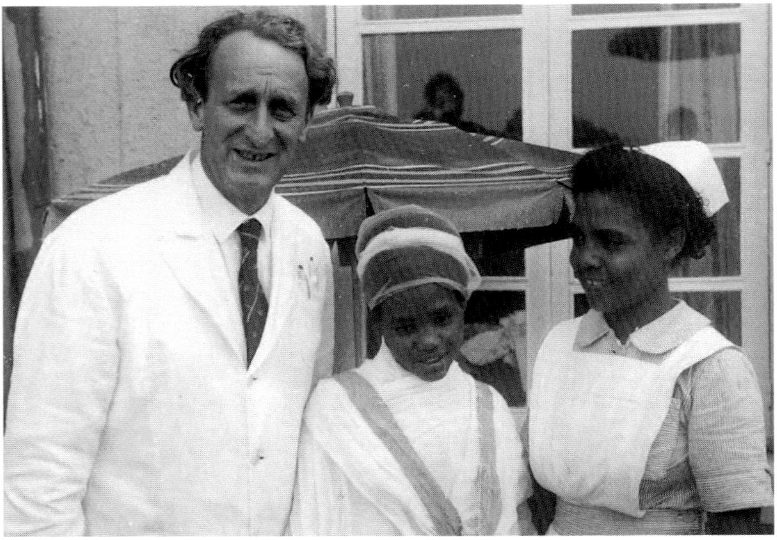

Reg with his first cured fistula patient. The nurse with them was one of the best in the hospital.

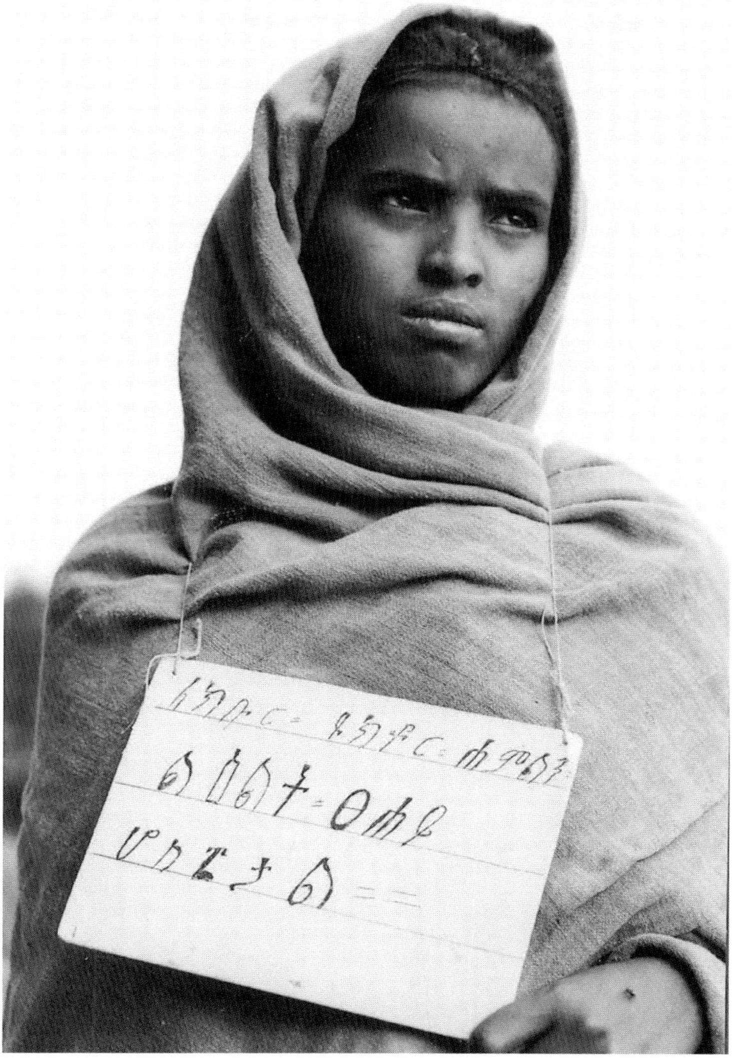

A young woman from a faraway province where another language is spoken, arrived with a sign hanging around her neck which read, 'Dear Doctor Hamlin, Princess Tsehai Hospital'.

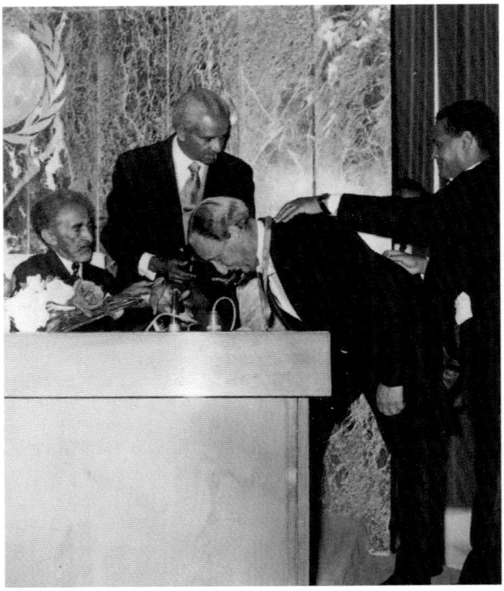

Reg (above) and I (below) were jointly awarded the Haile Selassie Humanitarian Prize by HIM The Emperor.

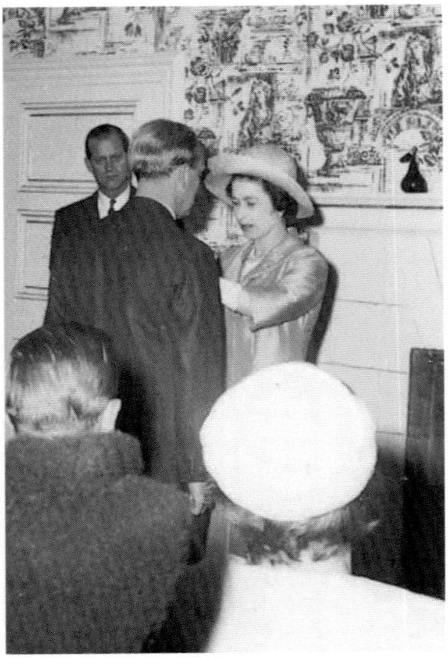

Her Majesty Queen Elizabeth II presenting Reg with the Order of the British Empire in 1965.

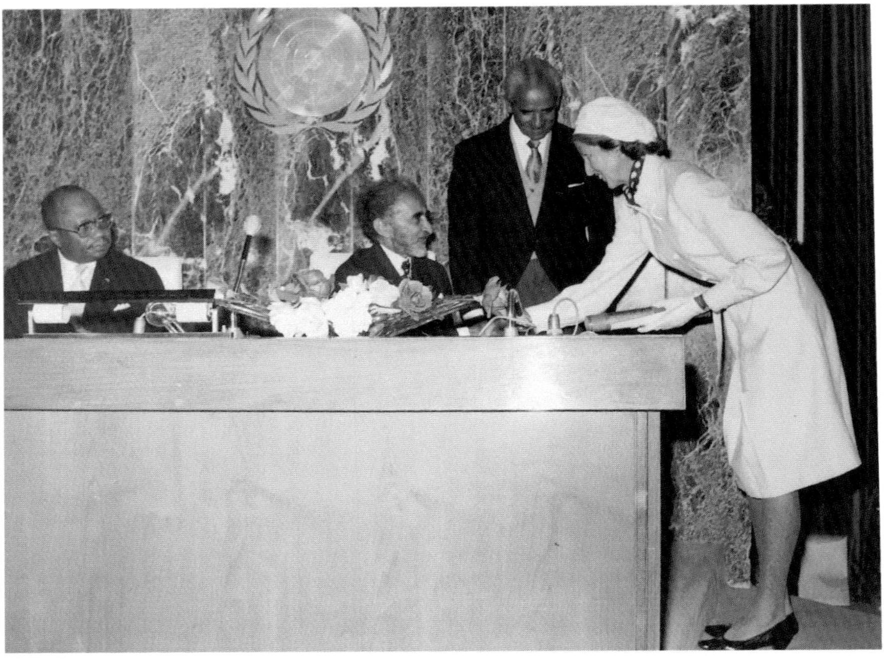

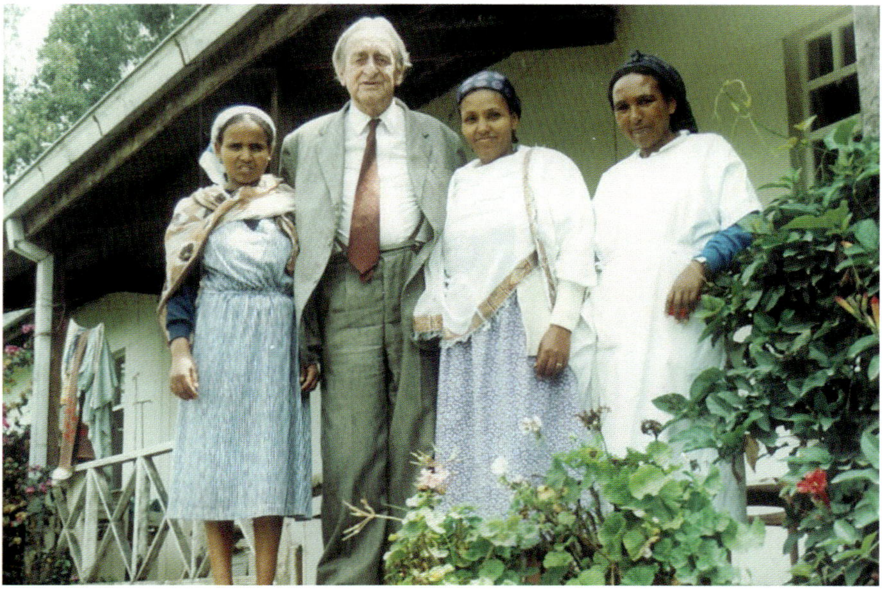

Reg with one of the cured fistula pilgrims (on his left), and Mamitu and Letekidane.

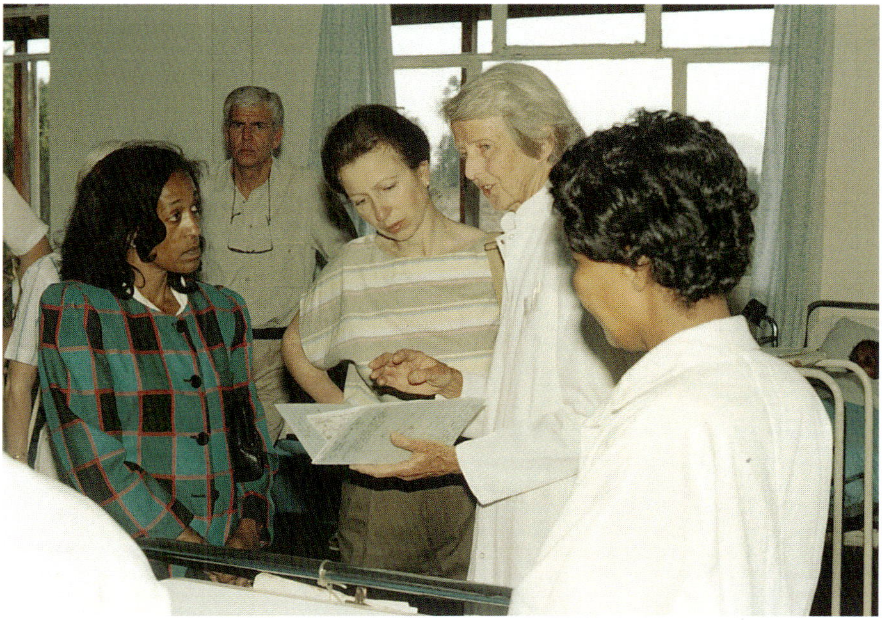

Princess Anne visiting the Addis Ababa Fistula Hospital.

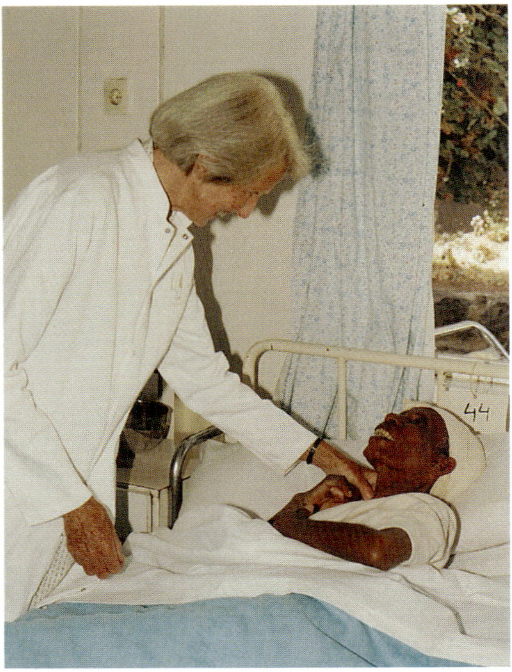

With a recuperating patient.

Operating with Mamitu as my assistant.

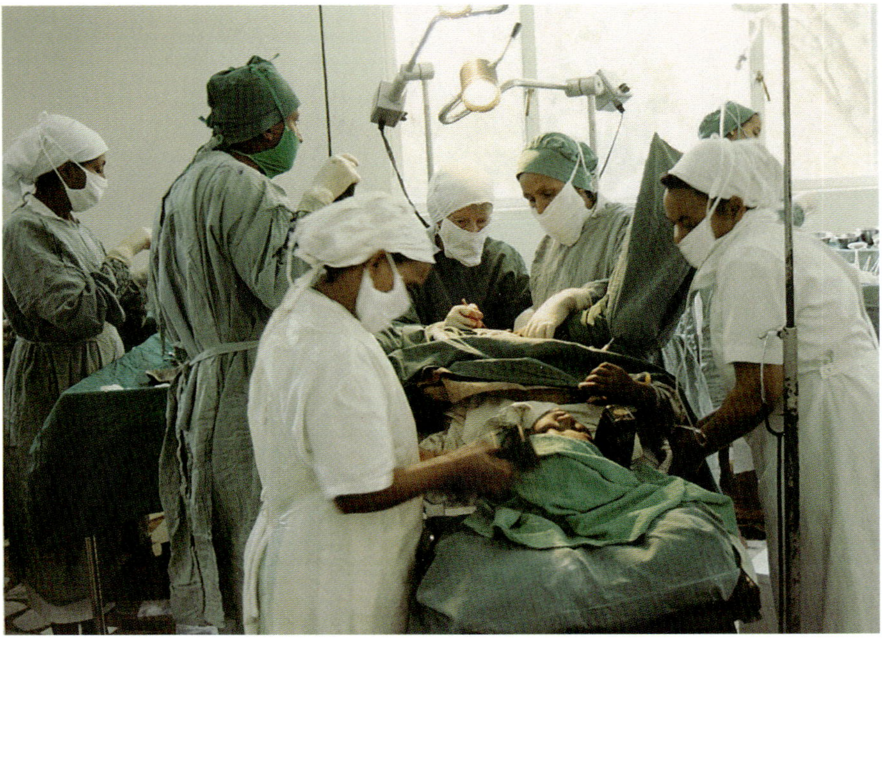

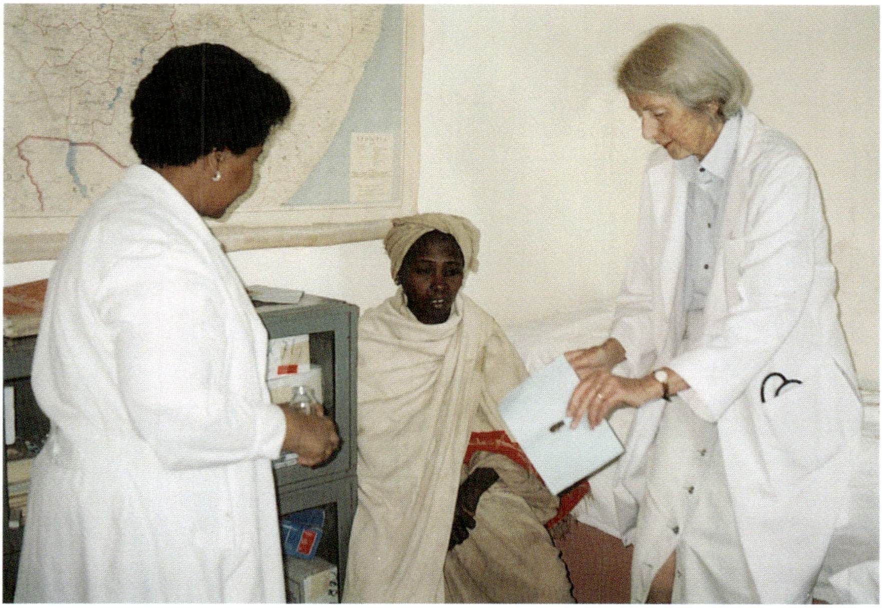

With the help of a sheet of paper with a hole torn in it, we explain to new patients what a fistula is and how we will repair it.

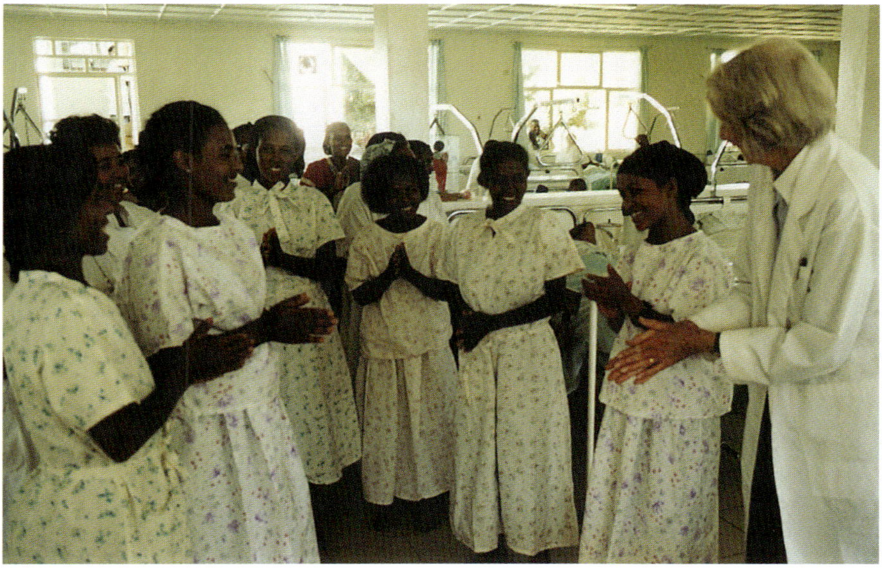

When the women are cured and ready to go home, we give them each a new dress and celebrate their recovery with a song and a dance of joy.

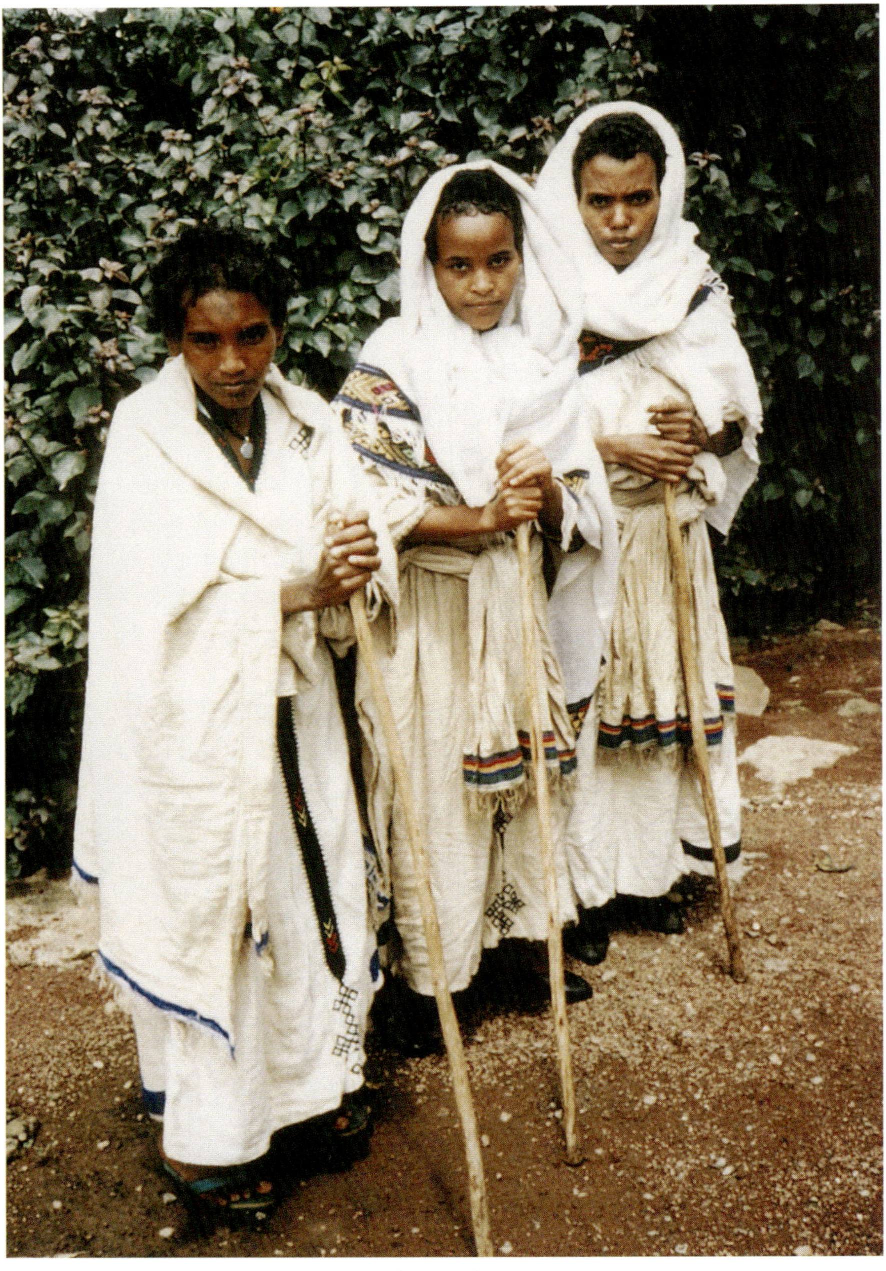

Three fistula pilgrims arriving at the hospital.

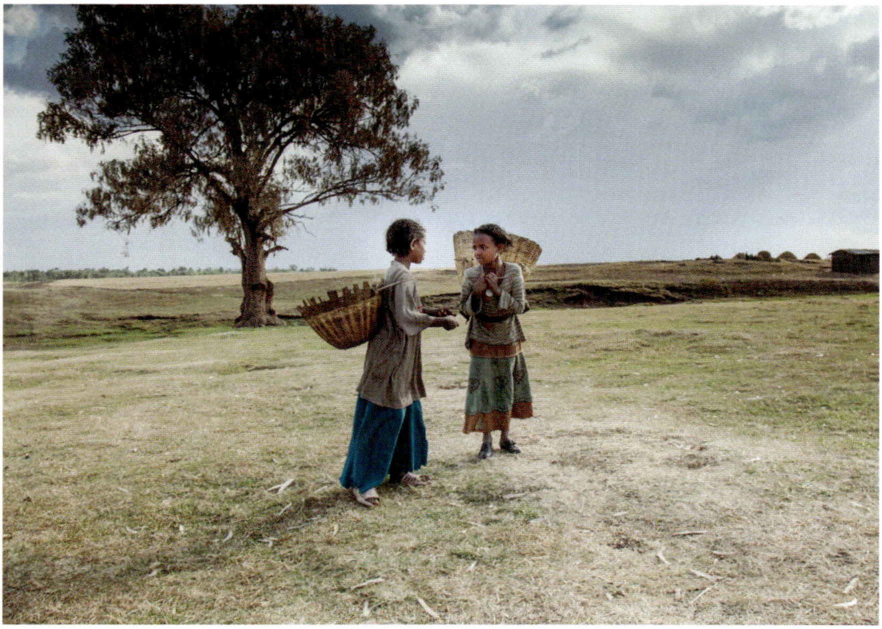

Joni Kabana

Ethiopia is a land of high plateaux, towering mountains and deep ravines. When I first arrived with Reg, I was reminded of the Australian bush.

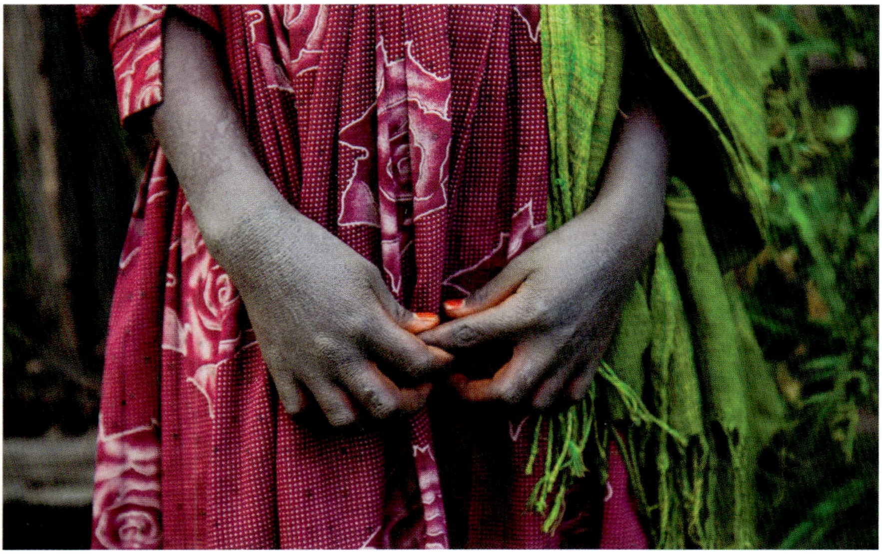

Joni Kabana

A young girl in rural Ethiopia often faces a life of physical hardships and a lack of education and medical services.

Joni Kabana

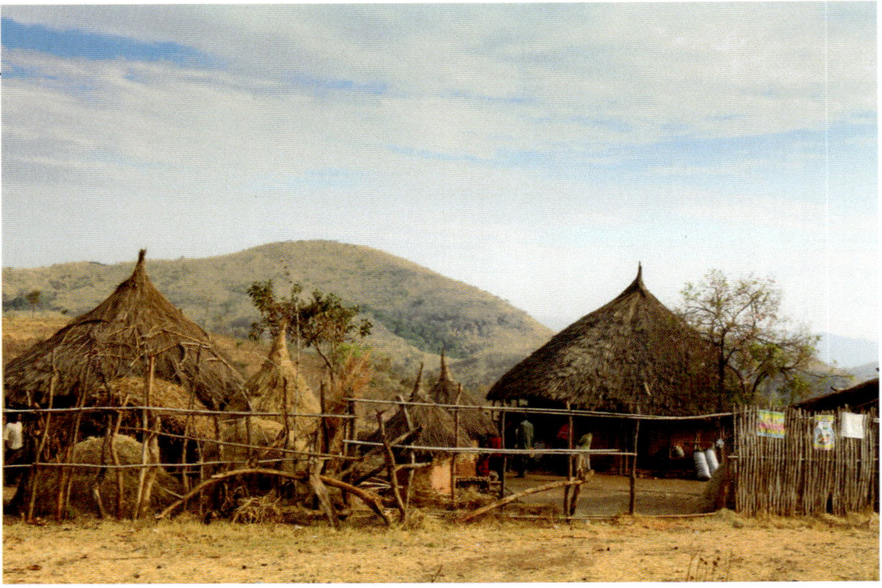

The beautiful landscapes carry a price of scarce roads and vast distances to medical facilities, leaving many women facing an obstructed labour in terrible trouble.

Joni Kabana

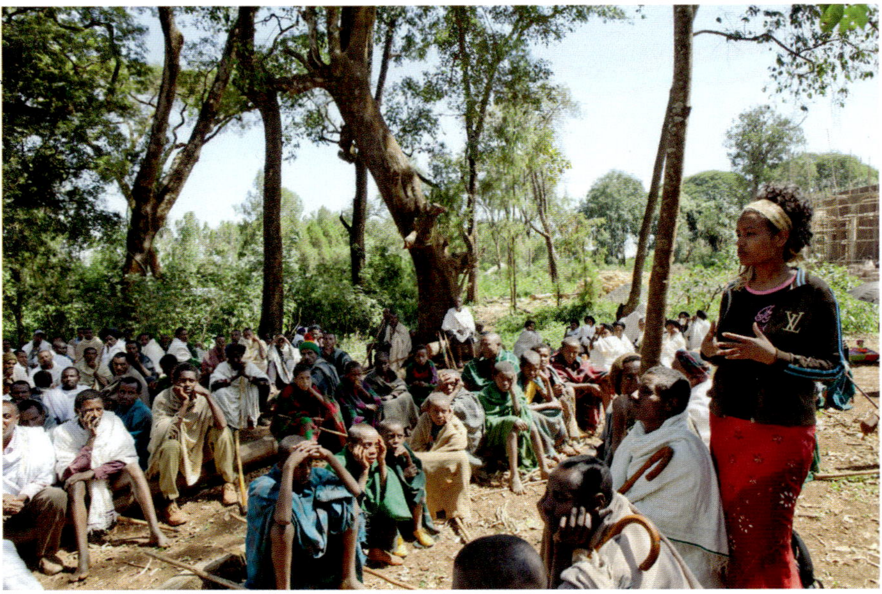

A young midwife teaches men about obstructed labour at a church service in rural Ethiopia.

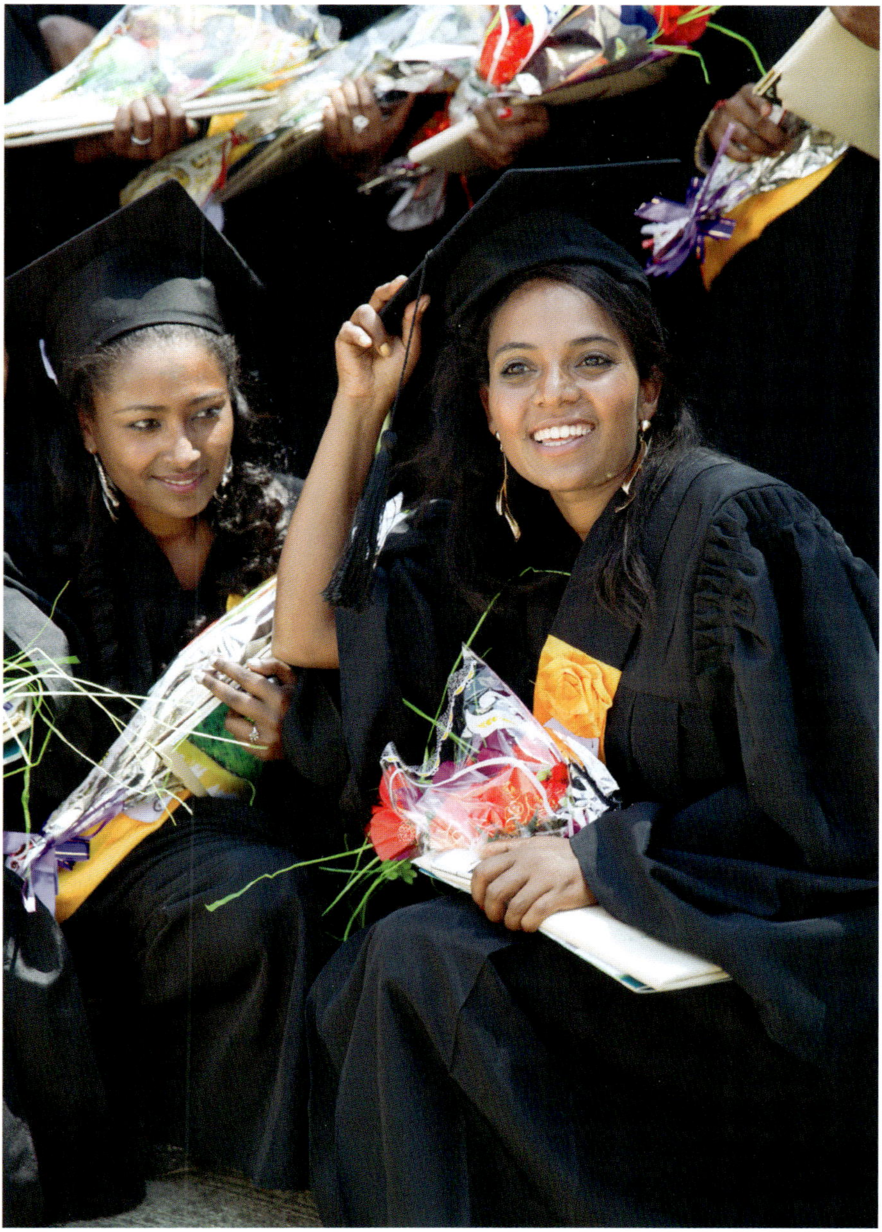

Joni Kabana

New midwives celebrate their graduation. Since the first graduates went into the field in 2010 there has been a marked reduction in fistula in those areas, with some midwives delivering up to 100 babies a month.

Joni Kabana

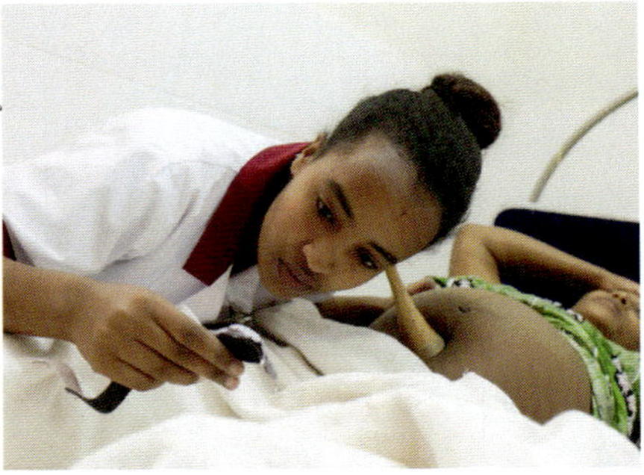

Joni Kabana

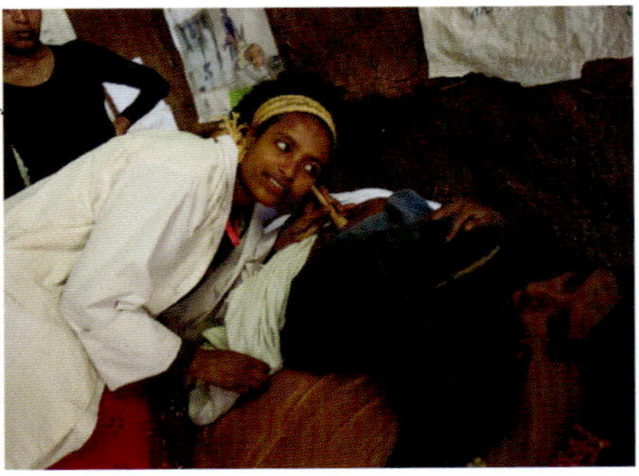

Joni Kabana

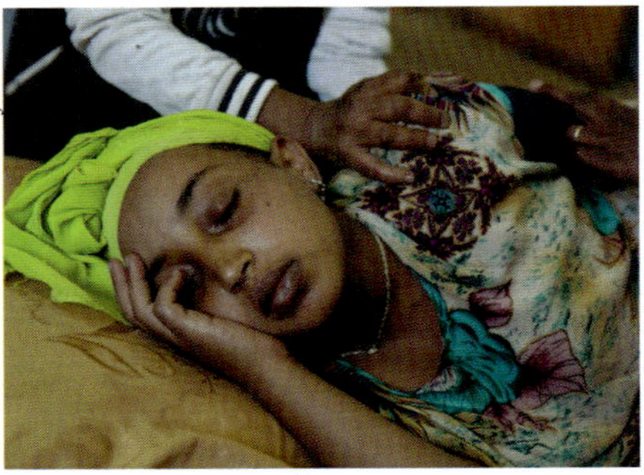

The midwives are sent to Atat, a Catholic hospital, to receive intense clinical training. They handle a number of abnormal obstetrics before being sent back to the area where they grew up.

Joni Kabana

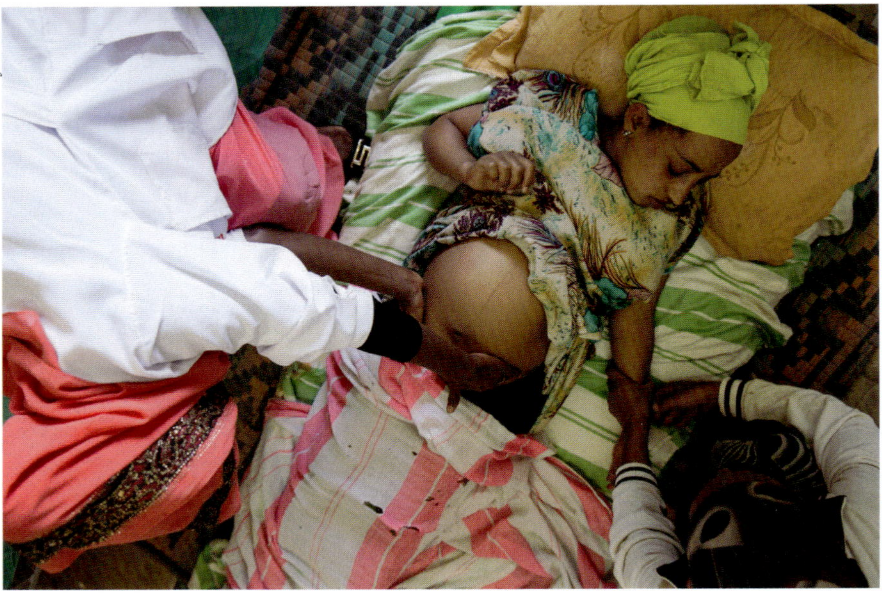

The need for qualified midwives is still critical. There are about 7,000 qualified midwives for a population of 100 million.

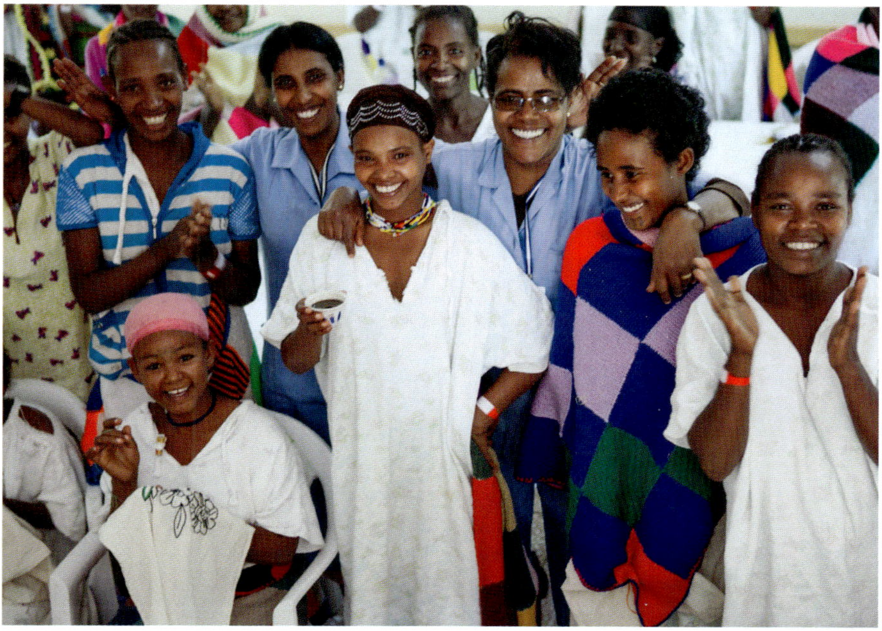

Joni Kabana

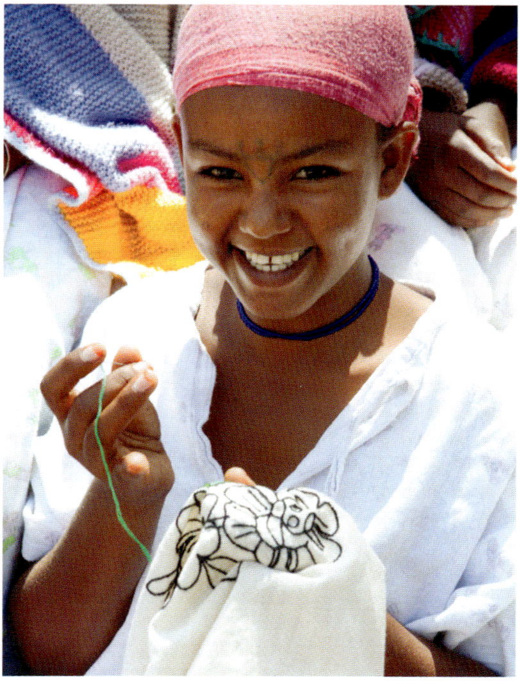

Joni Kabana

Recovering patients of the Hamlin Fistula Hospital celebrate their health by drinking coffee and stitching embroidery.

Joni Kabana

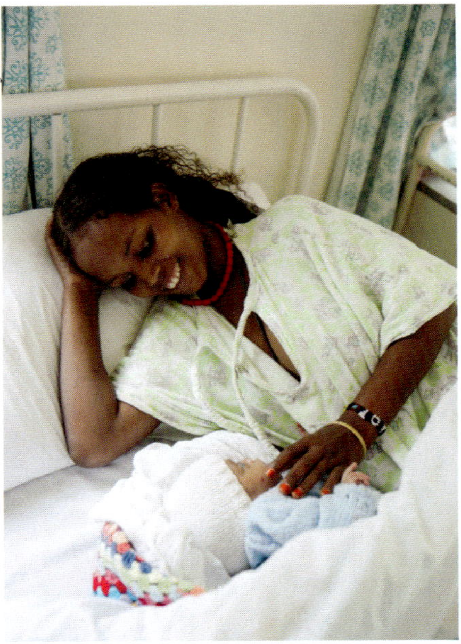

Joni Kabana

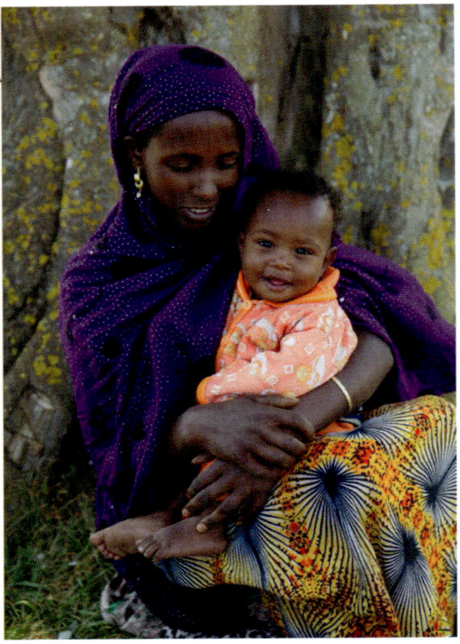

Joni Kabana

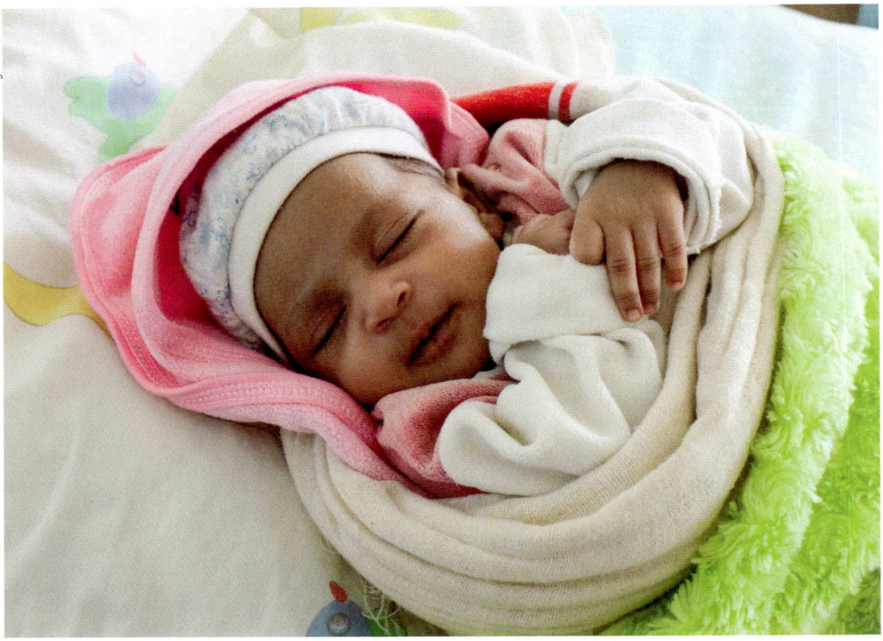

Since deployment in 2010, Hamlin midwives have seen a drastic reduction in the maternal mortality rate.

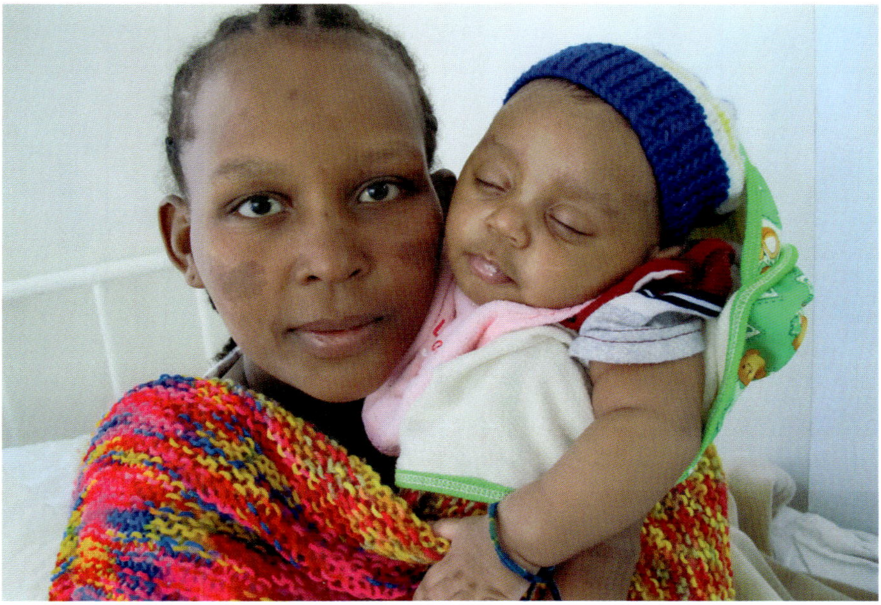

Joni Kabana

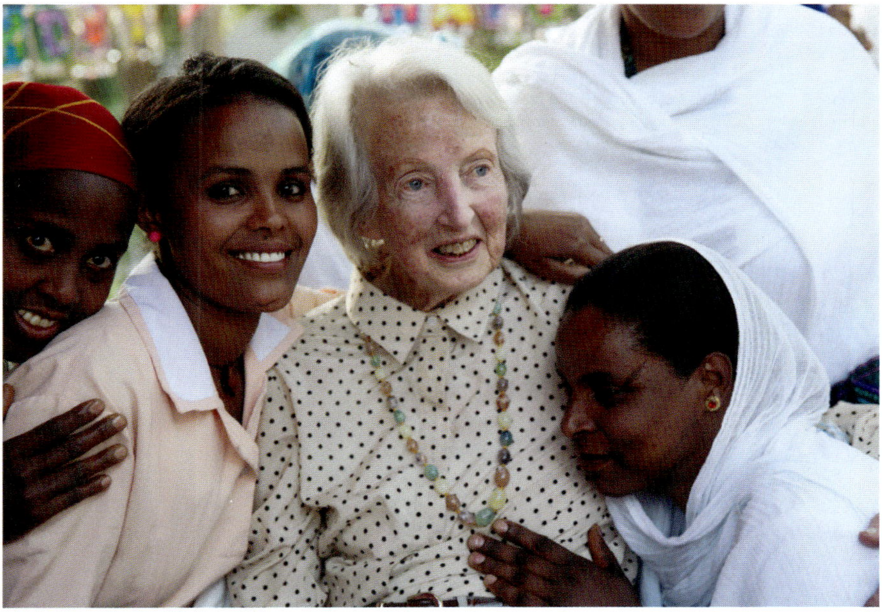

Joni Kabana

In their first five years, Hamlin midwives conducted 22,500 safe deliveries in the field. There are more midwives to be trained, more outlying areas to reach, but the progress is promising.

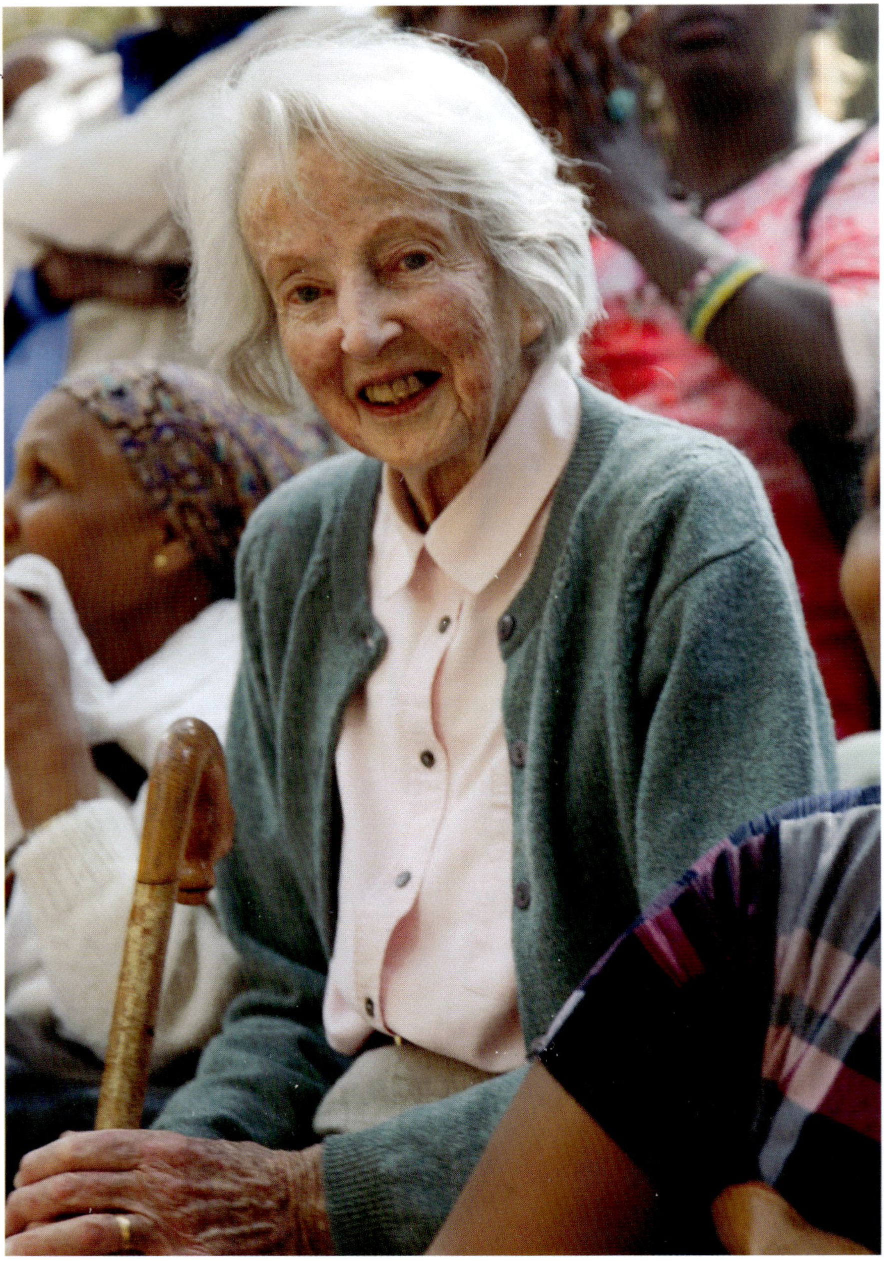

Joni Kabana

My original goal was to eradicate obstetric fistula in Ethiopia in my lifetime. I know that probably won't happen, but in ten to twenty years? It's a real possibility.

The idea of taking her to hospital before labour or in early labour is just not contemplated, and often after five or six days she is too exhausted to be moved. Maternal mortality in Ethiopia is high, almost the highest of any country in the world. But for every death, there are at least ten women who end up fistula victims, sometimes crippled as well through nerve damage from the long labour in a squatting position. These injured women often wish they had died – we know this from the stories we hear of suicides or attempted suicides.

Recently a law has been passed making the marriage of girls illegal before they are eighteen. This is certainly a step in the right direction, but such legislation is hard to enforce in a country where tradition is so strong. Even some of the priests, who have great influence over the lives of the peasants, encourage early marriage because they believe if a girl remains single for too long she will fall victim to temptation and be morally compromised. Among Muslims, too, early marriage is encouraged. We see constantly that the result of these policies for many women is a lifetime of misery and suffering.

The oldest fistula patient I have attended was 60. She came from a town called Keren, in Eritrea, and had been dripping urine constantly for 40 years. As usually happens she had been abandoned by her husband. For many years she did not know a cure was possible, then when she did hear about our fistula surgery, the war between Ethiopia and Eritrea made it impossible for her to travel. Hers was a simple case, which we cured in twelve days. When she was ready to go home she fell down and kissed my shoes, declaring, 'I love you next to God. To think I have been sitting alone, begging, for 40 years when I could have been cured long ago. I could have had babies, but instead my life has been wasted.'

Another older patient whom we cured had become a nun after being abandoned by her husband. I remember her well, as we took her catheter out on the day Princess Anne visited our hospital. She gave the Princess the most lovely smile, knowing she had been cured.

It may seem like an odd thing to say that these are the lucky ones. Often when women wait for many years scar tissue forms, making surgery difficult. Bladder stones are a complication when the free drainage of urine is prevented by the scar tissue. One very poor peasant arrived with a huge stone in her bladder and vagina. She told me that Dr Moriarty (an old doctor who was here many years ago) went down to a river and put this rock into her to try to stop the urine running out. She certainly had a vivid imagination!

Most stones can be removed fairly easily from the bladder, especially if the fistula is large, allowing the stone to be pulled out. I have seen huge ones where the whole birth passage is occluded, and once I had to deliver a stone with obstetric forceps, as if it was a baby's head. Imagine the suffering these women endure.

Chapter Fourteen

Early in 1965 Reg received an official letter from the British Embassy informing him that he had been nominated for an OBE (Officer of the British Empire) and asking him if he would accept. We were thrilled and surprised as we thought few people in the outside world were aware of the work we were doing in Ethiopia. Reg, naturally, accepted and a little later we were informed that the decoration would be conferred during a forthcoming state visit by Queen Elizabeth II.

Exciting days followed. The phone never stopped ringing as the news spread. We were pleased, too, to hear that the headmaster of the English School, Leslie Casbon, was also to receive an honour. Leslie was a friend of ours and his wife, Eleanor, was Mrs Sandford's eldest daughter.

The preparations in the embassy for the royal visit were full of drama. As the time drew closer, new furniture ordered from England had not arrived. New curtains were being hurriedly hung but the most nerve-racking thing was when new gold and white wallpaper was put on upside down. This was a disaster as the paper was patterned with Greek urns, specially chosen by the Ambassador's wife, a former Greek beauty queen. At the last minute the wallpaper had to be torn down and new paper flown out from England.

Another question that caused anxiety was that the Duke wanted thrones for the evening dinner party and the Queen did not. The Queen eventually had her way.

Reg, thinking he would need a morning suit, scoured the foreign community and tracked down a Belgian man roughly his size who had one. Then he was informed that a lounge suit should be all right, as there was to be a garden party after the medal ceremony and the Duke would be wearing ordinary clothes.

Fortunately I had a good dressmaker – an Armenian woman, who entered into the spirit of urgency and made a suitable dress and coat for the great day. I found the material in the market. It was not the silk I had hoped for, but a coarse-weave blue cotton, looking rather like linen and slightly shiny.

My next worry was how to curtsey without looking as if it was the first time I had done so. Fortunately, one morning after church the palace housekeeper, who had come out to prepare the way for the royal visit, obliged with a quick lesson on the church lawn.

The Queen was due to visit the hospital, so workmen were busily painting, cleaning and gardening to get the place looking spick and span. Our head of surgery, Dr Asrat, was rarely awed by foreigners. Being the Emperor's godson he moved in high society, and it took a lot to impress him. But he was more excited about the visit of the Queen than by any other head of state. He explained, 'She is not just like one of these jumped-up puppets from an African country, she is the Queen of England.'

On the day of the tour the Queen and the Duke arrived in an open car with a great cavalcade of officials. The senior staff of the hospital were lined up in the hallway in front of Princess Tsehai's beautiful marble statue, so I had an opportunity to practise my curtsey. Reg had to conduct the Queen around our department. During the visit to the nursery she paused beside our two recently acquired incubators and made a remark about the premature babies. After this Reg felt able to speak, as we had been told not to initiate a conversation but to wait for the Queen to speak first.

'Premature babies don't do very well here, Ma'am. We think it might be due to the altitude and the oxygen-lack.'

'Poor darlings,' responded the Queen. 'I'm feeling the altitude myself.'

Next day we gathered at the embassy in the main drawing room. The aide-de-camp came in and told us where to sit and what to do. He pinned a little hook on Reg's lapel and on Leslie's, to make it easier for the Queen when she presented the medals.

We sat quietly for about twenty minutes; the medals were brought in on a velvet cushion and placed on a table. The Queen and the Duke entered with the British Ambassador, and we all rose and bowed.

When Reg went up the Queen said, 'I did enjoy my visit yesterday. Thank you for taking me around.' She was sweet and gracious. We all noticed her lovely blue eyes.

As we left the room afterwards we all had to shake hands with Prince Philip. Richard was wearing a King's School tie, which I had bought in Sydney. After shaking Richard's hand the Duke enquired, 'What school?' pointing to the tie.

Richard replied, 'I don't know. Mummy just liked the colours.'

Richard again helped to ruin my reputation when he was reprimanded by the British Ambassador for trying to photograph the Queen coming out of the marquee at the garden party. He was kneeling near the entrance with his camera poised when suddenly he felt somebody seize him by the scruff of the neck.

'Richard Hamlin, I would have thought better of you.'

'My mother told me to do it,' was Richard's quick reply.

I had vainly hoped that Richard could secrete himself somewhere and not be seen, as photography was strictly forbidden!

Reg was terrifically bucked by receiving this honour. For the next few weeks he received letters of congratulations from all over the world – some from people he had not heard from for decades. In his replies he took care to say that the medal was for both of us, not just for him. This was untrue of course, but typical of him.

We had hardly recovered from the Queen's visit when we were invited to Dr Asrat's wedding. Dr Asrat had been sent to Edinburgh to train as a doctor, as at that time there was no medical school in Addis Ababa. After training in surgery he got his FRCS (Fellow of the Royal College of Surgeons). He became the first surgeon in Ethiopia and, indeed, a highly accomplished one.

His bride, Albastros, was from Tigray – a charming woman of great beauty. Her father was killed by the Italians before she was born, and the Emperor had made her his ward. With their education and social connections, they belonged to the most privileged class of Ethiopian society.

The wedding began with a church service at 5 am. This went on until eight, when the guests went off for breakfast. After that the bride and groom retired to their own houses until lunch. The bride gave a lunch party, then at four o'clock in the afternoon there was a reception at one of the big hotels. At about six the party moved to a huge marquee, which had been erected in the hospital grounds outside Dr Asrat's house, and celebrated until late. This exhausting day was typical of the weddings we attended in those days.

We did not attend all of the Asrats' receptions but were at the evening one, held in the marquee. A glittering assemblage from Ethiopian high society was there – women, elegant in their Ethiopian dress, men in either dark suits or the startling white national dress of a tunic over rather tight trousers. Many of them carried a horse-tail fly whisk and were attended by ancient retainers. Some of these appeared to be in their nineties. They were accepted as equals on this special occasion.

The food was laid out on tables, so much and of such variety that it was bewildering to behold. When we were seated with our already overflowing plates, sides of raw oxen were carried around on poles held by two servants at each end. They stood beside each table while these elegant, well-dressed men and women would inspect the meat, choose the portion they wanted and a man would slice it off onto their plates with a sharp knife. Then, after being dipped into various hot spices, the meat would be eaten raw. It was an astonishing sight to see Dr Asrat eating a piece of sirloin the size of his plate.

He told us later that when he was a student in Edinburgh, he and his Ethiopian friends would sometimes get a craving for raw meat but were careful to conceal any leftover scraps in case they alarmed their landlady.

After dinner a band of drummers assembled with a stunning array of percussion instruments. As they beat out typical Ethiopian rhythms, the guests got to their feet and began to dance. They didn't dance with each other but stayed in one spot, shaking their shoulders and clapping their hands in time to the music. The old ladies threw themselves into it with as much enthusiasm as anyone. We could not hope to perform like they did, but Reg joined in with the band, beating a huge drum, to the great delight of the musicians.

At about eleven o'clock I had to leave because the best man's sister had been admitted to the hospital in labour. The Ethiopians do not usually have a honeymoon, but stay in their home receiving visitors and going to banquets for about a week. As Dr Asrat lived near us, we saw a constant stream of cars coming and going, bearing gifts of flowers and food. I took some flowers and a plate of homemade Anzac biscuits one day, but there was so much food that my small contribution seemed superfluous.

These lavish wedding feasts made one realise the enormous gap between the rich and the poor.

Richard was about twelve at this time. One day he came to Reg and said, 'Daddy, before you die will you show me the secret of the fistula operations?' Reg was touched and secretly thrilled at the thought that our son might carry on the work we had begun. Not that we were thinking much about his future career at that age. If anything, we were more concerned about him growing up too fast.

When he was thirteen he went to the birthday party of a friend the same age. He came home at about ten o'clock, quite disgusted as there had been nothing but dancing and he had sat in a corner all evening. 'That is one thing I will never do,' he declared.

I had thought it was going to be the sort of children's party where games and charades were played. I felt disturbed that children were being pushed into adult life too quickly. This, even in the mid-sixties, was perhaps old fashioned, but it was something I felt strongly about. Childhood was too precious to be hurried through in the pursuit of adulthood.

Social events, though enjoyable, seemed incidental compared with our busy working life at the hospital. This was full of unexpected excitement and satisfaction, as in our field of obstetrics emergencies are sudden and dramatic. I vividly remember one evening, lying on my bed after a particularly hard day. Two hours earlier I had seen a patient in early labour. Everything had seemed to be progressing normally and I thought she would probably have the baby the next day.

She was not even in the labour ward at this stage, but suddenly I had a feeling that I should go to the hospital and check her. I went up to the ward and found the sister in a state of consternation. She said, 'I'm so glad you've come. I'm worried about the baby's heart.'

I listened and had a feeling of dread. I could not hear the heartbeat at all. It was obvious that the patient was in strong labour, so I quickly gave her oxygen and an ether anaesthetic to stop the contractions. As she stopped pushing the heartbeat slowly came back. I then had a chance to examine her and found that the cord had prolapsed, so was being pushed on with every contraction. After a lot of anxiety we delivered a beautiful, live baby. If I had arrived a few minutes later, the baby would have died. I felt quite certain that I was guided to go at that time.

Chapter Fifteen

After we had been in Ethiopia for a few years we no longer thought about returning to Australia to live. We loved going back every three years and seeing family and friends but we felt that Ethiopia was home. And we could not just turn our backs on the fistula pilgrims who continued to arrive at the hospital every day in increasing numbers.

Richard was growing up rapidly, and we had to make some decisions about his future. The English School in Addis Ababa only took students as far as O-levels. For his A-levels he would have to either go abroad or have a tutor. A private tutor was really beyond our means. The alternative was to send him to boarding school, in either Australia or England. We loved the Australian way of life, but England was closer so it would be easier for him to fly home for holidays. After a lot of soul-searching, we enrolled him at Epsom College in Surrey.

Leaving Ethiopia was a terrific wrench for Richard. At the age of fifteen, he exchanged space and warmth and freedom for the chilly dormitories and rigid discipline of a traditional English boarding school. As an only child he was very attached to us, almost to the exclusion of other relationships. Leaving his parents and the land he thought of as home was like going into exile.

In January 1967 we flew to England and took Richard down

to his new school. He looked almost grown up in his uniform of long trousers and dark grey jacket, wearing a house tie of black with a narrow, green diagonal stripe. His mind must have been seething with emotions but the only worry he admitted to was that the stiff collar and studs would give him trouble.

We drove up a long drive flanked by ancient beech trees and lugged out the trunk containing his things. His dormitory was rather spartan. He was sharing it with about ten boys, including an Italian, an Indian, a Ghanian and a Chinese, so he didn't feel too foreign. He was rather quiet and a little tearful as he kissed us goodbye and watched us drive away, but I am sure we were the ones more affected.

I was worried about him in England. London seemed a very different place since we were last there. The youth in the streets appalled me – the short, short skirts, men with long hair and untidy, awful clothes. Some were even wearing obscene badges – I would not wish to repeat what was on them.

In Piccadilly there were the flower people and others whom, in my concern, I thought must have been on drugs. All this depressed me and made me worried about leaving Richard in England. Secretly I wished he had been in Australia, which to me then seemed to be a much more wholesome place, possibly because I remembered it as it had been in my youth.

On a trip to Birmingham our view of things improved. We met old friends, did some fundraising and found generous and wonderful people. They were open, happy and approachable, and I have retained this love for the people of northern England and Scotland to this day.

Back in Addis Ababa the house seemed silent and empty without a noisy teenager. We missed him greatly. Even Rangi felt the change and would often pad into Richard's room wondering where he was.

In his first letter home he wrote:

> The boys in my house and in my class are all nice and there is no dirty talk or anything like that, even though a

> few of the more bumptious ones use words like 'bloody' etc. I am afraid I was a rather weak-willed Christian for the first few days and did not have the guts to get down on my knees at night and pray, but I remembered all you told me and what God thinks of me and have prayed on my knees every night for the last week.
>
> A few of the boys laughed at me when I was praying but they stopped when they realised that they were not going to shake me. In fact two of the boys, Thomson and Higginson, said the night before last, they would also pray, and last night Higginson did. I think Thompson forgot. So it shows that persistence and faith can accomplish great things.

I was very proud of Richard when I read that. In the letters which followed I could sense his homesickness, but as time passed he seemed to be settling in.

His exeats, or leave days, were usually spent with Reg's sister, Iris, who was one of the chief pathologists at the Royal Marsden cancer hospital in London, or with an old aunt, Auntie Mick, both of whom thoroughly spoiled him. The exeats he seemed to enjoy most were with a war-time naval friend of ours who had been stationed in Sydney in charge of catering for the whole British Pacific Fleet. Perhaps this was why meals with John Cook and his wife at their home seemed to feature prominently in Richard's letters to us. They lived fairly near Epsom so they frequently took the boy out and helped him through his first days as a boarder.

Meanwhile, work at the hospital went on at its usual hectic pace. Our work with the fistula patients did not mean that we could forget our other duties. We continued to see almost daily the catastrophic results of neglected childbirth.

On one awful day a woman arrived who had been in labour for eight days. The baby's head was out and obviously decaying. We delivered this dead child but, as so often happens, the mother was suffering from the worst type of septicemia, gas gangrene, and only lived a few hours after delivery.

That same day at midnight another woman was admitted with, again, a dead baby inside her in a late stage of decomposition. The smell was so overpowering that one nurse fainted as we pulled this baby out, and a medical student hurriedly left to be sick. The only one who seemed unaffected was the mother. We were amazed at her stamina. I could not imagine a European woman being so brave. She did well and next day was out of bed.

There was another especially interesting case from a medical point of view – one which, fortunately, ended successfully, in that the mother survived.

This patient arrived one morning in a shocked and collapsed condition. The baby's head had been born but the mother's abdomen was hugely distended and extremely tender.

Fortunately, we did not attempt to deliver the baby as we suspected that the woman's uterus was ruptured. We built her up with intravenous fluids and cross-matched blood for her. When she was fit enough, and her blood pressure at last recordable, we took her to the theatre.

I opened the abdomen, but it was impossible for Reg to deliver the baby. The whole abdomen seemed full of arms and bodies and another head. We realised that this was a case of Siamese twins, joined down the front.

This unfortunate woman had been in labour for days, her uterus had ruptured, and the two babies were in her abdominal cavity, but with one head delivered, outside.

As the babies had been dead for some time, it was a simple matter to remove the head that was outside and then easily extract the bodies through an abdominal incision. We then, of course, had to remove a hopelessly damaged uterus.

The medical students were excited, so the theatre was full of interested spectators. Later, one of the students sewed the baby's head on again, and we kept these Siamese twins for the medical museum.

Although the poor mother was desperately ill with severe peritonitis for many days, she survived. For this I was especially thankful, for as she had other children at home to care for.

Another patient who was a medical rarity arrived, declaring she had been pregnant for 18 months! At first we thought that she had a large ovarian tumour, but an X-ray confirmed her own diagnosis. Her pregnancy had developed out of the uterus to quite a late stage of gestation, being adherent to the bowel. The baby had finally died and become calcified.

When we operated we discovered an ovarian cyst as well, so both patient and doctor were correct in their diagnosis. She did well after the operation.

About this time, too, a most distressing case arrived one evening. The following story was related by her relatives. The girl was in labour with her first baby in her *tukul* in the countryside. The *tukul* caught fire, and so she was taken outside and put under a tree while her relatives extinguished the fire. When they heard her screaming they thought it was due to labour pains, but she was being attacked by a hyena just as she was giving birth. Her thigh and buttocks were badly mauled, and the baby was eaten.

When she arrived at the hospital she looked like the victim of a shark attack. We felt sure the surgeons would have to amputate her leg, but they managed to save it, and after months of skin grafts she went home walking normally.

On the days when we did not have operation lists we had outpatients' clinics. These were chaotic in the extreme, not through lack of organisation but because of the large numbers pressing to be seen. Working in separate cubicles, Reg and I had helpers to bring the patients down and prepare them for examination.

Sometimes I would hear Reg shouting next door, *'Tolu, tolu,'* which in Amharic means, 'Hurry, hurry,' as a patient leisurely clambered onto the couch. At least they were unencumbered by many clothes – usually one garment only and seldom any underclothes – so this saved time.

Often in the midst of this there would be the drama of a delivery on a trolley, when the patient arrived so late there was no time to get to the labour ward, or an ex-sanguinated woman having a miscarriage on the bench outside. And of course there were the ever-present fistula patients. Despite being desperate for help, they were ashamed to mix with the other patients, so hid away until the very end of the clinic. Soon word got around that if they could only catch hold of Reg as he emerged from his examining cubicle he would take pity on them, which he never failed to do.

On most clinic days we seldom had time for lunch. I often kept going on bars of chocolate.

One afternoon a week we had what was known as our private clinic. This was not because the patients were our particular private ones but because they paid for a private bed in the hospital if they were to be admitted. This was markedly different from the hectic morning clinics. Patients had the privilege of a pillow on the couch and even a clean drawsheet. They were given more privacy and examinations, with explanations, took longer.

I was particularly popular with some of the well-off Ethiopian women, as they often preferred a woman doctor. Some were quite shy, especially Muslims. At these clinics we also saw many expatriate patients – missionaries, nuns, diplomats' wives of many nationalities. We were expected to be present for their deliveries and to do their operations. Consequently we would be invited for the christenings of the babies we delivered and were sometimes given lavish presents by the wealthy ones – gold jewellery in the case of the palace women. Now, after so many years in Ethiopia, I often meet people in high positions who tell me they were delivered by me!

Ethiopians are naturally a most generous people. Even the poorest will bring an offering of a few eggs or a basket they have woven. Sometimes they bring a live chicken. I was sitting at the office desk one day when a patient presented me with one of the small local hens. We planned to eat it, but that night it laid an egg and its execution was delayed. Not for long, however, because one of our dogs finished it off soon after.

Operating days were hectic, with long lists interrupted by

emergencies. One special day I will never forget started at 5 am with an emergency caesarean section. The normal list got under way at 8.30 with a big cancer operation – a Wertheim's hysterectomy – followed by three fistula repairs and several curettes.

At 9 pm, when we were tired and looking forward to a rest, a woman with a ruptured uterus arrived. We took her straight to theatre. All went well, and I was just closing the abdomen when the anaesthetist announced that the patient was dead. She had suffered a cardiac arrest and her heart had stopped beating.

Reg and I waited with sinking hearts as the anaesthetist worked to revive her, keeping her oxygenated and pumping the heart. The minutes ticked by, seeming like an eternity, but gradually her circulation returned to normal. Our sense of relief was so great that all feelings of exhaustion were quite forgotten.

These dramas were vivid highlights in our working lives. Our family life with Richard, on the other hand, was confined to the impersonal medium of letters. In the middle of the school year he wrote saying he hated school and hated England and he wanted to come home *now*! We could only write back and tell him to keep his chin up and stick it out, that the holidays were not far away.

The separation was also hard for us. It was one of the prices we paid for making our lives in Ethiopia. We missed Richard so much, and the end of the year seemed a long way off. When December eventually arrived we began to get excited at the thought of once again sitting together in front of the log fire playing Richard's favourite music, the *Pirates of Penzance*, on the gramophone and eating his favourite steak and kidney pie. He wrote:

> I am counting down the days to the GLORIOUS RETURN TO PARADISE! Oh what a simply super marvellous day it will be when I arrive home at the land I have lived in for more than half my life, the land that is woven into me and can never be separated from me.

> I shall be mad with delight. I shall see you, the dogs, the servants, my friends, the countryside, the people, the horses, the compound and our dear old house.

On the big day we took Rangi with us to the airport.Back then we could watch from the balcony the plane arriving, and the passengers disembarking and walking across the tarmac to the terminal. Rangi seemed to sense the excitement, and as Richard walked below we had to keep a firm hold or he would have leaped over the railings in his joy – especially after Richard whistled to him.

Inside the terminal there was a gallery from where we could throw down the $10 note for the visa which Richard needed to visit us. This was such a simple procedure in those days. The note would flutter down, and Richard would catch it, Rangi all the time tense, with his nose through the bars and his eyes fixed on his playmate.

This became the routine for all Richard's holidays, and Rangi, I am sure, knew what was happening long before we reached the airport.

After two less than happy years at boarding-school Richard seemed to settle in and started to enjoy it, being elected a prefect in his last year. He had decided he wanted to be a doctor. During his final year he began looking around for medical schools and applied to several, including the one attached to St Bartholomew's Hospital in London.

When he came home after passing his A-levels, it was a great occasion. He was welcomed with tears and hugs, especially from Yeshi, who always wept whenever Richard left or came home. He spent the following days riding, going on camping trips with old friends and waiting for the mails with more than usual interest. One day he was informed there was a cable for him at the telegraph office. With thumping hearts Richard and Reg drove there and opened it up. He had been accepted into

St Bartholomew's. Richard went wild with joy, and he and Reg did a dance round the office, to the amusement of the staff and customers. Next day he went out with a blood bank team collecting blood and actually did some vein punctures. He said he already felt like a doctor.

From our first tentative operations, the fistula surgery had grown so much that the patients were taking up a great deal of our time. They were stretching the hospital's resources to breaking point, and it was becoming obvious that something would have to be done. We thought that fistula patients needed a hospital of their own, but as the government had no interest in providing one, the only way it was going to happen would be if we built it ourselves.

Reg and I mentioned this to the Emperor's daughter, Princess Tenagnework. She was so enthusiastic about the idea that she promised us a grant of land. We were grateful, of course, but were concerned that the land she wished to give us was a long way from the city and we knew the patients would not find their way there easily.

Towards the end of 1968 we were due for another long leave in Australia and New Zealand. This time we decided to combine the trip with some serious fundraising. In New Zealand we were invited to speak to an organisation called CORSO – the Council for Organisation of Relief Services Overseas.

We arrived in Wellington from Auckland on a cold, wet and windy day and found our way to an address in a run-down, semi-industrial part of town. Our hearts fell when we saw the place where we were to speak. We had expected something like a community centre or a town hall. This was more like an old warehouse.

Entering a cold, bare room, we made our way over to a corner where some elderly women were cutting up sandwiches. We introduced ourselves, but no one seemed all that interested. Reg said, 'I don't think I can be bothered showing my slides and speaking here, these old people won't be able to do any good for us.'

'We've come all this way,' I said. 'Just pretend the room is full of young enthusiastic people. Show the slides and talk as you always do.'

A few more people wandered in, and we all sat down at a table on a slightly raised platform. They listened at first with mild interest and then with rapt attention as Reg spoke movingly and showed the slides. I have seen this happen many times with Reg. His stories were so imbued with his own passion that listeners could not help being swept along with him. As he described the plight of the fistula pilgrims I looked around and saw tears in many people's eyes. After he had finished there was silence and then they broke into loud applause. When it died down, Reg called for questions. The head of CORSO asked him about our work and listened with interest as Reg told him about our idea for a special hospital just for fistula surgery.

'How much money do you need?'

We had not given any thought to this, so out of the blue Reg said, 'Ten thousand pounds.'

He said, 'You can have it tomorrow.'

Imagine our amazement and delight. The money, apparently, was already in hand from a special tenth anniversary appeal.

After the holiday we returned to Addis Ababa and plunged straight back into work. The promise of money gave us an added impetus to build our own hospital, but we felt that we would have to find a better place for it than the land we had been given.

One day when I was out riding I saw some beautiful land beside a river right on the edge of the city. It would be a perfect spot for a little hospital. Excitedly, we made some enquiries and discovered that it was owned by the Police College. Our excitement was soon dampened, however, when they told us it was not for sale.

A few days later I was out riding again and came across a piece of bare hillside running down to a disused canal with an old mill on the river below. At the top of the hill was an Italian-owned shirt factory. Reg went to see the manager, who told him that the land belonged to the Armenian community.

Armenians had come to Ethiopia at the beginning of the twentieth century when the Emperor Menelik granted them asylum from persecution by the Turks. They were a large community, heavily involved in the commercial life of Addis Ababa, and we knew many of them.

Sale of the land needed to be approved by a council of elders from the Armenian community. They agreed to discuss the idea, and so we were called to a meeting in a hall at the back of the Armenian church, perched on a hill near the centre of the city.

There were about ten of them, patriarchal-looking men in their sixties and seventies, some with long beards. Polite and grave, they were the fathers of their community. We knew most of them by sight and had met some in the various shops and businesses they owned. We had also treated some of their wives.

We waited while the elders deliberated in an inner room. After a short time they emerged and said that they were prepared to sell to us. We negotiated a price and at the same time asked for a smaller piece of steeper, rockier land nearer the river, which we would personally pay for as we did not want any building between the planned hospital and the river. This we were able to buy at a cheaper price and we eventually built our home on it.

We both saw God's clear guidance over this land for on the very day I discovered it when out riding and Reg determined it was available, we received a large donation from a foundation in America. Amazingly, this was exactly the amount the Armenians wanted.

But there was more to do. As foreigners we needed permission from the Emperor to own land in Ethiopia, so Reg had the rather difficult task of composing a letter to His Majesty. He wrote and rewrote it many times before he was satisfied with the wording.

7th November, 1970

His Imperial Majesty,
The Emperor Haile Selassie I

Your Majesty,

The writers, having long had close to their hearts a project to build (and to equip and to provide all the annual expenses of) a small free hospital of 40 beds for poor women suffering from the injury of childbearing known as the vaginal fistula, and having recently received from the people of the Dominion of New Zealand a gift of sufficient money for the building costs of such a hospital, now beg Your Majesty to grant us permission to purchase from the Armenian community for the Hospital site a block of land measuring 6000 square metres in the name of Hamlin Fistula Welfare and Research Trust, and also to purchase in our personal names a further 3000 square metres of land adjacent to the proposed fistula hospital's site, from the same community for our own residence from which we may direct the hospital and supervise the care of its patients.

Most graciously Her Highness Princess Tenagnework has consented to be the Fistula Hospital's Imperial Patron. The name of the Hospital would be The Addis Ababa Fistula Hospital, and the Trustees of the Hamlin Fistula Welfare and Research Trust are Woizero Mary Tedesse, Assistant Minister in the Ministry of Education, Mr. Olin Scott, Solicitor of Addis Ababa, and ourselves the writers.

To Your Majesty's Ministry of Public Health a written undertaking has been given by the writers that no financial responsibility arising from this project will fall upon Your Majesty's Ministry, and that every expense whatsoever will be the responsibility of our Fistula Welfare and Research Trust which has been duly established under Articles 516–544 of the Ethiopian Civil Code.

With humble duty we sign ourselves Your Majesty's most obedient and loyal servants,

Reginald H. J. Hamlin
E. Catherine Hamlin

While we waited for an answer we heard that Dr Asrat, now promoted to medical director, was using his influence with the palace to try to prevent this permission. We were amazed and disturbed, and could not understand his attitude. He argued that *ferenjis* should not be doing this work, and it should be done by an Ethiopian. Reg told him that he would be glad if an Ethiopian would do it, but there was nobody prepared to. I feel that as well as his underlying suspicion of foreigners, he was jealous of Reg's growing popularity and influence.

The Emperor, however, was not swayed by Dr Asrat's arguments, and we received a letter from the palace telling us we had permission to buy the land, but also saying we would need the permission of the Ministry of Health to run a hospital.

We now had the further delicate problem of breaking the news to Princess Tenagnework. As diplomatically as possible, we explained matters to her and said we would like to keep her plot as an annexe for the future. She quite understood and readily agreed.

Reg's excitement and enthusiasm were infectious. Soon we were both discussing plans and pooling ideas. We never thought of employing an architect as we were so sure of being able to design exactly the hospital we wanted.

Reg spent long evenings at the kitchen table with pad and pencil, drawing every detail. The main ward would be long and wide – the Florence Nightingale type which had impressed us at Crown Street, where all the patients could be seen from the sister's station at one end. It would hold 40 beds, twenty on either side of a low partition, with columns to hold up the centre of the roof.

At the far end was to be the theatre block, which would house a theatre big enough for three operating tables, a sterilising room, changing rooms, storerooms, a doctor's office where we could write up the operation notes and relax between operations, and an area for setting up the instrument trolleys.

We designed this section to be in full view of the ward, separated by sliding doors, so that the patients would be able to see people going in for surgery and coming out again, unharmed.

An important addition was a wide, covered verandah running the whole length of the ward. How thankful we have been for this over the years. We distribute meals from there and the patients love to sit in its shelter.

We also drew plans for a simple rectangular building to house the kitchen and laundry, and a small home where some of the staff would live. We wanted this to look as if it really belonged, getting the idea from the original British Embassy buildings which had been built as a collection of connected *tukuls*. We designed two round houses with thatched roofs, joined by a short corridor.

Obtaining permission to build was far from simple. I lost count of the many visits we made to government departments. There were permits to be obtained and endless forms to be filled in. Reg would set out from home with a bunch of medical journals to pass the time waiting in the anterooms of various officials. While allaying his impatience he was able to keep up to date with medical developments.

No one was willing to make a decision, so we were continually referred to someone higher up. Week by week we did the rounds of government offices, overcoming one barrier after another, until one final obstacle remained. The Ministry of Health had to sign a paper giving permission to begin building.

Reg visited the vice-minister, who was a particular friend of ours. He said he would like to help but it was really something the minister should deal with. So we wrote to the minister, and after a long wait Reg got an appointment to see him. He was gracious and friendly and promised to consider our proposal.

The weeks dragged by, and still there was no word. Reg saw the minister again and was told, 'It's all right. Go ahead and build.'

'But we must have a written document.'

'Don't worry, it will come in due course.'

Against our better judgement we called the builder and began work. The builders were personal friends and professionals of high repute. We had delivered the children of one of the two partners. We knew that our plans would be carried out according to our wishes.

Reg was down at the site nearly every day, and I was often there too, planning the garden and even planting some trees. Unfortunately they disappeared overnight, so we came to the conclusion that a fence was needed urgently.

The walls were almost up when we received a most disturbing message from the Ministry of Health. We were told to pull the hospital down and move to the land donated by Princess Tenagnework.

We never found out who was responsible for this command, but it was too much for Reg. He told the Ministry that we would both leave, that we would build our hospital just over the Kenya border and treat our patients there.

The next day a signed document arrived with the long-awaited permission to build and run the hospital.

It had been more than a year since CORSO in New Zealand had promised us £10,000. Now, just when we needed it, the money arrived. That got the main building finished, then we ran out of funds again. We still had the outbuildings for the laundry/kitchen and the nurses' home to build.

The story of how we raised the money for these buildings is an interesting one – especially to Australians. Sir Henry Bolte, the Premier of Victoria, had visited Ethiopia two years before on his way back from a trip to England. He spent a few days in Ethiopia at the invitation of the Foreign Minister, partly to investigate the possibility of trade between the two countries and also to invite the Emperor to visit Melbourne on his planned state visit to the Far East.

We showed Sir Henry and Lady Bolte over the hospital and met them socially at the British Embassy. We enjoyed their company. With their robust Australian manner they impressed us enormously, although perhaps not so much the British Ambassador and his very correct consort.

At the embassy Sir Henry was drinking a whisky and soda before the meal. When dinner was announced he took it with him into the dining room. The Ambassador's wife looked at him disparagingly as he put it down on the table, and he quipped, 'Brought it with me. Smart, aren't I?'

Lady Bolte was sitting next to Reg, and they were discussing the perils of being stuck next to someone boring at these functions. 'I know exactly what you mean,' she confided. 'Some of them are marble from the waist up.'

Later, we heard from one of the Emperor's grand-daughters, Princess Sybil, a delightful story about Haile Selassie's visit to Melbourne in 1966. Sir Henry had arranged a big reception in the Melbourne Town Hall. Wearing his gabardine cloak trimmed in red, the Emperor was standing in his favourite posture, holding both hands in front of him with his fingertips just meeting, looking highly dignified. Lady Bolte approached. 'If you think you are going to stand here in the corner like a lonely old gentleman, you're very much mistaken. Come with me, and I'll introduce you to the guests.'

Princess Sybil told us that the Emperor was tickled by this – a unique experience, I am sure.

Aware of these ties between Ethiopia and Australia, Reg had written to Sir Henry telling him of New Zealand's generous donation of £10,000 and suggested that Victoria might also like to contribute to the hospital. He probably emphasised that I was Australian and he was a New Zealander. Sir Henry sent $5000, which arrived in time to pay for the kitchen, laundry and nurses' home.

How straightforward it sounds when I write about these things – finding the land, designing the hospital, raising money, dealing with the bureaucracy. A few pages sums it up, yet it was four years from the time we got permission to buy the land until the hospital was built. During that time two important events stand out.

In January 1972 Brigadier Sandford died. On his last day he went out pottering in his orchard at Mulu Farm, seeming quite well. That night he went to bed at his usual hour. At 2 am he had a stroke and lapsed into a coma. He seemed to just lie there asleep. Mrs Sandford was by his side, holding his hand. He gave her hand a final squeeze and died.

The Emperor, who was on a state visit to Nigeria when he heard the news, immediately cancelled his engagements and flew back for the funeral. The service was held in St Matthew's the Anglican church the Brigadier and Mrs Sandford had helped found.

On this sad day the little church was packed to overflowing with the Brigadier's many and varied friends – foreigners and Ethiopians from every strata of society, from the highest in the land down to the humblest farm worker.

The Brigadier's coffin was draped in a Union Jack with all his medals placed on top. It was touching to see old Mrs Sandford walk in, with the aid of a stick, and take her place, surrounded by her children and grandchildren and all of her friends who had come to pay tribute. She bore her sorrow with British dignity and courage, and at the end of the service walked calmly to the piano, where she played the funeral march perfectly. She was a true soldier's wife.

The Emperor arrived at the British War Cemetery just in time to hear an Ethiopian bugler playing 'The Last Post' as the coffin was lowered into the ground. He had literally stepped off his plane and come straight to the cemetery. He bowed to Mrs Sandford, taking her hand, and expressed his sorrow at the loss of his friend. The Brigadier had indeed been his friend and champion, especially after the defeat of the Italians, when the British policy was to make Ethiopia a protectorate, with the Emperor just a figurehead. Brigadier Sandford had fought against this idea, wanting Ethiopia simply to be handed back to its rightful ruler without interference from the British government. His wishes eventually prevailed, thus Ethiopia and Eritrea were united under one monarch. We all felt a sense of loss as we came away from the graveside. It seemed as though an era had come to an end.

For Mrs Sandford and her family the mourning went on for days. Out at Mulu Farm a huge marquee was erected, and people came from kilometres around to pay their respects. Some sat silently on benches, some were weeping and wailing loudly and beating their breasts, while others just sobbed quietly. Ever hospitable, the family periodically handed round coffee and snacks of roasted wheat and peas. Before leaving, the mourners, in the Ethiopian tradition, would bow deeply to any members of the family who happened to be present. The Brigadier was 88 years old when he died.

Life went on. Richard was living in a hostel in London with other young medical students whose parents were mostly working overseas. From his letters home he seemed to be making friends and doing well at his studies. He helped in the hostel in various ways and at one time earned a little money as the stoker for the hot water system.

In November Reg learned that he was being considered for the Haile Selassie Humanitarian Prize. This was a medal and US$10,000. Several were awarded annually from the Emperor's personal foundation for achievement in different fields, such as literature, agriculture and industry.

The committee had to investigate each candidate to see if they were worthy of such an honour, writing to people all over the world as well as locally. The man who came to interview Reg was a charming and cultured Ethiopian with perfect manners. Sitting in an armchair in our drawing room he told us that all the reports had spoken of Reg in glowing terms, except for one man. Telling this he seemed embarrassed and upset.

Reg said, 'I know who that was – Dr Asrat.'

It emerged that, sure enough, Dr Asrat had been trying to blackball him, but he did not succeed, as the nominating committee took no notice.

We understood that his opposition stemmed from his intense patriotism, so this did not really affect our friendship with him or lessen our admiration for his many good qualities and his great surgical skill.

The prizes were to be given at a ceremony in Africa Hall, which the Emperor had built to be the headquarters of the Organisation of African Unity. Reg went to a lot of trouble writing his speech. The night before the ceremony he practised it aloud time after time so he would get it word perfect. In the morning he came in at six o'clock wearing his borrowed tails, asking, 'How do I look?'

Later that day we set off for Africa Hall, hoping we looked our best. We were nervous as we sat with the other prizewinners in the front row of the big circular hall. The tiers of seats behind were filled with friends and relatives of the recipients.

The Emperor entered and stood for a moment as we all rose and bowed low, then he seated himself on a high-backed chair, ornately decorated with gold and red plush upholstery. The Prime Minister, Aklilu Habte Wold, and other high-ranking Ethiopians stood behind on either side. In front of the Emperor was a polished table on which were the medals.

Reg's citation was read in Amharic by the head of the Emperor's charitable trust, Ato Abeba Kebede. He was a friend of ours and his wife, Tiruwork, had been one of our midwives. Reg rose to his feet and made a moving speech about the fistula pilgrims which eloquently summed up their plight:

> Mourning the stillbirth of their only child, incontinent of urine, ashamed of their offensiveness, often spurned by their husbands, homeless, unemployable, except in the fields, they endure, they exist, without friends and without hope. They bear their sorrows in silent shame. Their miseries, untreated, are utter, lonely and lifelong.

I felt proud listening to my husband delivering these touching words – words that came from his heart. The Emperor kept his eyes riveted on him, and I feel sure was swept up by his eloquence like everyone else.

Reg then stepped forward, mounted the steps to where the Emperor was seated and bowed from the waist. His Majesty placed the green ribbon around his neck with the impressive gold medal attached, thanking Reg for doing this work for his people.

Then it was my turn. A lovely smile lit up the Emperor's face as he handed me a scroll and the cheque. This smile will remain forever in my memory.

A band played the British national anthem, and our part of the ceremony was over. Later we gathered in front of the artist Ato Afework Tekle's famous stained-glass window in Africa Hall, where photographs were taken of all the recipients, with His Majesty in the centre. He then left in his Rolls Royce, but we and our friends, with many of our nurses too, attended a party in the spacious reception area. And so a wonderful day ended.

Richard came home for the holidays at the end of 1973, overjoyed as usual to be back in Ethiopia. He had developed a passion for cooking strange foods. He and Yeshi went off to the market and came back with a big bag of wholemeal flour. For the next few days the kitchen was a disaster as he baked loaves and for some reason or other made masses of yoghurt. I dislike yoghurt, but he was having a wonderful time, and Yeshi loved having him around, although he left her huge piles of washing up.

Despite all this interest in cooking he didn't seem to eat much and had lost a great deal of weight since we last saw him. He told me that he had been forgoing lunch to save money and that he never caught the tube or bus but went to and from medical school by bicycle.

I was worried that he was overdoing it. If only I had taken

more notice then, we might have been able to forestall what happened later. Helping me in the theatre one day he fainted. That, too, may have been a sign that all was not well, but neither Reg nor I saw it.

Richard was never overjoyed about going back to England. When we said goodbye at the end of the holiday we had no inkling that this time was any different. It was the beginning of a black period in his life, one which he was only able fully to explain years later. He knew he had to grow up and break away but emotionally he was still powerfully drawn to Ethiopia. He did not know where his identity lay. In addition to this he was beginning to doubt if he really wanted to do medicine.

When he was back in London he wrote asking if he might take a year off medicine to do a science course. Reg wrote back firmly advising him to complete his degree and do science later, if he still wanted to. In retrospect I can see that this was another warning that he was not happy.

Alone in London Richard worried about his future. Back in Addis Ababa we were completely preoccupied with the new hospital. As early as July 1972 we had written to the Ministry of the Imperial Court asking if the Emperor would open our hospital on its completion. The Minister replied:

> Regarding the opening of the Addis Ababa Fistula Hospital. As soon as you will let me know of the completion of the building I will be happy to arrange for a date convenient to his Imperial Majesty to open the hospital where the unfortunate patients will no doubt receive good care and treatment. I can assure you that His Majesty is very appreciative of your work and devotion.
>
> Sincerely
> Tafarra Worg Kidane Wold
> Minister of the Imperial Court

How good life seemed then. We lived in a country that we loved. Our work was satisfying; Richard seemed to be doing well in his second year of medicine; and we could look towards a future when he would perhaps one day take over. If we had cared to notice, there were signs that our cherished little world was about to be thrown into chaos, but in our single-mindedness and naiveté we did not see them.

Chapter Sixteen

Let me go back a little. In 1972, while we were preoccupied with building, the beginning of a devastating human tragedy was taking place 200 kilometres away, unseen by anyone in Addis Ababa. The Ministry of Agriculture produced a report saying that because of drought, the following year's crops in Wollo province in the north-east would fail. The message was clear enough, but they did not heed their own warning. By the beginning of the following year peasants began starving to death.

In February 1973 ragged, hungry people arrived at the outskirts of Addis Ababa, desperately seeking food. There was a meeting of the Organisation of African Unity taking place in the capital and the authorities deemed that the presence of these distressed people would be an embarrassment. The police turned them back then beat and ruthlessly dispersed students who went out into the country to try to bring them food.

News of the famine victims reached the Ministry of the Interior, which asked the Governor of Wollo for an explanation. He reassured them that while there was a slight drought problem, everything was under control.

It wasn't until six weeks later that bureaucrats in Addis Ababa began to realise how bad the drought was, and the government decided to ask for assistance. Perhaps they were too proud, even then, to reveal the full extent of the famine, but for whatever reason, the aid agencies were slow to react and when they did, the little food they sent was not nearly enough.

By the middle of the year people were dying in the streets of Dessie, the provincial capital of Wollo, and the bodies were piling up awaiting burial. There was a massive outbreak of cholera in another town, but news of this was also played down.

At this stage few people in Addis Ababa or the outside world knew what was going on. The Ethiopian newspapers did not report the disaster, and a documentary about the famine made by an Ethiopian television crew was banned from being shown. Without realising what a storm it was about to unleash, the Ministry of Information allowed a British television reporter, Jonathan Dimbleby, to film a documentary about 'Problems of Drought'. Dimbleby recorded heart-rending pictures of starving, fly-covered children lying in the dust with staring, hopeless eyes. Mothers with dried up breasts listlessly stared at the camera, too weak even to beg. When these images were shown in Britain, suddenly the world woke up. By now probably 100,000 people had already died. Before the drought was over that figure would rise to 200,000, and another million peasants would be brought to ruin.

I don't believe the Emperor knew the full extent of the drought until then. He had been fed the same rosy reports as his cabinet ministers. Once he did know he toured Wollo and saw for himself what was going on.

In February the following year there was a revolt in an isolated military outpost in the south of the country over wages and conditions. The government gave in and met the demands, but the unrest escalated to widespread disturbances among students and workers.

Although they were apparently unrelated, this incident and the drought together posed the greatest threat to the Emperor Haile Selassie's leadership since the failed coup of 1960. For the first time in his long rule people began to complain openly about the government and to demand that he step down. His answer was to promise political and social reforms. As a first step he formed a new cabinet, which immediately promised cuts in government expenditure and relaxation of press controls. But the Army had realised what power it had and, with its tacit approval, the strikes and demonstrations continued.

Although there was some gunfire in the streets there was no bloodshed – not at first, anyway. Rather, it was a creeping coup d'état. A group of young army officers, calling themselves the Armed Forces Co-ordinating Committee, arrested politicians, the Emperor's courtiers and advisers, members of the imperial family and many nobles and large landowners. The Emperor was almost totally isolated in his palace.

The final move was heralded on television screens on the night of Ethiopian New Year. The whole nation was invited to watch a TV documentary in which the producers cleverly juxtaposed images of lavish banquets alongside shots of peasants starving in the famine. One sequence showed the extravagant wedding of a nobleman's daughter at the time of the famine, where the centrepiece was a wedding cake flown out from England, allegedly at a cost of US$3000. Shots of the Emperor feeding his dogs were interposed with pictures of dying children.

They accused the Emperor of salting away millions of dollars overseas, which they said he had stolen from his country. There has never been any proof of this, and I and many others certainly don't believe it. Haile Selassie was 82 at the time of the coup – an old man nearing the end of his life. All he was guilty of was of being out of touch.

The day following the Emperor's humiliation on television, soldiers went to the palace to inform him of his dethronement. He stood with his usual quiet dignity, with only one close relative, Ras Imru Selassie, beside him. After listening calmly to the delegation he said, 'We have tried to serve our country in peace and war. If we must serve it now by resigning, we are willing to do so.'

He was then told that he would be removed from the palace

for his own safety. He was ushered outside, where a small police Volkswagen waited. The seat was pushed back for him to get into the back. He asked, 'What, into this?'

It was a cruel thing to do to him. In his confusion he waved to a crowd of students who ran beside the car as they drove him away. But they weren't paying homage, they were crying, 'You thief,' and 'Hang the Emperor.'

The Emperor's son, Crown Prince Asfa Wossen, was designated King of Ethiopia. He was living in England, confined to a wheelchair after a stroke and in poor health. Few people believed that he would ever take up the crown.

At first people thought the end of feudalism was a good thing. A provisional military government was set up, and all institutions, including the Parliament, were abolished. The Armed Forces Co-ordinating Committee, known as the *Dergue*, Amharic for 'committee', issued a flurry of proclamations promising land reform and a new constitution. They set up a committee to investigate the corruption of those they had arrested.

This was welcomed by the peasants, who had always had to give much of their meagre profits away to wealthy landlords, and by the students. Some people, though, worried about the *Dergue*. There was a disquieting air of mystery about it. Its members were anonymous. It was said to comprise about a hundred members of the armed forces, all young officers, none above the rank of major. Just who was in charge and what their political leanings were, we did not know.

We were both terribly upset about the Emperor – Reg especially. We had never been interested in politics but we believed he had been a good and benevolent ruler who cared for his people. He had done a lot for his country and didn't deserve to end up a prisoner. In those early days of the takeover everyone was confused about what was happening. Whatever the future held, there was nothing we could do about it. Our best course was to keep our heads down and continue working for our patients.

One of the first things the new regime did was to move the Princess Tsehai Hospital, lock, stock and barrel, to another hospital, the Black Lion. Princess Tsehai became an army hospital as it was next door to the military airport and the wounded could be transferred easily. The Black Lion had been built in the 1960s and was opened by the Emperor in 1969, to be called the Duke of Harar Memorial Hospital after the Emperor's son, who was killed in a car accident. After the coup it was renamed.

The hospital had stood empty for many years – a huge, modern edifice of eight storeys on a hillside dominating the city. The story went that one day the then Minister of Health had stood looking at the completed complex and, with his finger on his chin, was heard to say, 'And how are they going to run such a huge hospital?' thereby detaching himself and his ministry from any responsibility for it. In 1972 the Swiss Red Cross had taken over two floors and opened a private hospital. The rest was completely empty.

Although we were not quite ready to move into our new hospital, we were told one Thursday morning early in 1975 by the Ministry of Health that we had to be out by Saturday. Then began a scene of complete chaos and confusion. Everything that could be moved was taken outside onto the lawns. Porters, cleaners, gardeners, guards and even the patients' relatives all helped. Some semblance of order was attempted by the administrative staff, who tried to sort out items destined for the Black Lion from others that would not be wanted there. We were told that we could have anything from the latter group. In this way we were able to acquire much that was useful – beds, bed lockers and bed tables, a refrigerator, examination couches, chairs, tables, drip stands and so on. I even found Reg trying to detach a big commercial washing machine from the laundry wall, but he was not successful.

For the next few days a stream of fistula patients, relatives and our own staff could be seen lugging pieces of furniture down the road to our nearby hospital under the gaze of armed guards.

We were sad indeed to see the Princess Tsehai close as a

general hospital. It had been our home for so many happy years. We had hoped that it would be there as a mother hospital to us, its fledgling. Certainly, when choosing the site for our hospital a major consideration had been its proximity to a big general hospital where we could count on the use of an X-ray department and a sophisticated laboratory. Now these advantages would be denied us. Our own simple lab was small and only capable of doing the most basic tests. Only in the last three years have we had our own X-ray machine.

Of course there was now no question of the Emperor opening the hospital, and we were wary of drawing attention to ourselves by having a public ceremony. On Empire Day, 24 May 1975, Reg and I, alone, cut a ribbon strung between two chairs in the drawing room of our house and declared the Addis Ababa Fistula Hospital open. Next day we began treating our first patients.

We still had not built a house to live in, nor did we have space for the many waiting patients living in the hostels at the old hospital. However, the *Dergue* was helpful and allowed us to stay on in our old house for another six months and also gave us permission to continue using the hostels for our patients.

It seemed strange to be on our own with none of the backup of a big general hospital, but we were not daunted, as we both knew we had a more certain backup in a loving and all-powerful God. Almost at once unexpected things began to happen. The Red Sea Mission Team volunteered to help with the nursing. The mission was started by an English doctor, Dr Lionel Gurney, in 1951 to work in all the areas around the Red Sea. The Emperor had welcomed them into Ethiopia but the new regime forced many of them to leave. Those remaining came in from the country to stay at a house owned by the mission in Addis Ababa. They found themselves at a loose end and when we asked the nurses among them to help us out, they did so gladly. They even covered for night duty, until we were able to secure a permanent staff.

God took a hand with our missing autoclave, a device that

uses steam heat to sterilise such things as theatre drapes, gowns, gauze, etc, which can't be sterilised in boilers. We had ordered quite an expensive machine from England, but for months the shipping agents kept telling us that it had been off-loaded somewhere. Meanwhile we were using autoclaves at the old hospital for all our operating linen, instruments and gauze which needed to be sterilised. This was enormously inconvenient as it meant many trips to and fro in our small car.

One day Reg took a patient to the railway station for her journey home to Harar. As he wandered along the platform he noticed a large crate sitting at the far end with, DR HAMLIN, FISTULA HOSPITAL written on it. Imagine his joy when he realised that this was our long-lost autoclave. The stationmaster told him it had been there for months.

Before we moved our patients from the old hospital we had to be sure we could feed them. Reg spent much time with Birru buying in all the food supplies we would need. He would fill up the VW with sacks of grain, macaroni and lentils until there was barely room for the driver. One day I saw the car arrive filled to the roof with rolls of toilet paper he had found in a factory where slightly damaged rolls were being sold cheaply.

We had hired a cook a few weeks before the opening date and, with the help of some former patients who were not completely cured, good meals were soon being produced. The cooking was done on a stove run on bottled gas. This was occasionally in short supply, so we had an area constructed where we could cook over an open fire if need be.

The *injera,* indispensable in the Ethiopian diet and unique to this country, was cooked on two electric *injera* cookers, but could also be made over an open fire. Power cuts were frequent, and we had no generator.

The laundry, too, was at first staffed by ex-patients, but it was not long before we employed two women to take over this heavy task. Everything had to be washed by hand, as we had no washing machines. We used tubs and even an old bath. This was particularly useful for the gauzes used during operations. When washed, dried and autoclaved they could be re-used several times. In fact we still do this. Visitors are amazed and, I think, sometimes shocked to see washed gauzes lying on a big table drying in the sunshine. This is not only a great saving of money but also gives our patients something to do. They undo the tangles and fold each piece carefully, ready to be packed into drums and autoclaved. Another good reason for this economy was that the central medical stores would often be out of gauze. We occasionally resorted to buying and cutting up *shammas,* shawls made of similar material, which are worn by most Ethiopian women.

A month after we opened the hospital the rainy season arrived, presenting us with a serious drying problem. It was impossible to get the many sheets and theatre linen dry, so our staff hurriedly constructed a makeshift roof of corrugated iron supported by poles. Here, for the three months of the rains the clothes lines were never empty.

As well as our volunteer nurses from the mission, we had twelve of our own nursing aides – all ex-patients who had been trained by us at the Princess Tsehai Hospital. They helped out in the wards and outpatients and even occasionally in the theatre. Six of these women slept down one side of the ward, while I camped in the doctor's office in the theatre area to be available for any night emergency.

So our early nursing problems were solved. Then the Minister of Health arrived one day and told us he would release two nurses of our own choosing from their jobs at government hospitals. We picked two of our favourites from the old hospital to be employed full-time and were allowed another nurse part-time.

The theatre was always busy. Because we had no anaesthetist we gave our own spinal anaesthetics and could always supplement this when needed with open ether, administering it as we had been taught at Crown Street.

How different is the scene in the theatre today, with a full-time anaesthetist, often watching four operations proceeding simultaneously, longer-acting spinal anaesthetic agents, monitoring machines for recording blood pressure, a modern anaesthetic machine and drugs for general anaesthetics. The old ether-rag-and-bottle days are long-gone, however, it was a safe procedure and we never had an anaesthetic death. This, I am glad to say, is still the case.

In the early days of the *Dergue* life went on fairly normally in Addis Ababa. There was tension and uncertainty, but on the whole, people were optimistic about the change. The song of the revolution was *Ethiopia Tikdem Yalla Minim Dem* – Ethiopia first without bloodshed. And for a while it looked as though it had really been a bloodless revolution.

We heard that the *Dergue* was being led by three men – Major Mengistu Haile Mariam, a graduate of Holeta Military Training Centre outside Addis Ababa; Colonel Atnafu Abate, and Lieutenant General Aman Andom, a 51-year-old Eritrean, who had been made Chief Minister. General Aman was known as the Desert Lion because of his successful campaign against the Somalis during border fighting in the early 1960s. He seemed to be the spokesman for the *Dergue*, but it was rumoured that Mengistu was really the dominant force.

One of the first things they had to deal with was the age-old problem of the war with Eritrea. Eritrea, on the Red Sea coast, used to be an Italian colony. After World War II, Britain, with a United Nations mandate, assumed responsibility from their defeated enemy. In 1952 the UN agreed that Eritrea should become an autonomous state within the Ethiopian empire. The Eritreans would have a measure of self-government, leaving Ethiopia to control defence, foreign policy and finance.

Emperor Haile Selassie wasn't happy with this arrangement. He let things drift along quite peacefully until 1962 when he annexed Eritirea, declaring that it was just another province of Ethiopia. The Eritreans were not going to stand for that, and two separate independence movements sprang up. At first they spent as much time fighting each other as they did Ethiopia, but by the time Mengistu took over they were a serious force, sapping huge amounts of Ethiopian money and lives. If Mengistu was going to drag Ethiopia out of its endless cycle of war and famine he was first going to have to solve the problem of Eritrea.

General Aman Andom lived in a house next to the Princess Tsehai Hospital, sharing a common boundary fence. As a small boy Richard spent hours playing with the general's son. They were good friends and often rode their bikes together. One day Richard came back early from one of their expeditions saying that Michael was confined to his room for disobeying his father. The general was a strict disciplinarian and a wonderful soldier. Politically, he was a moderate, believing that Ethiopia should extract itself from the wasteful war with Eritrea. He wanted Eritrea to have some sort of autonomy so that the two nations could live together in peace. Being an Eritrean himself, he was well placed to negotiate with the leadership, and even went so far as to hold talks with them as a first step to bringing about a settlement.

Mengistu professed to regard this as a traitorous act, although he was probably just as worried that General Aman might take away his power. Things came to a head when the general refused to endorse a plan to shoot in cold blood 60 high-ranking political prisoners.

I remember it was a Saturday night in November when things reached a perilous stage. Mengistu surrounded the house with soldiers and tanks, and a terrific gun battle ensued with some troops who were loyal to General Aman. In our house we were deafened by the noise. After a fight lasting about two hours, a tank was driven through the already shattered house, and the brave general was shot. A few days earlier he had told a relative he would never submit to arrest but would 'die like a soldier'. And that is what he did, giving his life for refusing to submit to a murderous act.

That same night the troops had been to Menelik's palace, where the prisoners were being held in the dungeons. They led the 60 out to a convoy of trucks and drove them through the deserted streets to the Akaki Prison. There they lined them up against a stone wall and machine-gunned them. Among those murdered was the former Prime Minister, Endalkatchew Mekkonen, another former Prime Minister, Aklilu Habte Wold, and Haile Selassie's grandson, Eskender Desta, who had been head of the Ethiopian Navy. Tefarra Work Kidane Wold, the Minister of the Court with whom we had discussed the Emperor opening our hospital, and Ato Abeba Retta, the first Minister of Health when we arrived in 1959 and Princess Mary's father, were also killed. The bodies, along with that of General Andom, were all just thrown into a mass grave.

The city was in shock. In the days that followed we saw Mengistu's true colours as he put in train a revolution along classic communist lines. The big landholdings were all nationalised. The land was declared a national asset and given to peasants' associations to divide up as they wanted. Urban properties were taken over by the state, and people were only allowed to keep the home they lived in. Banks and businesses were nationalised. All the schools were closed. University students and the last two grades of secondary school were sent out into the countryside to explain the new ideology to the farmers. They were also ordered to carry out a nationwide literacy campaign.

Many of those who had become dear friends over the preceding two decades were affected, some losing homes, property, shops or businesses. Others were put in prison. Perhaps it was a good thing that Mrs Sandford, that indomitable Englishwoman who so loved Ethiopia, died just before the new regime took over her beloved Mulu Farm. She was 79.

Just before her death Mrs Sandford had the heartbreak of seeing three of her original four pupils, whom she had taught in her home prior to founding the English School, killed in the November massacre. All had risen to prominent positions in the government. Prime Minister Endalkatchew was one – a fine aristocrat who had been working on reform of the constitution when he was arrested. His distraught daughter, a university student, was forced to go out into the countryside with all the other students to spread the doctrine of communism.

After all this killing and the nationalisation of land, people began to get disillusioned with the new regime. It hurt a lot of rich people but it also hurt a lot of relatively small people, who were described as the petty bourgeoisie. They were not evil capitalists, just middle-class people who lived in Addis Ababa, some owning a few acres in the countryside as well.

Bambi, our Greek friend with the four daughters, had built up his business from a corner store into a big supermarket. When the *Dergue* took over, he and Helene were out of the country. Soldiers came to the supermarket, demanded the keys from his brother-in-law, who had been left in charge, and told him to leave immediately. He did not even have time to clear out his papers. It was many years before Bambi was able to return to the country where he had built his life.

All over Addis Ababa similar things were happening. Businesspeople had their assets confiscated. At a stroke, wealthy people were reduced to poverty with no means of earning a living. If they asked for permission to leave, in many cases they were refused. Bambi's brother-in-law only got out after a dangerous journey by camel to Somalia.

Our friends the Princesses – Ida, Sybil, Ruth, and Sofia – were arrested with their mother, Princess Tenagnework, and some royal cousins. The *Dergue* also arrested Princess Edjigayehu, the daughter of the Crown Prince, Asfa Wossen, from his first marriage. Eleven women in all, they were held under house arrest in the Duke of Harar's home within the military camp that had been used by the Emperor's bodyguard. Their children were taken to be looked after by relatives and friends but were closely watched. Princess Sybil's youngest child was only six months old when she was separated from him. We felt for her very much.

Mary Abeba was not imprisoned as she had never been recognised as a princess.

Princess Aida Desta could have escaped with her husband, Ras Mengesha, the governor of Tigray province in northern Ethiopia. They were both so popular that when soldiers came to arrest them local people armed with rifles surrounded the palace, defying the soldiers and foiling the attempt.

They were escorted out of Tigray, intending to leave the country, but meanwhile, Princess Aida heard a rumour that her mother, Princess Tenagnework, had been arrested and so decided to go to Addis Ababa to see if this was true. She was promptly thrown into prison with her mother and sisters. Her husband escaped to Khartoum in the Sudan.

Other grandchildren of the Emperor who were arrested to spend long years in prison were the sons of Prince Mekonnen, the Duke of Harar. The boys had been in the Emperor's care since the death of their father many years before.

In August 1975, about a year after the takeover, the regime announced that Haile Selassie had died in his sleep. They said when he became ill they had been unable to find his personal physician, Dr Asrat. This was strange because Dr Asrat had left word that he was dining at the British Embassy that night.

No one believed that the Emperor died of natural causes. There were persistent rumours that Mengistu had smothered him with a pillow soaked in ether.

Years later the Emperor's servant, Eshete, who had been allowed to look after him while he was in prison, was able to give his version of the story. Eshete said the night before the Emperor died he was not allowed to go near him. In the morning he saw Major Mengistu and two other men go into Haile Selassie's room. A short time later they came out again and ordered Eshete to take in his breakfast. Eshete went in and found the Emperor dead in his chair. There was the smell of ether in the room.

Mary Abeba, whom I had once saved from suicide, had already lost her beloved father, Ato Abebe Retta, a former Minister of Health, in the November massacre. Her husband, Seyoum Haregot, was in prison with her sisters. The death of her grandfather, the Emperor, was the final blow. Distraught with grief, Mary lost the balance of her mind and one morning cut her throat as she lay in the bath. I am sad to say that this time she was successful.

After the Emperor died no one knew where he was buried. He was given no public funeral. Many secretly mourned the passing of this great man but could not show it publicly. Everyone was afraid to express an opinion that could be construed as anti-government. The communists ruled by fear.

We discreetly hid our portrait of the Emperor, done in charcoal by a well-known Ethiopian artist. We were concerned that our newly established and smoothly running hospital might be taken over by the government as we had already seen happen to many mission hospitals. They even took over the large, well-run Seventh-Day Adventist Hospital in the city. I am sure we were left alone because we were a completely free hospital, with no fees paid by patients. As Reg used to say, we were true socialists.

However, keeping a low profile did not mean that we followed their policies. We continued our regular Bible classes for patients and staff who wanted to attend. These were conducted by missionary friends. They included some literacy as well, so we could truthfully say we were fulfilling the government's education policy if any questions were asked. We distributed Bibles to patients, hiding them in their small bundles of clothing when they left to go home. Later, Bibles were not allowed to be imported, and we heard that the Bible Society had a big consignment confiscated.

It was a time of uncertainty and constant anxiety. Every day there seemed to be some alarming new rumour, and each morning we would wake up wondering what the next development would be. We were terribly concerned that the hospital would be taken over. But far away in London, things were happening which would have worried us infinitely more, if only we had known about them. All of Richard's doubts about himself and his career were coming to a head, and we were not there to help him.

Chapter Seventeen

Richard's emotional crisis had been building up slowly for two years. While he had been studying hard he had been putting himself through a punishing physical regimen of squash and running. At the same time he was neglecting to eat, to the point where he was almost anorexic. He didn't realise how run-down he had become until he went to see the students' doctor. Shocked at his condition, the doctor told him that he had to put on some weight or he would make himself seriously ill.

The doctor was a sympathetic person and could see that Richard was a deeply troubled young man. He drew him out, and Richard confessed his doubts about continuing with his medical degree. As they talked they began to discuss faith. Richard was a believer through inheritance but, as he later put it, 'the penny hadn't dropped personally'. The doctor, a Christian himself, suggested to him, 'I happen to know you have faith. Let God in on this area.' Richard left his surgery and was walking down the corridor when he had a strong sense of God's presence. It was as if God had said, 'I care for you personally, you're in my personal protection and care. I love you as you are and will never reject you.'

This revelation had a profound effect on his dilemma. It

cut him loose from his exclusive tie to Ethiopia. His emotional roots shifted from a place to a person, Jesus Christ. He was in England, and that was good. Wherever he was, that would be good, too.

The question of whether or not to continue with medicine was still unresolved. He wondered if the whole thing was a mistake. Did he really want to be a doctor or was he only doing it to please his father? He had become so averse to medicine that sometimes the mere thought of having to face patients filled him with dread. He had already completed one part of his finals in April and May 1975. He was due to sit the rest in October and November. As the date approached he was filled with panic. He felt he could not go on any longer.

He wrote us a disturbing letter. I have kept it with all his other correspondence. It still upsets me to read it for it shows vividly the pain he was going through. He told Reg that there was a great need in his life for his love and he very much needed to see him again. Twice in the preceding month or two he had been overcome by the most excruciating grief, where he had wept uncontrollably. The first time was while visiting some friends of ours in Devon. And it happened again a few weeks later while he was at a church service at St Bart's Hospital.

'Daddy,' he wrote, 'I felt as if my heart was breaking. I know it was something to do with you and me.' He thought that these two episodes were not hysterical or emotional things with no substance, but were a deep longing for something that could be met by seeing his father again. He ended by saying that he was as committed as ever to being a doctor, but he wanted to come and see us.

Of course we told him to come. I believe Richard was experiencing terrible guilt at the thought of disappointing his father, and it was this thought that kept him persevering with medicine. Earlier on he had expressed a wish to change to a science course and give up medicine, but we had ignored that wish.

During many evenings in our home in Addis Ababa he tried to explain to us his fears and doubts. I, as his mother, could see he was profoundly disturbed and I longed to keep him at home, but Reg felt he should return and finish his course.

Looking back I realise that we did not fully understand the crisis he was experiencing, and to our shame and selfishness we failed Richard in his hour of greatest need. We listened to what he said but persuaded him that it would be foolish not to take the final step and complete his degree. He returned to London and, as he knew he would, failed his exams.

Even then Richard was still determined to persevere with his medical course but in the meantime he took a year off to try something completely different. He took a job as a delivery driver in London for a while, then worked under the Thames building the Dartford Tunnel. This was the first time he had ever earned his own living, and because of the danger of the bends while working in compressed air, he was highly paid.

I think he enjoyed this year. He was living in a community of Christian friends and was buoyant with his new-found faith, which evidently his workmates in the tunnel had heard about, too, for they used to greet him as 'Jesus man'.

There was one joyful note during this time. He met and fell in love with a nurse at St Bartholomew's Hospital. Diana Cliff had been brought up in Devon and came to London to do nursing. At first she had been shocked by the sudden change from a carefree country life to the crowded conditions of living in a nurse's home in one of the busiest hospitals in the centre of London. When Richard met her, she was sharing a flat with other nurses and had become more accustomed to city life, but she always retained a love of the countryside and open spaces.

Diana had been an agnostic, but one of her closest nursing friends was a Christian, with whom she had many long arguments. Determined to bolster her case, she had begun to read the Bible. Every time she reached the description of Jesus being crucified she found herself weeping. Curious about what was happening to her, she went with her friend Pam, to a fellowship meeting held at St Bart's. There her heart was touched by the Holy Spirit, and she committed her life to Jesus.

It was here that she met Richard, coming into his life and standing by him through all his troubles, just when he most needed someone with the character and loveliness that she possessed. I remember words used by Reg's sister Iris to describe their partnership. She said it was a marriage made in heaven, and this I believe, too.

At the end of Richard's year in the work force, he flew out to Ethiopia and once more raised the idea of leaving medicine for good. With Reg still so completely against it, he returned to London in October 1976 and back to St Bart's to study for his finals again.

I went with him this time to try to encourage him but I think I knew then in my heart that this attempt would not succeed, and that this was the wrong thing for Richard to be doing.

Back in the hospital environs all his aversion to medicine came flooding back. He was caught in the same quandary, dreading every day as he forced himself to go into the wards, unable to settle to study and wavering from determination one minute to resignation the next.

Poor boy. For months he tried hard to keep going, wrestling with competing emotions, his heart telling him he disliked medicine while his loyalty to us kept him going. He put pen to paper often – long, affectionate letters – but finally, with his decision made, he wrote and said that he was leaving medicine, and this time for good.

Reg, shattered at the news, rushed off to the post office and sent a telegram as a final attempt at persuasion, but it was too late for persuasion or argument.

I wonder now if things might have been different if Richard had spent that year off with us, or in Australia where he would have had my family around. His crisis took place far away, while we were caught up with moving into the new hospital, and Colonel Mengistu was killing people all about us, and we were not there to help.

Reg and Richard were both strong-willed and found it

hard to give up resentments. Reg was utterly shocked at seeing his cherished hopes and ambitions for his son shattered, while Richard felt that medicine had been imposed upon him against his will.

As a child he dearly loved his father, and their relationship was close. Reg had been very affectionate and protective towards Richard and in his mind had mapped out the future he wanted for him. Then all of a sudden Richard wanted to stand on his own two feet and work out his own future – which, thankfully, he finally did in the computer business.

It took some years for Reg to accept this, and for his old relationship with his son to be re-established, but it was impossible for Reg to stop loving him. I remember how excited he was whenever a letter arrived from Richard and the preparations he planned for his visits to us with his growing family.

For Richard this whole chapter drew him into the wonderful relationship he has with Jesus and which still dominates his life, motivating all he does. And for me – well, he will always be my Prince Charming.

Chapter Eighteen

At the same time as all this was happening in the life of our son in faraway England, the situation in Ethiopia was becoming more and more out of control. The members of the *Dergue* distrusted each other so much that when they had meetings, each man usually carried a gun in his waistband. About 50 of the original 100 or so members of the *Dergue* had vanished or been shot. One day nineteen were executed by firing squad for crimes that ranged from owning a villa to setting up a mafia-type organisation in the Air Force. A month or so later, two more officers were executed for allegedly planning a coup.

The Ethiopian governor of Eritrea, General Getachew Nadew, came to Addis Ababa for a meeting with Mengistu and argued strongly for a negotiated peace. Instead of talking with him, Mengistu sent soldiers armed with machine-guns to surround his house and kill him and his bodyguards. Another officer who argued for peace, Major Sisai Habte, was said to have been shot by Mengistu himself across the council room table. Major Sisai was one of the most intelligent and cultured members of the *Dergue*. He had been chairman of its political and foreign affairs committee and had led the Ethiopian delegation at the Organisation of African Unity.

Another of his victims was Brigadier General Teferi Bante, also a moderate. When the soldiers set out to kill him, he was hiding in a tank not far from the Black Lion Hospital. I was just scrubbing up for an operation there, with a Russian professor of gynaecology, when we heard the gunfire. He asked me, 'Dr Nicholson, what's going on?'

I said, 'We're in the midst of a revolution; you should know all about revolutions.'

I suppose I sounded bitter but I was annoyed at what was happening to the country I loved.

In 1977 an underground group called the Ethiopian People's Revolutionary Party began to oppose the military-led government. As far as we could make out, they were communists too, but apparently they wanted a different sort of communism from Colonel Mengistu's.

The EPRP distributed anti-government propaganda and assassinated a few public officials. Mengistu reacted ruthlessly, and a reign of terror began, known as the Red Terror. He split up the city into municipalities and put his henchmen in charge of them. He instituted a system of cadres and spies, just like in Stalinist Russia. All the big hospitals had these cadres on the staff, spying on people. Everyone was suspicious. People were frightened to talk in case their conversations were reported to the government.

We were not worried about our own people. They were not a big group, and we knew them all. There were faithful workers like Birru and Yeshi and our former patients who had worked with us at the old hospital and were now nursing aides. We knew they weren't spies. Our trained nurses, too, had been our colleagues and were our dear friends. They were completely trustworthy.

If the cadres thought you were an enemy of the government or if they even had a grudge against you, you could be shot in the name of revolutionary justice. It truly was a time of terror, with much shooting going on and loss of life. Driving through the city, we would often pass through pockets of gunfire. Or else we would see the results of some atrocity that had just happened – a body lying on the pavement or in the gutter.

Mexico Square, through which we had to pass on the way to the post office in the city, seemed to be a particular place where bodies were left lying on the pavement. The relatives were too afraid to move them. People just stepped around them, while vultures hovered overhead and dogs roamed among them.

There were curfews each night at ten o'clock, and on Sundays no one was allowed to drive without a permit. On all the main roads there were checkpoints. Being a doctor I could get permits to move around. One day I had to go out of the city to a fabric factory to buy sheeting material for the hospital. I passed through a checkpoint and came upon a pile of dead bodies, stripped naked and tossed onto a vacant piece of land. It shocked me so much I could not go on. I stopped the car and sat for a few minutes then turned round and drove home. I asked some people what had happened. They said these sad victims were workers from the factory who had received 'revolutionary justice'.

Sometimes people used this revolutionary justice to settle old scores. A lot of workers in a big printing works in Addis Ababa were picked out as being anti-government. They were taken outside and lined up to be shot. Among them was a woman who was eight months pregnant. She pleaded with the soldiers not to kill her until after her baby was born, but they shot her just the same, with all the others.

It turned out that they had not been anti-government at all. They had been betrayed by one of the factory managers, who had a grudge against them. He was caught in the end and hung.

Communism is an atheistic regime, so of course the *Dergue* hated religion. The Patriarch of the Orthodox Church kept an open dialogue with them, which some might view as collaboration. Because of this the Church was able to keep functioning.

The Protestant and Roman Catholic Churches stood firmly

in their faith and refused to co-operate with the communists. They were forbidden to conduct worship in their churches or to do any evangelising. Many pastors and priests were imprisoned and tortured. Some were killed and others fled. Many foreign missions closed, and their staff were expelled. In spite of this persecution the Christian faith spread and flourished in an underground 'church'. Services and meetings were held secretly by small groups in private homes.

We heard many stories of great bravery. One of our friends, a Christian woman, was arrested and put in prison where she was hung upside down and beaten. This torture went on for day after day. While she was being beaten the soldiers told her to raise her hand if she would renounce her faith. This she refused to do and never gave in. Finally, after two months the torturers relented, and she was released. There were many similar stories.

Some missionary friends, Colin and Hazel Maunsell, were living in Gondar in the north of the country. The major in charge of the town was convinced that Colin was a CIA agent. Close friends were tortured but would not denounce him. This same major kept the entire city in fear with only 34 men. If there was trouble in an area, the soldiers would drag out children from the houses and shoot them in front of their parents. After that there would be no more trouble.

St Matthew's Anglican Church was not closed as its congregation consisted almost exclusively of expatriates. Although it was safe, the government made it difficult to attend because of the Sunday driving ban. Every month Reg and I had to renew our permits just to be able to go to church. Because many expatriates had left, the congregation was greatly depleted.

Colonel Mengistu decided that he wanted to crush the Eritreans once and for all. Fifty per cent of government expenditure was going on armaments. While he bought up MiG fighter planes and guns and bombs, the roads fell to pieces, clinics and schools were starved of funds. In 1984 there was another terrible famine. This time a million people starved to death, but still he threw more and more people into the war. At one stage he was conscripting boys as young as fourteen.

In Addis there were shortages of everything. There were long bread queues, and it was difficult to buy sugar, oil and the staple grain, *tef*, for *injera*. Of course no imported food products could be found in any grocery stores.

Reg had an experience that would have been amusing if it wasn't so tragic. He went into an Armenian shop where we used to buy our stationery. At each request the shopkeeper responded, 'I haven't got that. I haven't got that.'

Finally Reg said, 'What have you got?'

With an expressive gesture he replied, 'Nothing but the shelves.'

Reg asked him why he did not close. He was not allowed to. He could not dismiss his workers and was slowly using up all his capital.

There were shortages of everything we needed for the hospital. Obtaining essential medical supplies was a major undertaking. Once a month Reg or I, or both of us together, would go to the central medical stores, taking Mamitu with us. Mamitu was a former patient who had stayed on to work at the hospital. Among many talents, she had a way with men – she was pretty, with a winsome manner, and extremely patient.

We would arrive with our long list and begin the tedious process, visiting each separate department that dealt with the many different categories of medical items. There was a department for antibiotics, another for surgical sutures, another for intravenous fluids, and so on.

Reg, perhaps seeking intravenous fluids, would approach the head of the section and say, nicely, 'I need 300 bags.'

There would be a great rolling of eyes and shrugging of shoulders. 'Impossible. They are all going to the Army.'

They both knew that this was just the opening gambit. Reg had dealt with these people for years, and they all liked him. He would chat with them about the weather and their families, all the while politely insisting that he simply had to have the drips.

With obstinate cases Mamitu's charm and quiet persistence were invaluable. It was impossible for any man to refuse this persuasive combination. A great saying in most departments is, 'Come back tomorrow'. She had a way about her that would melt the coldest heart. We frequently needed to make several trips in our VW to collect the stores we had bought, so the monthly visit always took up a whole day.

However, as difficult as it was to keep supplies up, and also to find donors willing to give to a hospital in a communist country, we were thankful that the *Dergue* did not interfere with us and that we were left alone to run the hospital as we wished.

After Mengistu had been in power for some years I was surprised one day to be asked, or rather ordered, to examine his wife as he was anxious for another son. He already had three children but only one boy.

I drove to the old palace, which was the seat of government, and where there was a clinic in the grounds. I had to leave my car at the entrance and be taken up the long drive in a military jeep. Once in the clinic I felt on familiar ground and actually knew the nurse in charge.

Mengistu's wife was a simple country girl of considerable beauty, with the natural charm of her peasant background. I felt sorry for her being thrust into such a position. Perhaps it was fortunate that she never did have another child.

Six months after the Princesses and their relatives were placed under house arrest they were taken to the main prison. Here at first they were crammed together in a small, vermin-infested cell with hardly room to move. Later they were housed in a special section for political prisoners. The eleven women were placed in one room, where at night they slept on mattresses on the floor, rolling them up during the day so they had some space to move around. Outside there was a tiny area where they could exercise and where in time Sybil coaxed a few herbs to grow to enhance their monotonous diet.

Sybil soon emerged as the leader, organising activities each day so that there was always something to occupy their time. At first this was tremendously difficult, almost impossible, for they were not allowed to have anything sent in from the outside except their food. After a while the rules became more lenient, and their life improved. Books were now allowed in. Sybil's first request was for a Bible, then she sent me and others lists of books that they wanted, and soon a library was organised. This was indeed their greatest boon.

Other activities that helped to fill in their days were sewing and knitting, tapestry work and basket-making. Their creative talents blossomed and we, their friends, received quite unconventional presents at Christmas.

Fortunately the Princesses had old school friends in England who never forgot them and who sent out a constant supply of things for them to work with which we, in Addis Ababa, could never have obtained from our empty shops. Tapestry, wool, books – and much else besides – all came from England.

Sybil's husband, Dejazmach Kassa Wolde Mariam, was with other male political prisoners in a dungeon under the palace. They, too, found it hard to fill in the time. One wrote a textbook on mathematics, which I think is amazing. I don't know how he could do such a thing while he was locked away, never knowing what his fate would be. He was the former mayor of Addis Ababa and one of the fortunate ones who was finally released.

Every Sunday after church I would take food to the prison, usually cakes and biscuits or jams and marmalade that I had made. I knew they liked these from their English school days.

I would have to queue with hundreds of others waiting with food for their relatives, and often it was a long wait. Sometimes I was fortunate to be taken to the front of the queue by one of the guards, as the Ethiopians are universally polite to foreigners. Nobody ever complained.

Once inside the prison gates, the food would be placed on a long trestle table to be inspected. Occasionally a soldier would poke his bayonet into a cake if he happened to be suspicious, but later they came to know me and this horrid habit ceased.

I never saw the Princesses face-to-face, but Sybil and Ruth became clever at secreting notes in food containers they were returning, and in this way I learned their needs. I tried my best to supply them – sometimes it was special books or a request for something from their friends in England. I soon felt that I knew these friends well through corresponding with them so often.

Sybil occasionally managed to smuggle out longer letters. Usually they were cheerful, telling me of their activities – a Christmas service they had held, singing from a hymnbook I had sent in; which herbs she had managed to grow in their tiny garden; a visit by one of them to the prison doctor.

But in one letter, six years into their internment, Sybil asked me to pray for her as she was losing her faith. She wrote that her life had been destroyed, she was eaten up by anxiety about her children and she did not know how she could face more years in prison.

She asked me to pray also for her husband because she had heard that he had been taken from the prison with eight others to an 'isolated place' and she was desperately worried.

It was impossible for me to write long letters back. I could only send brief notes with the food. But in these I tried to encourage and comfort her. I was able to send her a devotional book that I had found helpful and the *Pilgrim's Progress*, which she asked for. Surely, like Pilgrim in the book, she was going through a 'slough of despond', but like him, God would bring her out to the 'delectable mountains'. This He did, for I never again had a despondent letter from her.

Some of the Princesses' children were safe overseas, but there were still ten left in Ethiopia. Four of them were being looked after by an American missionary couple, Denton and Jodie

Collins. The other six belonged to Princess Edjigayehu and were living with relatives. While she was in prison Edjigayehu had died of an intussusception, or bowel obstruction. It had been misdiagnosed, and the operation done too late to save her life.

The Collins's situation was precarious. Mission properties were being confiscated all the time, and many had either fled the country or been forced out. Church leaders were disappearing. Now and then rumours swept the city that the children were about to be arrested and all the royal prisoners put on trial and executed.

The couple began thinking about how they could get the four children in their care out of the country to safety. They were held back by the thought of reprisals against the prisoners. Before they tried anything they wanted to know what their mothers, Princesses Sybil and Aida, thought.

A Dutchwoman, Mariette van de Loo, was closely connected to the Princesses. She had established the Ethiopian Women's Welfare Organisation and visited the prison regularly. She was sometimes able to see the royal prisoners in person.

Miss van de Loo also took a keen interest in the children. Sometimes she would bring them down to the hospital, and I would take them out for picnics. They weren't allowed to leave Addis Ababa, but there were one or two nice spots within the city limits where we could go.

Mrs Collins asked Miss van de Loo to find out what the Princesses thought of getting the children out of Ethiopia. At first she was shocked that Mrs Collins was even contemplating such a thing. She said if she had any plans not to tell her the details – for her own safety. Because of her close ties to the royal family, her own position in Ethiopia was tenuous. Indeed, eventually she was expelled from the country.

For a while Jodie heard nothing, then one day Miss van de Loo called on her at home. She declined refreshments and waited until the houseboy had left the room before leaning over and delivering her message in a whisper. The Princesses had told her that they would pay any price for their children's liberty. Jodie was free to make plans.

In early 1977 Jodie and her own two children flew to London, leaving Denton and the four others behind in Addis. There she made contact with Ras Mengesha, Princess Aida's husband, and his son Michael, who was the older brother of one of her charges. They decided to try to find a pilot who would be willing to fly from either Kenya or North Yemen into Ethiopian airspace and rendezvous with Denton and the children somewhere outside Addis Ababa.

Leaving Ras Mengesha to organise the search for a pilot, Jodie and Michael then caught the train to Oxford to visit a former British Ambassador to Ethiopia, Sir Thomas Bromley. Sir Thomas was a good friend of Ethiopia. In the early days of the revolution a member of the royal family had given him some jewellery, with instructions to use it for the benefit of the children.

When Jodie outlined her plan, Sir Thomas agreed immediately to help. He had been given seven pieces of jewellery, he said, which would probably fetch about £10,000. He had assumed that he would be spending it on the children's education, but as soon as the escape plan was mentioned he said there could be no better use for the money.

The Collinses were sure their phone in Addis would be tapped and their mail opened so they arranged a code to communicate with each other. They would pretend that they were talking about a relative, named Catherine, who was having an operation. If they said 'Catherine' was due for surgery on such and such a date, that was when the escape was planned. Jodie and her Ethiopian friends hoped to send someone back to Addis Ababa to convey the details of the 'surgery' to Denton. The contact man would be referred to as the 'doctor'.

Shortly after she had visited the former ambassador Jodie received a phone call from the wife of Prince Asfa Wossen, the Crown Prince of Ethiopia, who was also in exile in England. She asked to meet her at a restaurant in a London hotel.

As they politely sipped coffee, the matriarch of the royal

family explained the reason for her call. She was worried, she said, about the six children of her late step-daughter, Princess Edjigayehu, who were still being looked after by relatives in Addis Ababa. She wondered if Jodie would be able to help get them out of the country.

That would make ten children. Somewhat stunned at the enormity of the idea, Jodie gave her word that, if it were possible, she and Denton would do their best.

Two weeks after Jodie had arrived in London, Michael phoned with the news that the jewellery had been sold and that Sir Thomas had a cheque ready. Plans had been made for someone to go to North Yemen, where they thought there was a pilot who would be prepared to make the run. They suggested that Denton get permission from the authorities to take the children on a holiday to a missionary friend's house in the north of the country. On the pretext of going for a picnic they were to go to the mission airstrip. An aeroplane painted in mission colours would fly in from North Yemen and pick them up. The 'doctor' was ready to leave for Ethiopia to tell Denton about the plan.

Happy that everything was at last falling into place, Jodie flew with her two children to her parents' home in Oklahoma. As soon as she arrived she booked a call to her husband in Addis. Anxiously, she wrote down the coded conversation so that there would be no mistakes when he came on the line.

Connections to Ethiopia always took hours. When he finally answered, Denton sounded depressed. Mrs Collins held up her crib and read aloud, 'Catherine's surgery is scheduled for April 22. The doctor will contact you with all the details about Catherine's surgery.'

The line went quiet for a few moments. Then Denton said, 'Jodie, listen to me. Cancel Catherine's surgery.'

She shouted into the phone, 'What are you talking about, Denton? I can't cancel Catherine's surgery. Don't be silly. If I cancel her surgery, she will die. What do you mean?'

'Jodie, listen. Catherine will die if you don't cancel her surgery. Cancel it! I will write the details. Trust me.'

With that, he hung up.

It wasn't until she received a letter from Denton that she learned what had happened. He had been subjected to repeated harassment from government officials and forced to take the children to the security headquarters, where they were interrogated for hours. Later he had been called in to see the top security officer, a man named Timken, and asked point blank if he was planning on taking any children out of the country. It was right after this that Mrs Collins had phoned saying 'Catherine's operation' had been scheduled. He was sure he was being watched and his phone tapped. To go ahead then would have been too risky.

Soon Michael in London got in touch with Jodie with a new plan. This time Denton was to take the children south to Lake Langano on the pretence of a weekend excursion. A plane would fly in from Kenya and pick them up. Michael said the 'doctor' was standing by to go to Addis to convey all this to Mr Collins. When he arrived he would call and invite him to play a game of tennis.

Once again Jodie had to convey this to Denton by telephone in code. She explained that 'Catherine's operation' had been rescheduled and the 'doctor' was coming. She suggested that he should 'try and have a game of tennis'. It was frustrating having to speak in code like this. She could only hope that when the contact man called, Denton would understand what Jodie had been talking about.

A few days later he was at home when the telephone rang and the caller asked him if he would like to play some tennis today. He immediately understood what it meant.

Denton agreed to meet the 'doctor' at the Hilton Hotel. He arrived carrying his tennis gear. The contact showed him a letter of introduction from the Crown Prince, on his private letterhead, and they sat in the coffee lounge while he told him about the new plan. With ten children, Denton and the 'doctor', there were twelve all told. They had arranged for the aeroplane to fly to Lake Langano, the popular weekend retreat for expatriates, land on the beach and take them over the border to Kenya.

To Denton, isolated in Addis Ababa all this time, the plan seemed to be getting out of control. He was fearful and extremely reluctant to go ahead. Surely they could not all fit in one little plane?

The 'doctor' nonchalantly replied that if there wasn't enough room, then some would have to wait on the ground while the plane dropped off the first load and returned. The thought of hanging around waiting for hours struck fear into Denton's heart. It seemed madness to him. Nevertheless, he agreed to talk to his wife about it. After another guarded phone call to Jodie in America, he agreed that 'Catherine would have to have surgery.' It was set down for three weeks' time, Sunday 17 July.

The day before 'Operation Catherine', Denton picked up a Volkswagen mini bus that he had hired from the Ethiopian Tourist Association. To his alarm it was painted in garish black and white zebra stripes. He could not have chosen a more conspicuous vehicle if he had tried.

As they approached the checkpoint, one of the children, Menen, shyly told him that she had forgotten her identification card. This was a serious setback; the soldiers always thoroughly examined everyone's card.

Denton had his American passport, and all the other children had their correct papers. He decided they would try to bluff their way through.

They came up behind a queue of about 50 buses carrying troops down to the Somali border. He drove cautiously past them and slowed down to stop at the checkpoint. Sometimes these searches took hours as the soldiers examined everything, opening up and going through each piece of luggage. To his astonishment they just waved him through.

That night the twelve escapees stayed at the hotel. At nine next morning, as planned, they drove around the lake to a beach, parked the car and waited.

There was the faint drone of an aeroplane. The pilot did a couple of circuits and landed on the beach. As he watched it taxiing towards them, Denton's heart sank. The plane did not look nearly big enough to take all of them. Then he heard another faint sound. He searched the sky and out of the clouds appeared a second aeroplane.

The children quickly tumbled in. In one of the planes the seats had been taken out and the floor covered with mattresses so they could all fit in. They hung on as best they could and took off, heading south-east towards the Kenyan border.

Just over the border the pilot of Denton's plane pointed out a large salt lake and began to descend. The lake straddled the border between the two countries. They had flown up there the day before and dumped some fuel drums just over on the Kenyan side. The planes refuelled and took off again, their destination this time a game park about two hours drive from Nairobi.

When they landed they were greeted by an Italian tourist operator, Giorgio, who had organised the whole thing. Giorgio drove them to Nairobi and booked them into a hotel. From Nairobi the children went to Sweden and then to America and freedom.

I was delighted to hear that the children had escaped although worried that Mengistu might take reprisals against the Princesses still in prison.

After five or six years, nine of the men who were imprisoned in the dungeon were suddenly taken out and shot. One of them was Sybil's husband, Dejazmach Kassa Wolde Mariam, who had been the popular chancellor of the university and before that, governor of Wollega. We heard that he had had the opportunity to escape at the beginning of the revolution. He had served his country honourably and with distinction and thought, justifiably, that he had done nothing to warrant arrest. How sadly mistaken he was.

Another victim was a man we also knew well and admired, Ato Ababa Kebede. He ran the Emperor's Trust and it was he who had read out the citation when Reg received the Haile

Selassie Humanitarian Prize. I was bitterly angry when I heard he had been killed. He was a sweet-natured man, truly good and upright, with a deep Christian faith.

His wife, Tirawork Asfaw, or Terry as we called her, was also a good friend. She had been with Sybil and Ruth at school in England, did midwifery there and came back to Ethiopia to work at the Princess Tsehai Hospital in the maternity wing. She and I had much in common as we both loved gardening, and in our exhibits at the twice-yearly shows, often won prizes. She suffered great hardship as she was stripped of the wealth she had inherited from her father. Her way of life changed and she endured these years of uncertainty with great courage.

Terry used to go to the prison every day with food for her husband. One day they simply told her not to bring food any more but gave her no reason. She presumed he had been taken to some other part of the country and for years thought he was still alive.

Sybil, under the same illusion about her husband, wrote to me once asking me to pray for him. I came upon the letter again not long ago and was saddened to read her words, 'Pray for him that he'll be all right. We don't know where he is, he's somewhere in the country.' It was not until she was finally released that she learned the truth.

Year after year the Princesses endured imprisonment, with its privations, uncertainty and humiliation. They displayed, throughout, the patience under hardship that Ethiopians possess more than any other race I know. They were kept going by their tremendous fortitude and, I feel sure, their faith.

As time went on the *Dergue* came under considerable pressure, mainly from the British and Canadian governments and Amnesty International. After fifteen years the Princesses were told one morning to get up quickly and prepare to leave. They thought they were probably going to be shot. Instead, they were escorted out of the prison gates and told they were free.

They were provided with a house in town (their own homes had long ago been confiscated) and allowed to live together under some restrictions but with freedom to move about the city. They were not allowed to travel to other provinces, or to leave the country.

Sybil soon came to visit us at our hospital. It was an emotional meeting for us all. We threw our arms around each other and shed many tears. Over the years Sybil had got used to the cakes that I had taken to her in prison. There are only a limited number of recipes that work at this altitude, and I am sure she had tasted them all. When I served one of her favourites, we both laughed with delight at the simple pleasure of taking afternoon tea together in freedom. We talked about her experiences in prison and what had been happening in Ethiopia during her long internment.

One day Sybil invited me to meet Princess Tenagnework, the Emperor's daughter. I went to their home and sat in the drawing room waiting to be received, just as if we were in the palace. When we met, she still had the same regal presence I remembered from visits in happier times. The years of imprisonment had not changed her a bit. She thanked me for being a friend through their difficult years and for staying in Ethiopia.

Above all else Sybil longed to see her children again. She had four daughters and one son. She called her son Amaha, after a brother who had died as a young boy. Amaha was six months old when she was imprisoned. By the time she was released he was sixteen and living in America. She had missed his entire childhood.

Sybil told me what happened when she spoke to him on the phone. Both were so overwhelmed and crying so much that neither could hear what the other was saying. Another year was to pass before Sybil was allowed to go to America to meet her children.

There is a beautiful monument and memorial garden in the grounds of Selassie Cathedral in Addis Ababa, built by the families of those who were killed. They commemorate the 60 who were shot on that fateful November night in 1974 and the nine others who were taken from prison five years later, Sybil's husband among them.

You enter a nicely kept garden through a little gate opening onto a paved stone path that leads to the main monument. Just inside the gate, and on either side of the path, are two tombstones, one in English and the other in Amharic, reading, 'In memory of those brutally murdered by the Dergue.'

The monument at the end of the short path consists of a slightly curved wall. Upon it, embossed in copper, are figures in prison garb chained together. This wall partly surrounds a low dome, below which is a large excavated cave. As you enter you pass a brilliantly lit gold crucifix in a glass case, and on the opposite wall are two large paintings. One shows the 60 being executed by firing squad. The other depicts the nine who were taken from prison and strangled, then thrown into a mass grave. A man sits on a chair with his hands and feet chained together and a cord around his neck, being strangled by a soldier, and in the doorway is the next waiting victim. On the other walls are large framed photographs of all these people, with their title and rank written below each.

I visited this sad place with my friend Tirawork. As we gazed silently at the pictures of these men, many of whom I personally knew, the horror and cruelty of those dark days was brought back vividly to me. I am thankful that these victims are not forgotten.

About six months after the hospital opened we had moved from our old home at Princess Tsehai to a house we had built in the grounds of the new hospital. The Red Terror was just beginning, and many anti-government students were being killed by Mengistu's soldiers.

Yeshi's son, Yohannes, who was in the twelfth grade, became involved with an anti-government organisation that was distributing pamphlets. I remember one of them said,

'Everything is becoming more expensive, only life is cheap.' Because of his activities he became a marked boy. He moved around all the time, never staying in one place for more than a night. Yeshi was terrified that he would be captured and shot.

To comfort Yeshi I told her that we would hide him. Our house was unlikely to be searched, in fact few people knew that it even existed. We had built it without any permission and it never had a number. It was hidden among trees below the hospital looking out over the river, so we had no neighbours and were secluded.

Yeshi was relieved, and for several weeks Yohannes camped in our laundry, hardly venturing out even into the garden. We were sure that nobody in our hospital would betray him, but as the Red Terror increased in intensity the staff became worried. One day Birru, as their spokesman, came and told us of their concerns. He explained, 'If Yohannes is discovered hiding here, you will be thrown out of the country, the hospital will have to close, and we shall probably all be shot.'

This was much too risky, so we reluctantly told Yohannes that he would have to go. We asked him to ring every day or two to assure us and his mother that he was all right. This he did twice, and then we heard nothing from him.

Yeshi was arrested and taken to the local detention centre with a number of other women. Here she was pushed to the floor, and soldiers threatened her with guns. Fortunately Yeshi was not tortured. As she could truthfully say that she did not know where Yohannes was, she was released in three days.

Yeshi believed that he would be all right, but I had doubts. There were too many stories of students being hunted down and killed. Their bodies were disposed of in mass graves or thrown over high cliffs on the outskirts of the city as food for the hyenas.

When I suggested to Yeshi that she must accept that he might be dead, she replied, 'I know he is all right, and that Christos will look after him as I've been praying for him.' This she did every day, and it was touching to see her faith.

A year passed with no word. I'd given up hope that he was

alive, then one day when I was lying on my bed Yeshi came running in in a state of great excitement with the news that Yohannes was back. The government had issued a proclamation of amnesty, and he had decided to give himself up.

We later heard how he had spent the last year. Disguising himself as a beggar, he had travelled to the northern province of Wollo, where he joined other beggars around a pool of holy water. A farmer's wife spotted him and knew at once that he was not what he pretended. 'I know you're not a beggar,' she said. 'Come home with me and I'll look after you.'

In the countryside the hunt for students was not so intense, and so for the next year Yohannes was safe, working as a labourer on the farm. If soldiers or police came, the farmer kept him hidden. Yeshi was enormously grateful to the farmer and his wife, and she was able to visit them one day and thank them. On the way she went into the famous monastery of Debre Libanos to give thanks to God for keeping her son safe.

Yohannes spent a short time in prison after he gave himself up. This was more of a formality than anything else, and he was not ill-treated. After his release I managed to get him a job with Orbis, the Mercedes dealer. Yohannes is now in charge of the spare-parts department.

It was still a hard time for young men. Soldiers would go into houses, drag out any boys of military age and send them away to the war with Eritrea. One of our nursing sisters, who had three boys, moved them every night to a different location.

Mengistu tried his best to force communist ideology on the people. One method was to hold indoctrination classes in all the government factories, schools and hospitals. Attendance was compulsory. We never had classes inflicted on us, probably because our staff was not big enough, or perhaps we were just fortunately forgotten. Nobody was ever able to tell me what they learned at these sessions. When I quizzed nurses from the Black Lion Hospital, they told me, 'Nothing. We don't listen.'

Certainly all the so-called reforms, literacy campaigns, indoctrination and liquidating 'enemies of the state' made no difference to the lives of the women we were seeing. The peasants were still desperately poor, ill-fed and uneducated. Medical care in the provinces did not improve, and travel was made even more difficult because of the escalating war with Eritrea.

Our poor, neglected fistula patients still came flocking to our door in rags and smelling of urine, hoping that we could give them a new life. People asked me why we did not leave. How could we turn our backs on so much need?

Chapter Nineteen

We cured so many thousands of women that most of them have become a blur. When I reflect back over the years, however, certain faces come swimming unbidden out of the tide of memory. Even though everyone's story was amazing, some were even more so. One young woman arrived at the hospital and handed us an envelope with a letter inside that had been written by a missionary doctor down near the Kenyan border. It introduced her and asked us to treat her fistula. There was nothing especially unusual about her. Like so many of our patients she was dressed in rags and weak from hunger. The sealed envelope was so worn and grubby you could hardly read it, but inside the clean letter was legible enough. To our surprise it had been dated seven years ago.

'Why has it taken you seven years to get here?' I asked.

She told me she had been begging at the bus station for her fare. That was how long it took to raise the money.

Fifteen-year-old Mahoubar was orphaned at the age of seven. Her relatives sold her into virtual slavery. She was raped and beaten. When she was seven months pregnant she ran away and returned to her relatives. Far from being sympathetic, they forced her to work in the fields until her labour began. She told us that it started one Wednesday, then another Wednesday passed. On Saturday the baby was born. It was a dead boy, and Mahoubar was left with fistulas in her bladder and rectum.

As so often happens with these girls, she was sent to live alone, away from any contact with her village society. In this case it was an empty hut in a desolate area. Soon hyenas, attracted by the smell of her condition, began to circle the hut. Mahoubar was so afraid that she dragged herself to a mission clinic and was eventually brought by them to our hospital.

Poor child. Not only did she have fearful injuries but also damage to the nerve routes in her pelvis from the long pressure of the baby's head, resulting in crippling injuries to both feet. This type of nerve palsy is quite common and can lead to further crippling. Not being able to walk easily following the long labour, many lie in bed curled up, hoping against hope that the urine will dry up if they keep very still. As a result of weeks and sometimes months of immobility, their leg muscles waste, then joints become stiff and contractions occur. Then their condition is pitiable indeed. We see them being carried through our gate on the back of a father or brother. I have even seen them alone, crawling on hands and knees. These patients are with us for months, sometimes years.

Mahoubar was one of those who had to learn to walk, at first with a walking frame, later with sticks and special boots to keep her feet from dragging. Now she is on our staff as a nursing aide, walking normally and cured of her fistula injuries. She has no home to go to, so we have given her a home with us in the hospital. Mahoubar has learned to read and write. Through her contact with others and by reading the Bible she has become a Christian.

It is hard to convey to people in the developed world how poor these patients are. One woman, who was divorced by her husband because of her fistula, had a calf as part of her settlement. It was her only possession. She had to wait until it grew big enough to sell in order to cover her bus fare to Addis Ababa.

As I browse through old photographs I am reminded of two girls who arrived together. They declared that they had to have their operations on the same day as they had ridden together on a horse from their distant village and needed to ride home together. The horse was being held by a man down the road.

We did what they asked, and they rode home as they had come, this time each in a new dress and with joy in their hearts. A few years later one of the girls returned to be delivered safely of a live baby. We took a photograph of mother and child on one of our own horses as a reminder of how she had first come to us.

As our work became known and our reputation grew, gynaecologists and surgeons from other developing countries came to visit us. Some would stay a few weeks to watch and learn our techniques. They began by assisting at operations, then attempted surgery themselves, starting with simple cases. We had a small guest *tukul* in the grounds where they could stay.

Reg and I attended to every aspect of the hospital. For years we never had anyone to do the administrative tasks. During the day we would examine the new patients in our small outpatient room, admit them, do our ward rounds and, on three days every week, operate in the theatre. In the evenings after dinner, Reg would retire to a primitive little office he had built onto one end of the house to do all the accounts and write up the records, filing them all with meticulous care. He did everything in beautiful longhand, although if he was appealing for funds or writing to someone special he would ask a friend to type the letter for him.

Almost from the start of our life in Ethiopia Reg was constantly on the lookout for likely donors and would scan the newspapers or note the names of wealthy people who came up in conversation. On most mornings he would be up at five o'clock to write letters of appeal before starting work for the day at the hospital. The letters had to be short and unusual enough to capture attention.

To the Chairman of British Petroleum, Sir Henry Drake, in London, he wrote, 'While you have been drilling holes in the Middle East and making a profit, we have been mending holes in the Horn of Africa and making a loss.'

Sir Henry wrote back and said that unfortunately their trust did not operate in Ethiopia but, because it was such an unusual appeal, he was sending £500 himself.

The search for funds never stopped, as we needed money coming in continuously if our work with the fistula pilgrims was to continue. Recently, looking through a little book of Bible texts that Reg used to read, I found written in the margin for 20 December, 'Money arrived today for fistula patients, 1,000 pounds from Aunt Jean, 500 pounds from Eric Vincent, 220 pounds from New Zealand.'

Eric Vincent was one of our most generous donors in the early days. We called him the Blue Bird Toffee Man because that was how he had made his fortune. Another generous British benefactor was Sir Julian Hodge, a multi-millionaire financier, socialist and philanthropist who had founded a bank in Wales.

It was while on holiday in Malindi that Reg first heard of the Jane Hodge Foundation. Casually scanning a newspaper in Lawford's Hotel lounge, he came across a small paragraph with news of this charity in Wales. Sir Julian's response to Reg's appeal letter was immediate. Ever since he has contributed generously, rescuing us from time to time from financial difficulties. He continues in his old age to show an interest in all our activities and corresponds regularly from his home in the Channel Islands.

It soon became obvious that if we were ever going to raise enough to meet expenses, we would have to go to America. The first time we tried to tap into America's wealth was during our long leave in 1973. When I look back on it I realise how naive we were. We bought a book called the *Foundation Grants Index*, a big, heavy hardback of 292 pages giving basic data about American foundations.

There were 5254 of them. In our hotel room in New York we started ringing those that were interested in Africa. In fact we hired two rooms so we could each have a phone. It was tedious and frustrating, and we were discouraged by the lack of interest. It was hard to convince anyone that we had more merit than the hundreds of other supplicants they had to deal with. One after the other they fobbed us off until we were beginning to think it was a complete waste of time.

After spending most of the day on this fruitless and exhausting effort and achieving nothing, Reg had an inspirational thought. 'Let's just ring World Vision before we give up,' he said.

We had no idea of the phone number, but the hotel operator amazed us by the speed with which she connected us to World Vision Canada, in Toronto, and not to the US office in Seattle as we had expected. This was fortunate, as Reg was able to speak at once to the head, Don Scott. He said, 'Tell me your story quickly.' Reg did and received immediate encouragement. Mr Scott told him that there would be someone going to Ethiopia from World Vision Canada in the next few weeks and he would arrange for this person to visit us.

Sure enough, soon after we got back a representative arrived at the hospital, and as the result of this visit and Don Scott's enormous sympathy with what we were doing, we received a huge donation from World Vision Canada. This generosity has continued over the years.

While we were in Sydney before leaving for New York we had looked up an old friend, Bob MacBeth. He had been assistant medical superintendent at Crown Street while Reg was superintendent. He was also Reg's closest friend and had been his best man at our wedding.

When Bob heard of our fundraising plans he suggested we visit his uncle, James Duncan, in Bermuda. Mr Duncan certainly seemed a remarkable man. He had been born in Scotland and sent to be educated with a relative in France. When he left school he went to Canada to seek his fortune. He rose to be head of the big tractor manufacturing company, Massey Ferguson, and then got involved with building the St Lawrence Seaway, which connects the Great Lakes to the ocean.

Mr Duncan was a millionaire many times over. He moved in fabulously wealthy circles, was a friend of Winston Churchill and knew many captains of industry. Bob contacted him, and we received an invitation to visit. Before we left, Bob warned, 'Reg, don't rattle the moneybox under his nose as soon as you get there.'

We made arrangements to visit him on our way home from the United States. Mr Duncan suggested that before we went to Bermuda we might like to have some time to ourselves at another house he owned in Jamaica. It was built in a millionaire's enclave – a beautiful little bungalow with a balcony overlooking a picturesque bay. We spent a few days there, being looked after by the servants and having a rest in idyllic surroundings.

This pleasant interlude was only a foretaste of what was to come. In Bermuda, Mr Duncan lived in a two-storey mansion with a colonnaded front, called Somerset House. There were endless expanses of immaculate lawns and beautiful gardens, a swimming pool and lots of servants padding about to attend to our every whim.

Our host always dressed in a cream linen suit. In his seventies, he was married to a Spanish woman, his second wife, who had been a dancer. They had three children. For two days we had a wonderful time, swimming and going out in boats on a calm, azure sea. Over lunches and dinners we told him all about our work in Ethiopia but, mindful of Bob's warning, we refrained from asking him for money.

Shortly before we were due to leave, he made it easy for us by saying to Reg, 'Tell me, why have you come to see me?'

Reg told him we were hoping he might be able to help us raise money for our work. He agreed that he would, but no mention was made of any figure.

Many months later a letter arrived from Mr Duncan. He had contributed some money himself, personally approached many of his friends and set up a trust for us in Canada. Enclosed was a cheque for US$50,000.

Some time later Mr Duncan called to see us in Addis Ababa on his way to China to gather material for a book he was writing. We arranged for him to meet the Emperor. He said this was the highlight of his visit, but what I remember most about it was the awful bout of food poisoning Reg and I suffered after dining with him at his hotel. We both thought we were dying, and it was with trepidation that we rang Mr Duncan next morning thinking that, because of his age, he might have been seriously ill. Instead he cheerfully told us he was perfectly well and looking forward to the lunch party we were giving him that day.

We were helped in all sorts of ways on our next trip to America. For our visit to New York we were provided with a fabulous home all to ourselves, lent to us by a kind family. This good fortune came about because their gynaecologist son-in-law, Park Gray, had worked with us on a WHO scholarship for six months while we were still at the Princess Tsehai Memorial Hospital. We had got to know him well, also his wife and two small boys. When he heard of our proposed trip he suggested we might be able to stay at one of his wealthy father-in-law's houses, thus saving big hotel bills.

The family had a house on Long Island Sound in Connecticut that stood empty for much of the year as they preferred to live in their New York apartment. It was there that we had to go to meet them to be appraised.

They approved us, and we moved into their beautiful home. The garden was one I shall never forget. There were stretches of lawn with rhododendrons, azaleas, dogwood trees and elms in profusion. The grounds were practically surrounded by water. The house, built of white timber with grey shutters, a shingled roof and covered with wisteria, was right on the water's edge. It was furnished with exquisite taste and fitted with every luxury you could imagine. The bedroom we slept in was painted a pale blue with blue and white cretonne curtains and a cream carpet; it had its own bathroom and a sitting room with French doors that opened out directly onto a white jetty with a boat.

We were unused to such luxury and all the wonderful appliances that did everything at the touch of a button. Our only concern was the housekeeper. She was a Scottish woman who had been with the family 30 years. We enjoyed talking to her and listening to her broad Scottish accent, but her great weakness was alcohol. Reg found her one night sitting in the car completely drunk. She wanted to drive home, but we persuaded her to come inside and spend the night in the house.

Every day we would go up to New York on the train to tell our story to some foundation or charity. Our British benefactor Eric Vincent, the Blue Bird Toffee Man, had recommended us to a friend of his, John Loeb, a wealthy New York stockbroker. One day Mr Loeb organised a lunch for us at his apartment on Park Avenue, inviting twenty of his wealthy friends.

His lavishly furnished apartment took up two floors of the building. It was spacious and grand, and perfectly suited our tall, distinguished host and his elegant wife. After being warmly greeted, we were introduced to the other guests. In the dining room three round tables, spread with starched damask, sparkled with cut glass and polished silver. Overhead hung a beautiful chandelier. One of the guests was the attractive actress, Joan Fontaine. She took Reg by the arm and said, 'You're sitting next to me, baby.'

I sat next to the widow of Roger Hammerstein, the composer. We ate a delicious lunch, and then Mr Loeb asked Reg if he could tell his story in ten minutes, as New Yorkers were very busy and impatient to get back to their work.

Reg shot back, 'I can do it in five, if you like.' He made a brief but moving speech, which evidently touched the hearts of this sophisticated group as we walked out of Mr Loeb's apartment with $24,000.

For years afterwards, every now and then we would receive a cheque from Mr Loeb or sometimes from his daughter's trust, for $15,000 or thereabouts. It would be accompanied by a note that read, 'I had a feeling you might need this.' And often it came just in time to pay the bills.

Another appointment we managed to arrange was with the Rockefeller Foundation. We were excited about this as we knew of their immense wealth and generosity. Looking like commercial travellers with our briefcase of photographs and brochures, we arrived at the Rockefeller Building, caught the lift to the forty-seventh floor and were shown into an office, where a group of people received us warmly. They seemed to be dying to hear what we had to say.

We brought out the photographs and began our talk. They had never heard about the fistula problem and seemed incredulous until we mentioned that it was an American, Dr J. Marion Sims, who was the first to show that it was possible to cure sufferers. Then they became especially interested and began asking questions.

The meeting went on for more than half an hour. They seemed so fascinated and eager to know all about the work, that our spirits rose. The Rockefeller Foundation had assets of $757 million. We felt sure they were going to give us a big donation that would set us up for life. Finally we reached the point where we asked for money. The secretary said, 'In all my time here I have never heard of such a worthy cause. We are just so sorry, but our charter doesn't extend further north than Uganda.'

Reg and I were amazed at the wealth in America. Two millionaire doctors, husband and wife, invited us to dinner at their home in Connecticut. In front of their magnificent house were parked four Mercedes-Benz cars and an Oldsmobile. We went in expecting to find a large group of fellow guests – but we were the only ones. The five cars belonged to our hosts. They also had two light planes, a yacht and a ski lodge near Canada. We went home confident that a large cheque would soon arrive. No cheque has ever come, although for many years they sent us Christmas cards illustrated with an etching of their ski lodge.

In Seattle we were invited to go to the cathedral and speak

to the diocesan staff. Leaving our hotel we tried in vain to find a taxi. We moved from street to street hailing to no avail. Suddenly a big car pulled up, and a lady stepped out saying, 'It must be four years since I last saw you both.' She was an American tutor–sister who used to work at the Ministry of Health in Addis Ababa.

She drove us to the cathedral. Inside the hall well-dressed ladies were cutting up sandwiches and putting out coffee cups and cakes on trestle tables. Reg asked one of them if she had a projector.

'No. Whatever for?'

He was just about to answer when every eye turned towards a glamorous-looking woman, who had just arrived. She was greeted warmly and kissed on both cheeks by the Bishop. Reg asked his sandwich-making friend who she was.

'That is Mrs Waddell. She has flown from New York to be our guest speaker.'

It seemed there was some sort of mix-up. We were not the guest speakers, we were simply guests.

After this muddle had been explained, the Bishop asked us to speak as well, and Seattle has since been extremely generous to us.

We arrived in San Francisco late on a Saturday afternoon to give another talk. After greeting us our host said, 'You are to preach at the Episcopalian Church at 11 am tomorrow.'

'Did you say preach?' said Reg.

'Why, yes, of course.'

'But I don't preach.'

'Oh, dear. I understood you were missionaries. Do you think you can manage? It has been advertised in the church newsletter.'

Reg didn't turn a hair. He preached on the lesson for the day and, I thought, did it rather well. But he also managed to bring in the needs of our patients and reduced many in the congregation to tears.

In Chicago we arrived fifteen minutes early for a Rotary luncheon to make sure everything was set up correctly. It was just as well because they had forgotten the slide projector that we had asked for. Someone rushed out and hired a machine that was so sophisticated we had no idea how to work it.

One of the Rotarians volunteered to take care of it. The lights were dimmed, and the coughing and scraping of chairs died down as the audience turned their attention to the screen. The first slide showed a pretty Ethiopian nurse.

'Here we have one of our beautiful nurses,' said Reg. 'You can see how lovely she is.'

For an instant the beautiful nurse appeared on the screen, then a metallic click came from the projector and the nurse shot up towards the ceiling, leaving only her legs and ankles in view.

The audience shifted restlessly. Reg kept talking while the volunteer fiddled with the machine. After a minute or two the nurse appeared again.

'As I was saying,' resumed Reg. 'Here is one of our lovely nurses.' The machine gave another click, and the nurse disappeared once more. Four times this scenario was repeated. Every time Reg started to speak, the slide disappeared again.

Towards the end the all-male audience was calling out, 'She's a sweetie. Hold her there. Hold her, hold her. Come on, baby, don't go.' They were laughing so much that they were falling out of their chairs.

In the end Reg gave up the slides and did the talk unaided.

My impressions of America were influenced by the tremendous contrasts between their way of life and that which we had become accustomed to in Ethiopia. In America everyone seemed to be in a hurry, the fevered activity mostly centred on making money. That sense of frenzy and the fabulous riches we saw were all so different – even shocking.

We would visit doctors in their homes, and there might be four cars in the driveway – one for every member of the family – but they never seemed to eat together. The parents would take us out to a restaurant, and the children would be out somewhere else with their friends. The family seemed to spend very little time together. It was a completely different way of life to the old-fashioned existence we were used to.

We were entertained by gynaecologists whom we knew or were acquainted with through our work. Meetings were arranged for us at medical centres, where the audience often responded to Reg's talks with a standing ovation. Their enthusiasm was so great that it filled us with hope that they would surely help. But in spite of promises and pledges we seldom raised much money. It was usually only enough to pay our fare to the next centre.

Some doctors gave us surprising advice, advocating birth control to solve all the problems of obstetric fistulae. Others suggested that we should sterilise our patients after the repair operation to prevent it happening again, as in any case, there were too many babies being born in the developing world.

This was bad advice, to be condemned at once. Such sweeping statements reflected their ignorance about the patients' needs, even if well meant. These people were just thinking of American society and they didn't understand the position of women in Ethiopia. Most of our patients are young peasant women in their teens or early twenties, with little or no education. For many it is their first pregnancy that ends in tragedy – a dead baby and a fistula. To condemn such girls to a childless future would be abysmal, for their happiness depends on being able to have a husband and family. They wouldn't be able to marry again if it was known that they couldn't have a baby. They would be forced to live alone, trying to earn their living with no education and without the comfort of having a family.

When we were working at the old hospital, where we did a lot of obstetrics as well, we often saw these repaired fistula patients coming back to us pregnant, and were able to look after their labour. Some needed a caesarian section, others an assisted delivery, while some were even delivered normally. I have many treasured photographs of them smiling and holding their babies. Reg would frequently comment, 'For these girls, the wheel of fortune has turned full circle. They have what every woman wants, a live baby in their arms.'

Our fundraising trips always included a week or two in Australia, where I would catch up with my family. My sister, Ailsa, was married to a farmer, Graham Pottie, near Molong in New South Wales. In her later years my mother moved to a little cottage on Ailsa and Graham's farm, with Bertha, the housemaid who had been her faithful companion and friend ever since we were children.

Bertha never ate a good meal; she lived on apples and wheat biscuits. I am sure that without my mother's care she would have faded away. I often heard my Mother say, 'Bertha, if it wasn't for me, you would have been dead long ago.' This sounded a blunt way of expressing her concern, but Bertha would be persuaded then to drink the frequent cups of Ovaltine and milk that my mother prepared for her and to take the vitamin pills that she gave her.

In early June, 1982, I was stunned to get a phone call from my mother announcing, 'Oh, Catherine, I've got the cancer I always dreaded. And already it is in my liver, so I'm going to die.'

She had always been a strong person with great vigour and enthusiasm for life. It was hard to believe this awful news. I told her I would come straightaway.

Under these circumstances the formalities of leaving the country were speeded up, and instead of the usual wait of weeks to get an exit visa, I had it in 24 hours. Ethiopians are amazingly sympathetic and kind in such emergencies. I was booked on Ethiopian Airlines to Bombay where, the following day, I would catch a Qantas flight to Sydney.

As I left Bombay Airport to go to my hotel, a man dressed as a porter approached me and took my bag. I thought this was normal, but as we reached the pavement a policeman grabbed him and placed him under arrest. He was not a porter but a thief, despite the uniform.

Next day I arrived in Sydney and drove straight up to Molong. My mother was cheerful and firmly determined not to go to hospital. Quite rightly, she knew that nothing could be done. All her family gathered around her. Sheila, our eldest sister, and her gynaecologist husband, John, came from Sydney, also my brother Peter, with his wife Pat. Peter had recently been made a doctor of engineering, and we were all proud of him.

Two other brothers came – Donald, a forester from Atherton in Northern Queensland, and Jock, a farmer from the Tamworth district. Jock and his wife Louise had two small children, and they were a particular delight to my mother. She made a tape for them giving a short history of her life so that they could remember her voice.

Jock was the youngest in our family and therefore a special son to my mother. He had been her companion for many years after my father's death. They lived on a farm, also in the Molong district. Mother converted the small dilapidated farmhouse into a lovely home with an exquisite garden. It is difficult to say whether my mother provided a home for Jock or vice versa, but whichever it was, it was a delightful place. Reg and I spent many happy days there when on leave in Australia. It was only after Jock fell in love and got married that my mother moved to Ailsa's cottage.

Mother joked that she could only get all the family around her when she was on her deathbed.

For the next few days relatives and friends came to see her, and my mother entertained everyone as though nothing was amiss. She would get up each day and sit in the drawing room, incredibly brave and serene, demonstrating to all of us how deep and sure was her Christian faith. It was impossible to feel sad and depressed when she was so bright. But soon her appetite failed, and she became weak and unable to leave her bed.

I had a bad cold at the time, and even when she was so ill she was concerned for me because she heard me coughing at night in the next-door room. A nurse came to help us when my poor mother was too weak to help herself. Towards the end I slept on the floor beside her so I was able quickly to give her injections for pain relief prescribed by the local doctor.

She never became unconscious, she just lay there with her eyes shut, listening to us talking around her bed, reading passages from the Bible to her or singing her favourite hymns. I am so thankful we were able to look after her in her own home and that she was never left alone for a minute of the day. She always had one of the family and Bertha, too, to sit beside her, hold her hand and comfort her during her last lonely fight with death.

On the night of 25 June I gave my mother an injection for pain at about 10 pm and she drifted off to sleep peacefully. Her pulse was feeble and her breathing shallow, so I knew she was dying. I rang the family in the main house and told them to come down to the cottage. Suddenly my mother sat up, opened her eyes and exclaimed, 'Jesus,' as though she had seen Heaven open and Jesus there to welcome her. She then sank back on the pillows and was gone.

We stood around her bed and prayed and cried. We had lost someone who had been at the very centre of our lives, who had shared our experiences, joyful or sad, for as long as we could remember. For all the years that I had been in Ethiopia, my mother had written at least once a week and often more frequently – long letters, which kept me in touch with Australia and my family. Life would seem empty without her.

I only had two weeks leave. Before returning to Ethiopia I was able attend the moving service taken by her godson and nephew, the Rev. Broughton Knox, and to see her buried beside my father in a garden cemetery. At her graveside her brother, the only surviving member of her large family, made an emotional speech about his 'little sister', recalling their happy childhood on the sugar plantation in Bundaberg, Queensland. My mother was in her eighty-fifth year when she died.

Chapter Twenty

Before I go further I must mention some who have become, in a special way, my Ethiopian family. I speak of our nursing aides, who are all important to me. Perhaps it is because of the suffering they have endured with such courage or the years they have spent with us. Perhaps it is because of their devotion to the fistula patients or just their endearing personalities. More often it is all of these reasons combined.

Each and every one of these women has a distressing history. Some have endured numerous surgical operations, and many still have medical problems. For this reason they have not been able to return to their distant villages. They live in the hospital compound, and some have been with us since the Princess Tsehai days.

Letekidane Gebre Yohannes is one. She arrived 30 years ago from northern Shoa province with a dead baby inside her and a history of being in labour for five days. A craniotomy, or compressing of the baby's head, was done, and the decomposing baby delivered. Lete's injuries were severe – a fistula into her rectum and a hole into what remained of her bladder. Most of the bladder had been destroyed and it was reduced to the size of a thimble.

Lete underwent many repair operations but was never cured of her urinary incontinence. For many years she did her hospital work with a ureteric catheter in one of the strictured ureters, wearing a test tube strapped to her leg or an empty drip-set bag, where the urine from that kidney would collect. Gradually her kidneys became diseased, and her life was endangered.

Dr Gordon Williams, a urologist from the famous postgraduate Hammersmith Hospital in London, is a friend to Ethiopia and to our hospital particularly. He agreed to come out and operate on Lete, in spite of the opinion of other surgeons who saw her and predicted that her kidneys would surely fail with any further surgery.

As her condition was life-threatening without surgery, Gordon bravely said he would go ahead. He did what is known as an ileal conduit operation, where a segment of small bowel, or ileum, is separated from the rest of the gut and used as a reservoir for urine. The two ureters from the kidneys are implanted into one end of this segment, while the other end opens with a stoma on to the abdominal wall. To this stoma a collecting bag is attached that can be emptied periodically through a small tap.

Thanks to Gordon's surgical skill and speed, Lete withstood the surgery well and has been healthy ever since – the life of a very special person saved, and saved to serve. This Lete has done ever since, with faithfulness, always cheerful and extremely competent. She runs the outpatients' department and one of the hospital stores.

Lete is a small, limping figure, from a congenital partial dislocation of the hip, about 1.6 metres tall, with a rather solemn expression, working quietly and obviously loving her job. Nothing is ever too much trouble for her.

Over the years she has saved up enough money to build herself a little house so that when she is too old to work she will have somewhere to live.

Another who has built herself a house is Enatanesh Demisse. Like Lete, she arrived at the Princess Tsehai Memorial Hospital with terrible injuries. She, too, needed many operations to finally cure her fistula. We used a muscle from her leg to rebuild a destroyed urethra, and this thankfully restored her continence. It is easy to pick her out as she quietly goes about her job in the wards because of the distinctive tattoo marks she has around her neck, in the form of a perfect choker – many rows of small dots, all evenly spaced, obviously done by an expert.

Tattoo marks, often a Coptic cross on the forehead, usually denote that patients are from the provinces of Gojam or Gondar and that they belong to the Orthodox Church, which is strong in these regions.

Enatanesh, like all the other nursing aides we employ, goes once a year to visit her family. On one holiday she became critically ill with peritonitis arising from a pelvic abscess. At first we despaired for her life, but with blood transfusions, urgent surgery and powerful antibiotics, she made a remarkable recovery. Perhaps because of all she has been through she is particularly kind and sympathetic to all the new patients.

Lete Birhan sleeps in the first bed of our main ward, with all her worldly possessions beside her in a small chest of drawers and a wheelchair in the corner. Lete is one of our dearest and oldest workers. She arrived from Aksum in Tigray Province with a fistula only a few years after we had begun working in Ethiopia.

Her fistula was unusual. It had not been caused by childbirth. Lete was betrothed when she was a young girl, then it was discovered that she had an inperforate hymen, so to remedy this and prepare her for marriage a *wogesha* was called. During the 'operation' he cut through her urethra and bladder, thus causing her complete incontinence and a fistula. We mended her injuries, but the experience she had suffered was so traumatic that she decided she did not want to marry and stayed on at the hospital to help. Some time later she was knocked over by a car and broke her back. She is paralysed from the waist down.

For many years Lete helped in the operating theatre, but her special forte is our new physiotherapy department, where she has been trained by Jenny Bassford, a visiting English physiotherapist. She helps the many patients who are crippled through nerve damage or disuse atrophy of the muscles and contractions of the joints from long immobility in bed. She is tireless in the encouragement she gives these girls and in the exercises she teaches them. Many owe their ability to lead normal lives again to Lete's perseverance.

Lete is a familiar sight in her wheelchair, propelling herself through the hospital or along a special path to the physiotherapy room. Despite her disability I have never heard her complain. Her contentment and serenity are obvious to all those who work with her, and her courage is an example to us all. Even when sitting quietly on the verandah in the afternoon, Lete is usually busy, perhaps cutting and folding gauze, knitting garments for her nieces and nephews or for my grandchildren. Often when I go up in the late evening to visit the ward I find a group of her friends sitting round her bed laughing, gossiping and knitting.

It is a happy scene, one that characterises the spirit of our hospital. Much of that spirit is due to our nursing aides. Despite their permanent afflictions, they display an innate serenity and consistent grace, which I am sure spills over to the patients. They are never rude or abrasive and treat even the most abject peasant woman with courtesy. I am constantly hearing from people who work in other hospitals how special ours is, and I am sure that this is so because of our wonderful staff.

I have watched Birru, who started working for us as a teenager the first year we arrived, grow up, marry, have a family and send his own children out into the world. About seventeen years ago his wife, Edjigayehu, developed a rare sarcoma in the lung. It was unfortunately inoperable, so we brought her to the hospital and nursed her in a little room on her own for two or three weeks until she died. And so Birru was left a widower, with five young children to bring up by himself – four sons and a daughter. He has applied himself to this task with consistent devotion.

We employ his eldest boy, Getahun, at the hospital as a clerk. This is a responsible job, as he is often the first person to welcome the new patients. He treats them with courtesy and sympathy, taking their history and filling in the cards before they go to the outpatients' department to be examined by the doctor.

Getahun does lots of other jobs as well and is constantly at everyone's beck and call, running messages willingly, helping in the pharmacy and keeping the records store-room in order, with all the cards filed properly.

We are all pleased to see him working so well because when he joined the staff he had a problem with drugs. He picked up the habit in the Ogaden, an arid area near Somalia. There it is common to see people chewing a herb called *chat,* which causes hallucinations and is addictive.

This upset Birru terribly, and we were all concerned for Getahun's future. Everyone rallied to the young man's support, and with his willing co-operation, this wretched habit has been cured.

Another son, Tsegai, is a carpenter. I am pleased to be able to employ him from time to time when we need a piece of furniture made, as I helped put him through an apprenticeship with a big woodworking firm. When he finished his apprenticeship he got a job with a builder but now he prefers to work on his own and he is making a great success of it.

Birru's third son, Tesfaye, is a soldier in the Regular Army. Recently he was fighting at the front line in the war with Eritrea. How relieved we all were to see him return home safe and sound when this long, wretched conflict came to an end in August 2000.

Tesfaye's best friend, a boy who grew up here in Addis Ababa with him, was an Eritrean and so fought on the other side. This bizarre situation was common in the war, as

Ethiopians and Eritreans previously lived together side by side and were like brothers.

A great sorrow in Birru's life has been the tragedy of his fourth son, Mesfin, born with Down's Syndrome. Birru has been marvellous the way he has never complained and he has looked after his boy without a wife's help for many years. Masfin was able to attend a small church school and has since learned some spinning and weaving skills, which he uses with other disabled people in a workshop financed by the Catholic Church.

Birru's only daughter, Zawdiresh, has just left school and is doing a sewing course. She also helps in the home. Zawdiresh is the light of her father's eyes. Although she is still young, she acts as a little mother to her family.

Birru is devoted to his children and has never remarried. His life revolves around his family and our hospital. His official position is the hospital storeman, but he is also my faithful adviser and friend.

Mamitu Gashe, the quietly charismatic woman who used to help us obtain our medical supplies during the Mengistu years, is also someone very special and, as with Birru, I cannot imagine life in Ethiopia without her. She was sixteen when she came to us in 1962 – a beautiful Amhara girl, whose whole life was suddenly and irrevocably changed because of something that went wrong during her first labour.

Her home was in the province of Shoa. Its northern part is a lovely, fertile, high plateau. On the eastern edge of this plateau is a steep escarpment dropping down thousands of metres to the Danakil Depression and Awash River Valley. Mamitu's home village was on the plain at the foot of this great escarpment.

As a child she lived with her mother, father, four brothers and five sisters in the family *tukul*. Mamitu's father was a farmer, and she was his favourite daughter. She loved him very much. Every day when he came in from the fields he would sit outside the *tukul* and call Mamitu to him. Lovingly, she would wash his feet and kiss his knee and they would talk about the day's events together.

Mamitu's marriage was arranged while she was still a child. She met her husband for the first time on her wedding day at the age of fourteen. Suddenly her carefree childhood ended, and she was taken away from her family to live with her husband in his own village.

She was sixteen when she became pregnant. When her labour pains began there was no thought of seeking professional care. In any case there was no hospital or clinic nearby. Everyone expected her to be like the other village girls and to have her baby quickly and normally. Days passed, with Mamitu often crouching on the floor straining to deliver her baby. She recalls few details now of that horrifying experience; mercifully, it is no longer in her memory. She has a vague recollection of her mother being with her and of the *wogesha* being called in to help.

Four long days of agony passed before her dead baby was born. As a result Mamitu was left with shocking injuries to her bladder, rectum and birth passage.

For three weeks she lay in her *tukul* without help, feverish and shivering and incontinent of urine and stool. She had a sister living in Addis Ababa, and her family thought if they could get her to the capital she might be able to find medical assistance. Her brothers and an uncle fashioned a stretcher out of goatskin stretched between two poles and set off. Mamitu was unconscious for most of the three days it took to carry her to the nearest town, Debre Sina. From there they took a bus to the capital.

Her sister did not know what to do. She had never heard of our work, but her godmother worked at the Seventh-Day Adventist Hospital, so they took her there. Here she lay for two more weeks, still with a fever from puerperal sepsis, before being sent on to the Princess Tsehai Hospital for us to deal with her vaginal injuries.

Reg's heart went out to this sorrowful little girl. He put her into the special ten-bed room we had for fistula patients in the obstetric ward and saw that she had every comfort and care. It would be many weeks before she was strong enough for surgery.

Then began a series of operations as we attempted to repair the extensive damage to her whole lower urinary tract – ureters, bladder and urethra – and to her rectum as well. Reconstructive major surgery involved muscle, fat and skin grafting to try to give back anatomical and functional normality to organs that were grossly damaged. Mamitu stood these operations with courage and the optimism of youth.

But as the years went by she realised, as we did, that she could never be made completely normal again and that she would always suffer from incontinence. She was, nevertheless, grateful that her rectal fistula was eventually cured and her temporary colostomy closed.

Her husband at first came to visit her, but as the months passed and she was not cured he drifted back to the country. Mamitu stayed on at the Princess Tsehai Hospital, living with other women in the hostel we had built, with her few possessions in a box under her bed. She soon became a natural leader among the others and a favourite with the nursing and domestic staff of the hospital.

Reg sensed that Mamitu was somebody special, with talents hidden because of her peasant upbringing. She was intelligent and quick to learn, with a maturity beyond her age but with a soft and tender heart and winsome ways. She was the natural one to choose when there was a shortage of nursing staff in the wards or in the outpatients' department.

She was soon able to make beds in the professional nursing way. Sister Garret, the senior staff nurse in the obstetric ward, was her great mentor, and Mamitu learned all her nursing skills from this well-trained Anglo-Indian nurse. Even now she often says, 'Sister Garret taught me that.'

Reg took her to the hectic and crowded outpatients' department and there taught her to test urine, boil up the gloves, and prepare the patients for examination.

Despite her lack of schooling she picked up English in a remarkably short time and before long was acting as Reg's special interpreter. Reg gave her copybooks to practise her writing and simple reading books. Her life took on an added dimension as she became imbued with a desire to excel in all the new things she was learning and in her work at the hospital.

Mamitu took pride in doing everything well, emulating Reg in his enthusiasm and hard work for the fistula patients. Reg became a second father to her. She loved him devotedly and would do anything for him.

It was not long before she graduated to helping in the theatre, where Reg taught her to assist him at the fistula repair operations. At first she was merely cutting stitches and swabbing under guidance. She had to stand beside him on a box because she was so short.

I remember an amusing incident during one surgical procedure when the peritoneal cavity was opened during the dissection and the fallopian tube dropped down, obstructing the operation area. Mamitu remarked, 'This soft thing is getting in the way.' She did not know its name but knew it should not be there, so neatly pushed it back through the opening and packed off the area to prevent it happening again.

Reg, being a natural teacher, was excited by her ability. Soon she was familiar with a large medical vocabulary and was able to identify the relevant anatomy of pelvic organs, just as if she was a bright medical student.

In our theatre in the new hospital there were frequently three operations being performed simultaneously. If Reg was busy and wanting to start the spinal anaesthetic for the next patient or was perhaps called to some urgent matter in the ward, he would ask Mamitu to finish the operation for him. This she did perfectly.

Her fingers were dexterous, and her handling of the tissues gentle and careful. I was always pleased to have her assist me and still want her help at any difficult operation. Her skill at passing ureteric catheters into the tiny openings of the ureters seen on the edge of any big bladder fistula is impressive. Her ability to find these openings in any injury where the anatomy is distorted or scar tissue has formed is superb. I have heard all our surgeons on occasions call Mamitu to help when they are in trouble. Once I asked her how she always seemed able to find these hidden ureteric orifices, and she replied simply, 'I ask God to help me.'

Her operative training was not intentionally planned, it just seemed to develop over the years because of her ability and talent. So now Mamitu has become a confident and competent fistula surgeon, and her record of successful operations is well over a thousand.

In 1989 Reg was awarded the Gold Medal of the Royal College of Surgeons. Mamitu and I were included in the citation. The President of the College, Sir Ian Todd, came from London to present the award. He wanted to see an operation, so we arranged for Mamitu to do a big case with Reg assisting. There she was with this eminent surgeon looking over her shoulder, and he was amazed that she could do it perfectly.

Mamitu took it all in her stride. I asked her afterwards if she had been nervous and she answered, 'No, I wasn't nervous. I didn't want to let you down.'

The next day we were invited to lunch and a reception at the British Embassy to be awarded our medals. Mamitu was allowed to take a guest with her so she asked Letekidane. They both looked charming in national dress, I think bought new for the occasion – Lete with her limping gait and solemn expression, Mamitu with her open smile and that natural dignity.

We gathered together in the lovely drawing room of the residence, and Sir Ian, standing beside the Ambassador, made a short speech then presented Reg with the medal and a parchment scroll. Mamitu received a beautiful bunch of flowers and bowed sweetly to Sir Ian.

Then we were shown into the dining room, where we were seated at a long table set with cut glass and shining silver. On the walls were oil paintings of former kings and queens of England, looking down sternly as though they were just waiting for someone to make some social faux pas. Lete had never used a knife and fork in her life, and Mamitu had only occasionally, but by carefully watching everyone else around them they managed so adroitly that one would have thought they had been going to occasions like this all their lives. I am sure the kings and queens would have found no fault with their behaviour. We felt exceptionally proud of them.

Even when earning her first small salary Mamitu always saved a little each month and helped her needy family. Later Reg increased her salary and opened a bank account for her so that she began to earn some interest on her savings.

A dresser from the Princess Tsehai Hospital happened to suggest that she should buy a block of land. Mamitu had never dreamed that she could do such a thing. Gradually the idea blossomed and she eventually came to me for advice, too shy perhaps to ask Reg. I thought it was a wonderful idea, and we began to search the outskirts of the city. In time we found a little wooded hillside with a gully below, not too isolated and yet not crowded. Here she was able to buy a small plot about 30 metres square. Her excitement as she started to get her little house built was infectious. She would come to me and report, 'I've paid for the cement for the floor,' or, 'We've started to build the *chika* walls.' Then the day came when it was finished, and we were all invited from the hospital to go for a special meal to celebrate. Mamitu was the first of our nursing aides to build herself a house. Lete, Enatanesh and many others followed her example.

During the famine years in 1972–74 some of Mamitu's family came to Addis Ababa. Among them was her mother, who was now a widow and partially blind. She was installed in the house with Zawde, Mamitu's sister, who had come with Mamitu when she was so ill and stayed through all the years of surgery.

Zawde's husband had recently been killed in the war with Eritrea, and she had a baby son, Daniel, only six months old. It turned out to be a fortunate arrangement, as the communist government would have certainly taken the house if it had not been occupied.

Mamitu supported her family for many years. Daniel was a particular joy for her, and she lavished love on him like another mother. Her love and devotion have been amply rewarded, as Daniel has turned out to be a young man of rare qualities.

Mamitu paid for his schooling, and later I helped by paying for driving lessons. He is now employed as one of our hospital drivers and is a favourite with all the staff and the visitors who need a chauffeur. He has an unblemished safety record.

Reg loved Mamitu and looked upon her as his own daughter. He left her a legacy in Australia which was earning interest in the bank for many years. She eventually brought the money to Ethiopia because one of her brothers was living with his wife and three children in a tin shack in the street. She built him a little house and has added a little flat onto her own house which she says is for her old age. The rest of her legacy and her own savings are in the bank earning interest.

Mamitu has dedicated her life to looking after the fistula patients and has put her heart and soul into the task. Often I have seen tears in her eyes as she welcomes a particularly sad young girl arriving with nothing in this world but her urine-soaked clothes and the hope that we can cure her. I have seen her many times pour out love from her heart to these patients. Her achievements, with all her own disabilities and medical problems, have been remarkable.

Because of her surgical skill she is frequently given the responsible task of teaching new postgraduate doctors fistula surgery, assisting them in a gentle and unassuming manner, which I know they really appreciate. She also acts as senior nurse in charge of the whole hospital every fourth weekend, taking her turn with the trained nursing staff. This task, like everything else Mamitu turns her hand to, she does perfectly. Mindful of her lack of education or any formal medical training, she is always respectful of those in positions of authority at the hospital. Even so, she is not slow so speak out if she sees something that is wrong.

Mamitu has several photographs of Reg in the big room at

the hospital that she shares with two friends. Whenever she talks about him, tears well up, and she starts to cry. For that reason it is hard to get her to talk about her life. If you can persuade her to tell her story, it is sometimes a little confusing because she refers to Reg as *Abaye,* which means my father, and she calls me, *Inate,* my mother.

If Mamitu had been educated and formally medically trained she would have undoubtedly been a first-class surgeon who could have practised anywhere in the world. But then, there are so many stories like that in Ethiopia.

Chapter Twenty-One

The years of drab Marxist rule dragged on. Petrol was rationed, and permits continued to be needed to go out of the city or to drive on Sunday. There were long bread queues to be seen everywhere, and many of the grocery shops were almost empty. Fortunately fruit and vegetable stalls still operated, and with their trays of oranges and bananas they added the only bit of colour to an otherwise dreary city.

The press was controlled, so we soon gave up buying the local papers – they were filled with propaganda and denunciations of the West, particularly America. Crude anti-American posters appeared at strategic spots. There was one near the American Embassy showing a picture of Uncle Sam being hit on the head with a large Russian sledge-hammer and dollars pouring from his top hat.

The East Germans were in charge of security and ruthlessly imposed a system of repression. We were friendly with a charming East German woman who was the Professor of Obstetrics and Gynaecology at the recently established medical school in Gondar, run by her countrymen. One Christmas we invited her to dinner, which she greatly enjoyed. She was relaxed and happy as we talked and sang carols with friends. I asked her to stay to have cake and mince pies – a luxury in those days – which

Richard and Diana had posted to me from England. She regretfully refused, saying she had to go back to the East German Embassy to sign the book, as she had been out with Westerners.

In the countryside, state farming was attempted but largely failed, as did the villagisation scheme, where peasants were taken from their long-established little farmhouses and herded together in soulless communes down either side of a main road. Many who refused to go were forcibly evicted, and their homes burned behind them.

We still needed to have our life-restoring annual holidays in Kenya, but leaving the country was even more difficult than before. A friend of ours wrote a ditty about the bureaucrats' response to visa applications. It went, 'Our hearts are filled with sorrow but come again tomorrow and then we'll tell 'em *yellum*.' (*Yellum* means no in Amharic.)

Nevertheless, we did manage to get exit visas and take our lovely holidays on the Kenyan coast. Every three years the Ministry of Health continued to honour their commitment in our contracts, and paid our fare to our 'country of origin' and back. So we were able to go to Australia and New Zealand to holiday and to fundraise.

I had also been to England several times to visit Richard and Diana. They now had two children, Sarah aged five and Paul, three, but Reg had not seen them or met Diana and Richard for many years.

In 1984 we arranged for them to come out for Christmas. It was a very special holiday, and even with all the restrictions we managed to have a wonderful time together. I shall never forget the excitement of meeting them at the airport. In those days we were not allowed to wait anywhere near the terminal building, so we were standing on the other side of the road when they emerged from the exit – Richard coming back to the country he loved, looking so happy and proudly bringing his wife and family. We rushed across the road to greet them, and none of the soldiers stationed there seemed to mind. Time had healed the wounds, and the past was forgotten in the joy of reunion.

At the hospital another welcome awaited them from Yeshi and Birru and all the others who had been part of Richard's childhood. Birru had erected a swing and built a tree house for the children, and I had a new small pony for them. Although we were not allowed to go for any extensive safaris, there was plenty of novelty and excitement.

We had saved some petrol from our ration, so we were able to have a few picnics. One special place was the Sudan Interior Mission holiday compound – on a crater lake about 70 kilometres south of the city. Here we could swim and go boating and enjoy the beauty of a tropical garden full of frangipani, poinsettias, guava trees and paw paw.

The holiday went by all too quickly, but as Richard was now in a big computer firm, they had only a limited amount of time with us. Fortunately, the visit has been repeated many times since, more recently with two more children, Catherine and Stephanie. They have all been introduced to the joys of camping at Langano, a favourite Rift Valley lake, where there are lovely campsites and a huge expanse of water to explore and swim in.

By now there was a full-scale civil war going on in Tigray Province in the north. A confusing alliance of rebel forces, whose initials all sounded like each other, were fighting the Ethiopian army. There was the EPLF (Eritrean People's Liberation Front), the EPRDF (Ethiopian People's Revolutionary Democratic Front), and the TPLF (Tigrayan People's Revolutionary Front).

In 1987 Mengistu sent a large force north into Tigray. Whenever they reached a town, all the inhabitants turned out and welcomed the Army, but this was just a sham, as they were really on the side of the rebels and giving them all the support they could. The TPLF never fought the Ethiopians head on, but used guerrilla tactics with great success.

All the big hospitals in Addis Ababa were crammed with

injured soldiers from the front. There were so many that they were lying in the corridors and on the floors in the wards. One day I was at our hospital doing a round and Reg was down at the house, when several bus-loads of wounded soldiers arrived. I ran down to Reg and said, 'Come quickly. They are taking over the hospital.'

Reg ran up the path through the garden to the hospital. When he arrived he approached the major in an unhurried manner and shook his hand. Taking him into the ward, he showed him all the beds occupied. I stood by, admiring Reg's tact and quick-thinking as he said, 'Perhaps we can put stretchers down the centre of the ward, but do you have any broken limbs? Will they need X-rays?'

'Oh, certainly,' replied the major.

'I am sorry, we have no X-ray department,' Reg replied truthfully.

And so this crisis was resolved amicably, and the buses took off down the road several kilometres to the leprosy hospital, where there was an X-ray department.

The civil war continued. Every day we heard conflicting news of success or defeat for the Ethiopian Army, and great loss of life. Secretly we hoped that Mengistu's army would be defeated.

In early 1991 we began to hear that the Tigrayan rebel groups had combined and were marching towards Addis Ababa. Every day a new town was captured, and the advance of the rebels seemed assured. Little resistance was offered by the Ethiopian Army, which was falling back before the onslaught. We all suspected they would make a final stand at the capital.

Gradually towns all around the city began to fall. At first it was Debre Birhan in the north, then Ambo only about 150 kilometres west, then Debre Zeit, 100 kilometres south of the city. The capital was virtually surrounded.

We all wondered what sort of fight the army would put up now that they were virtually trapped in the city. But we need not have worried. No resistance was offered; the army just disbanded. The soldiers decided it was time to look after themselves and disappeared, mostly taking their guns with them.

Mengistu knew his time was up and chartered a plane to take him south, deceiving the pilot by telling him he was on his way to inspect an army camp in the country. Once airborne he ordered him at gun point to fly to Nairobi and then on to Zimbabwe, where his friend, President Mugabe, gave him political asylum. His wife and three children were already there.

On 28 May the city was blacked out. We could hear gunfire close by. We didn't leave the hospital, but friends told us that people were throwing flowers at the tanks as they rolled into the city. One tank pulled up near our neighbour's house. A soldier popped her head out and asked him, 'Which way to Addis Ababa?' When he told her she gave him the thumbs up sign and trundled off towards town.

The soldiers in the rebel army, although ragged and poorly dressed, some even without shoes, were extremely polite and anxious to allay our fears. A few of them came down to the hospital and told us they were assigned to protect us, and gave us a number to ring in any emergency. Others stood outside shops to prevent any looting. It was amazing to see how well organised this seemingly rabble army was. We were impressed.

But this was not the case with the Ethiopian Army. These soldiers were now leaderless and shooting indiscriminately. Some just fired into the air as if to get rid of their ammunition. Several stray bullets fell into our compound. One went into the hostel and landed on a pillow. Fortunately it was daytime, and the bed was not occupied.

I was sitting in the drawing room knitting in my usual seat on a sofa when the phone rang. It was Pippa Sandford, the headmistress of the English School, asking me if we were going to the British Embassy to shelter, as we had been advised.

'No,' I replied. 'We feel safe here, and in any case I do not wish to leave our patients.'

Just at that moment a bullet came through the ceiling and

lodged in the cushion where I had been sitting. Pippa, still on the other end of the line, heard the noise and my exclamation of alarm. 'Oh, Pippa,' I said, 'you may have just saved my life.'

That same evening, soon after we had finished dinner, a massive explosion shook the house. We rushed outside thinking that the whole city was being bombarded. From the garden we could see the sky south of the city lit up with a great conflagration, and sporadic explosions sounded every few minutes. Some of them blew out the windows of the Augusta shirt factory next door, but the hospital, being further down the hillside, was not damaged.

The night sister on duty had a reporter friend who told her it was the ammunition dump being blown up, evidently by Mengistu's supporters. Later we viewed the devastation caused by this wanton act of destruction and heard that many people had lost their lives, mostly from the fire that engulfed the community living around the dump.

So that was the end of Colonel Mengistu's rule. Seventeen years of terror and waste and repression. There was a peace conference in London between all the factions, and a new government was formed, composed largely of people from the TPLF. Many of Mengistu's people were jailed. A few of those who attended the peace talks in London decided that it would be better for them if they did not go back home.

Some of our old friends who had fled during the Mengistu regime returned. New businesses slowly sprang up, and old ones were revived. Bambi, years later, was given back his home and his supermarket. He endured several years of hardship and considerable expense as he struggled to re-establish his business. At first he was forced by the new government to keep on 40 staff, even though there was no work for them to do. But now his supermarket is again flourishing.

Although he and Helene miss their four daughters and their grandchildren, who are still in Greece, they are happy to be back and able to carry on the business which they spent so many years building up.

Even with businesses being returned and homes restored to their rightful owners, there are still many who have not come back. Plenty have settled in other countries and become prosperous. In America there are over one million Ethiopians, some in high business or academic positions. It is unreasonable to expect such people to give up their lucrative jobs and comfortable lifestyles to return to one of the poorest countries in the world, with a huge unemployed population and few jobs available.

Old wounds are slowly healing, and I am pleased to say the Emperor has been exonerated of the scandalous accusations made against him. The mystery of where he was buried was solved when the man who dug his grave was brought from the prison to show where it was. The body lay beneath the floor of Mengistu's office. The remains were removed, put in a coffin and placed in Ba'ata church.

In November 2000 there was, at last, a fitting funeral in Holy Trinity Cathedral. All the remaining Ethiopian royal family came from overseas to attend. It was supposed to be low-key and not official, but a big crowd turned out as the procession wound its way to the cathedral, and there were many speeches. The Patriarch took the funeral service, attended by a colourful ecclesiastical hierarchy. Unfortunately, people like Nelson Mandela, the British royal family and some others who wanted to attend were told not to come.

As the coffin was being lowered the Patriarch took the Ethiopian flag with which it was covered and handed it to Princess Tenagneworke, the Emperor's only surviving direct offspring. The Emperor is buried in a tomb inside the cathedral beside the Empress, a position that had been evidently reserved by him years ago.

I sent some red roses to the family, and all those at the hospital who knew His Majesty signed the card. I wrote on it, 'In memory of our beloved Emperor from all at the Fistula Hospital, who were privileged to have enjoyed the golden years of his reign.' Haile Selassie will long be revered with other illustrious kings of Ethiopia. He was surely the most enlightened and benevolent of them all.

In August 1991 we managed to get away for a few weeks holiday in Kenya where Richard and Diana and their children joined us for a very special and exciting holiday. A short time after we returned home, Reg noticed a mass like a haematoma on the medial side of his right thigh. He took no notice of it and went about his work as usual. One day there was a visiting surgeon in the theatre watching operations, so Reg said to him, 'I've got this mass here. I wonder if you would look at it?'

He examined the lump and said, 'You must have knocked your leg without knowing because you've got a big haematoma in the muscle.'

Reg said, 'I can't understand it. I would know if I'd knocked myself.'

We knew a good orthopaedic surgeon working at the Black Lion Hospital, a Scotsman named Mr McQuillan. He agreed to do a needle biopsy for the mass but he was not successful in getting any tissue. He then suggested that he should remove it and send it to the pathologist.

Reg went into the theatre and had a spinal anaesthetic. While they operated I waited outside. The surgeon came out and informed me that it was an encapsulated tumour which was growing in the fibrous tissue between the muscle layers. 'We've taken it out and we'll have it sectioned. It's probably a simple tumour of some sort.'

Reg had two uncomfortable days at the Black Lion, then the British Ambassador, James Glaze, invited him to come to the embassy clinic to convalesce. The embassy had their own clinic in the grounds with several big bedrooms, a minor theatre and treatment rooms. We knew the two nurses in charge because they had been at Princess Tsehai Hospital, so Reg was welcomed and treated as a VIP.

Mamitu went over to help while I stayed running the hospital.

There was no kitchen in the clinic, but the ambassador's wife kindly sent food to Reg from the residence, and I visited every day, taking over titbits that I knew he enjoyed and lots of reading material.

It was an anxious time as we waited for the results of the pathology. After some days Mr McQuillan came to our home. As he sat down in the drawing room I knew it was bad news by his manner and his face. He told me the tumour was malignant, a fibrosarcoma, growing from the connective tissue between the muscles in the thigh.

I asked him what he thought the prognosis was.

He replied, 'The tumour was completely encapsulated, and as we removed the whole of it intact, I am hopeful that it will be cured and that it will not recur.'

I drove over to the embassy and told Reg what Mr McQuillan had found. He heard me out then said, 'Well, I hope it's all out.'

He was very brave, but I could see he was upset. He was mainly troubled because he couldn't get back to work. He stayed in the clinic for about two weeks until the wound healed, then returned and carried on as if nothing had happened, doing administrative jobs and running about the town getting supplies.

After about three months the lump started to grow again. There was nothing more that could be done in Ethiopia, so we went to England to see the experts there.

We contacted our very good friend Gordon Williams, whom I have mentioned before. He is the chief urologist for the famous Hammersmith Hospital, who saved Letikidane's life and that of many other Ethiopians since then. Gordon is a much-loved surgeon, who gives his time, money and talents to help these poor peasant women, usually visiting once or twice a year to operate and teach our doctors. Sometimes he will even come specially for some emergency. Recently he arrived at 10 am on a Saturday and came straight into our theatre, where he operated on a girl who would certainly have died without his intervention. He took eight of us to dinner that night and flew back to London the next day to be ready for work on Monday.

Now, because of his concern for Reg, he again came to our aid, finding a bed for him in his own ward. It was the same room Reg had been in three years before when he had had an operation for a prostatic obstruction and, as then, Mamitu was allowed to sleep on a camp bed in the corner as a 'special nurse', surely unheard of in most hospitals.

The orthopaedic surgeon who came to see Reg seemed brusque and unnecessarily blunt as he gave his opinion – 'The only solution is a hindquarter amputation.' This means amputating through the hip joint. Reg was 82 years old, and this was radical surgery even for a young man. Also it is extraordinarily debilitating because you cannot sit after it has been done.

Reg was quick to give his answer, which was that he did not want such an operation. The reply from the doctor was equally quick. 'Oh, well, take it or leave it. If you do not want it, there is nothing else I can do.'

His bedside manner was certainly not his strong point.

The oncologist was a different character – most sympathetic and caring. He was a famous man in his specialty, but particularly humble. His opinion was given with obvious concern, but it was not encouraging. He told us that this type of sarcoma was seldom radio-sensitive, but it was worthwhile going through the radiation treatment as it may do some good.

The course would take a month, but there was no need to be in the hospital during this time. Richard and Diana lived in a northern suburb of London, and an ambulance trip would take at least one-and-a-half hours each way, and more in the rush hour. So we decided to stay in a little hotel recommended by the oncologist and run by an Armenian who had relatives in Ethiopia. This was only a ten-minute drive away and was next to a large park where we could take Reg in his wheelchair for outings. Richard and his family could join us at weekends for picnics.

There was a funny little rickety lift, which would just take Reg in his wheelchair with Mamitu and I squashed against the walls. We were on the third floor so we made this precarious trip down to the waiting ambulance every day.

We always had the same husband and wife team running the ambulance. Soon we became firm friends and quite looked forward to these daily excursions, as the hotel accommodation was fairly cramped.

One day, four of the Emperor's granddaughters and their mother, Princess Tenagnework, came to see Reg. Now that they were allowed to travel freely after the overthrow of the *Dergue* they were on their way to America. We were embarrassed having to entertain royalty in such a small room, but they did not mind in the least and all sat happily on the beds while Mamitu and I made tea with an electric jug in the corner.

We were touched by this visit, but I am sure they knew it would be the last time they would see my husband alive. I still have the lovely soft tartan rug that the Emperor's daughter gave Reg. It was on his bed always.

It was wonderful to have Mamitu with us during those sad and rather gloomy days. She looked after Reg as she would her father, washing his clothes and seeing to his every comfort. Together we managed to keep his spirits up and talked daily about getting back to Ethiopia.

When the month's course was finished, we were offered the British Ambassador's house in Reigate. It was empty because he and his wife were still in Ethiopia. Here Reg was able to convalesce in comfort and even walk about a little in the garden. He still needed a few more deep X-ray treatments, and we were also able to consult other experts on his condition. One told us that this type of sarcoma was common in people in their eighties, especially men. Although this was interesting it was not particularly cheering.

What heartened Reg more than anything were the visits from Richard and his family and the good meals I was able to prepare. With so much available in the nearby shops and a spacious, well-equipped kitchen, cooking was enjoyable. Friends travelled from all over England to see us, and we were really spoiled. But Reg was longing to get back to Ethiopia, so as soon as the course was finished we booked our flights and came home – back to our hospital and a warm welcome from our wonderful staff.

It was good to be home again, and Reg was happy. Every day he would go up to the hospital and he refused to use a stick. 'People will think I'm old,' he said, but he had the help of a slender young nursing aide named Fatima, whom he called his walking stick. She came down to the house each morning and walked beside Reg, helping to support him as he negotiated the steep steps to the hospital. Birru ran ahead with a chair, and if Reg felt faint or weak he could sit down for a few minutes, so it was quite a procession.

He enjoyed going to the hospital every day. Just as he had done all his life in Ethiopia, he would talk to the women who were going to have their operations and tell them not to be frightened. When patients were ready to go home, Reg would gather them together in their new dresses and talk to them as they sat in a row on an empty bed in the ward. Often there would be a little group of six or eight women, looking so happy. He would tell those who had been deserted by their husbands to search for a new one but not to marry again for three months. Those whose husbands were still with them, perhaps because they had children and family, he would advise to wait for three months before again sleeping together. Then if they got pregnant they must be sure to have the baby in the hospital. 'When you feel the baby walking around in your stomach, that is the time for you to start walking to a hospital.'

Usually the nurses would gather round for this talk, and when it was over they would take part in the traditional dance of joy with the patients, clapping their hands and sometimes singing as well. Reg enjoyed this simple ceremony and even when he was very weak he still joined in the clapping. It usually ended up with the women hugging him and often trying to kiss his shoes. He was greatly loved by every one of them.

Reg had a wonderful way of welcoming every patient being admitted. He never treated them as just another case, but took time with them, showing that he cared and explaining in a graphic way what had happened to them during their long labour. He would take a piece of paper and tear a hole in the centre, so that the flap was still attached and could be folded back. He would pour water though the hole, telling the patient that this was what had happened to her bladder. Then he would fold the flap back and make the paper look normal again with no hole in it. 'Now, this is what we will do with your bladder. Just a few stitches, and the hole will be mended and no more urine will run out.'

It was touching to see how often this humble ceremony caused a smile, and eyes to sparkle, as hope was born again in the patient's heart. Just to be loved and cared for means so much to these women who have suffered rejection and isolation.

At about this time, late 1992, a BBC film crew arrived to make a documentary about the hospital. In England Gordon Williams had used his influence and convinced the BBC that our work would be a worthwhile subject. We owe him an enormous debt of gratitude. This documentary, and later a second one, raised an astonishing amount of money.

I was so glad that Reg, although terribly ill, could co-operate with the photographers, be interviewed and filmed with the patients. The BBC crew were here for a month and came down to the hospital nearly every day, usually bringing a picnic lunch with them, which they ate in the garden. The enormous effort Reg made during the film-making seemed to sap his resources considerably. After the New Year and in early 1993, he seldom had the strength to walk up to the hospital and spent most days at home, sorting through his files and getting things in order for the time when he would not be here.

When visitors came he would sit in his usual chair in our drawing room and talk. Later, when he felt too weak to get up, he received them in his bedroom. Bambi flew out from Greece to see him and sat on his bed reminiscing about the old days. At that stage he had not yet been given back his properties, although he was hopeful, and negotiations were in progress.

Another who came especially to see Reg was one of his old students from Princess Tsehai Hospital, Dr Ogba Selassie. He flew all the way from The Gambia in West Africa, where he was now a Professor of obstetrics and gynaecology. Seldom did a day pass without either a phone call from some concerned friend or relative or a visitor to our home.

Mamitu was released from her hospital duties and devoted all her nursing skills and her loving nature to caring for Reg. She was with him constantly, as I inevitably had to spend time in the hospital or in the town on business. I often came home at lunchtime to find Reg sitting in a comfortable armchair, which Birru put out on the lawn every day, enjoying the sunshine. Richard arranged for a television and VCR to be sent out from England. Many friends lent us videos and, as we had quite a good library of books at home, Reg had the opportunity to catch up on some of the reading that he had never had time for previously.

Every evening we would gather around his bed, pray together and read the Bible, with Reg often choosing a favourite passage. Once, near the end, when he was terribly weak, I heard him murmuring a prayer asking God to give him 'His robe of righteousness,' and then falling peacefully asleep. He had a simple, almost childlike trust and faith and never seemed to be upset by doubts.

By July 1993 he was almost too weak to get out of bed. Our nursing aides, under Mamitu's expert eye, would come down each day to help make his bed, rub his back and generally look after him. He stayed at home with us through all these weeks of declining strength as he could not have had better care in any hospital.

Many of our doctor friends came to see him. When Reg finally lapsed into unconsciousness, one in particular, Dr Mesfin, came every day. Our doctors, nurses and other members of the staff would sit quietly around his bed, many of them sobbing. They all loved Reg deeply and knew that he was dying.

In the early hours of the morning of 5 August, I was sitting beside his bed. I felt sure he squeezed my hand as I said to him, 'You are going to be with Jesus,' speaking close to his ear, hoping he could hear.

At 2.30 am Reg just stopped breathing and was gone to his eternal home.

Having lived in Ethiopia so long I knew what would now happen. Crying and wailing began at once, many of the staff beating their breasts with grief. Mamitu was hysterical with sorrow and could not be comforted. My friend, Norah Landells, the wife of Professor John Landells, professor of pathology at Addis Ababa University, was with us that night and was a great support as she tried her best to calm the girls. I was able to be alone with my darling husband for some hours before he was placed in the coffin, a coffin which Birru had thoughtfully bought ten days previously.

That day everything was taken out of my hands in the wonderfully sympathetic way in which Ethiopians care for the bereaved. Quickly and efficiently, matters were arranged for the funeral service next day and the burial. This included the printing for the church service of a folded card with Reg's photo on the front and the story inside of his years in Ethiopia.

I had already asked our friend Colin Maunsell, a missionary in Ethiopia for many years, to take the service, as our own rector was on leave. Together, before Reg died, we had chosen the hymns and Bible readings.

August 6 dawned with sunshine, despite August being the wettest month of the rainy season. St Matthew's Anglican Church was packed, with many standing outside and some even out on the road. Colin spoke movingly in Amharic as well as English for the benefit of the large number of Ethiopians who did not understand English. The singing of the stirring Easter Hymn rose to the rafters of the little church as a triumphant testimony to our faith.

Jesus lives! thy terrors now
Can no longer, death, appall us;
Jesus lives! by this we know
Thou, O grave, canst not enthrall us.
Alleluia!

At the end of the service a friend with a beautiful soprano voice sang 'I know that my Redeemer liveth' from Handel's Messiah. Reg used to sing this as a solo when he was the leading boy soprano in the Christchurch Cathedral choir in New Zealand. Later I had these words inscribed on his tombstone.

I had permission from the British Embassy for Reg to be buried in the well-kept British War Graves Cemetery. Some of our friends were already there, including Brigadier Sandford and Dr Fitzherbert, as, of course, were all the British Commonwealth soldiers who had died in Ethiopia fighting the Italians during World War II. It is a peaceful place, with lawns and gardens surrounded by a high stone wall, nestling below the western arm of the Entoto Ranges which partly encircle Addis Ababa.

Here my husband was laid to rest, surrounded by a huge crowd of mourners, including all our staff wailing and weeping as they realised that 'their father' had left them. The sun continued to shine as wreath after wreath was piled high over his grave.

Back at the hospital Birru and our other men arranged for a large marquee to be erected on the lawn. For three days people came to sit quietly and mourn. I went to the tent two or three times each day to greet these friends, some of whom I hardly knew, but who had come out of deep respect for my husband and sorrow for me. At times little cups of strong, sweet coffee would be handed round and plates of roasted grain, *kolo,* which is a custom at every Ethiopian *likso,* or funeral. The hospital lawn was soon a sea of mud, for the rains had returned and kept on continuously for three days.

Down in my house I was seldom alone. At night we had a big fire burning in the drawing room, where many of our senior hospital staff spent the nights wrapped in blankets and resting on pillows. Often I would retire to my bedroom to be alone with my thoughts and prayers, but it gave me some solace to know that I was surrounded by people who showed their care and love by being willing to spend so many nights in relative discomfort. Nothing was too much trouble for them. Food was provided, and everything was done for my well-being. One has to live in Ethiopia to appreciate and admire this ancient tradition of displaying respect for the departed one and sorrow for the bereaved.

I got back to work fairly quickly. The hospital still had to keep going, and I was glad to have things to do. But at night, when Yeshi had gone home and I was on my own in the house, it was sometimes hard. Reg and I had done everything together, and it was difficult suddenly to be alone. At times I felt like just giving up.

One morning, not long after Reg had died, I rose at 6 am and went out to sit on the verandah in the dawn to meditate and to pray, as had lately become my habit. On this occasion I was suddenly overwhelmed with the feeling that everything was too much for me and that I would never be able to run the hospital by myself.

I was not crying but evidently looked as though I was, as Birru appeared and knelt by my chair. He took my hand in his, kissed the back of it and said, 'Don't leave us; we'll all help you.'

I was so touched that I really did cry then but partly from relief and joy.

Birru's words and actions were just what I needed. They dispelled any thoughts of not carrying on. I began to realise the enormous blessings that I had, and the future seemed suddenly bright and exciting.

I knew I had a hospital to keep going and that I would have to continue to raise money, but with a staff so devoted and talented I was not alone.

Chapter Twenty-Two

Reg's death brought about some changes at the hospital. I had to take over a lot of the administrative work that he used to do and become much more involved with fundraising. With these added responsibilities I thought I would need some more help on the medical side. An American urologist, Steven Arrowsmith, had been working as a missionary doctor in Nigeria and had come over to study our techniques. He wasn't happy with the mission-based hospital where he was working, mostly because they would not admit fistula patients.

Dr Arrowsmith was keen to work with us and seemed just the right person I was looking for. He said he deplored the trend in America for doctors to forget their original calling in the interest of making money, but in Ethiopia with the fistula pilgrims the motivation could not be clearer. The chance to do good in the world really excited him.

I therefore suggested that he should ask his mission, the SIM, to transfer him from Nigeria to Ethiopia. It took some months to arrange things with the Ministry of Health and to draw up a contract between the mission and our hospital. One great advantage for us was that we would not be called on to provide a salary because Steven would still be funded by the mission while working for us.

A friend who lived in London but owned a house not far from the hospital was more than happy for Steven and his family to use it rent-free as he wanted someone to occupy it and look after the servants. So Steven and Jan, with their three little daughters, moved into this quite luxurious home, built in the style of a grand *tukul* with a thatched roof and a big central room with a large fireplace.

We had a happy Christmas together as Richard and Diana were here too, with their children. But early in the new year of 1994 the Arrowsmiths had a frightening experience, which I feel sure coloured their outlook on Ethiopia.

One night at one o'clock seven armed bandits broke into the house after overpowering the guards. They tied Steven up with the telephone cord, which they had cut, and his own belt. Jan and the three girls were imprisoned together in one room. Poor Steven did not know what was happening and feared they might be raped, but they were really quite well treated. When one of the robbers thought the youngest child looked thirsty he brought her a Coca-Cola from the refrigerator.

The bandits demanded money. When Steven told them they were missionaries and had no money, one of them crossed himself saying, 'We are Christians, too. We only kill Muslims.'

After ransacking the house, taking watches, jewellery and what money they could find, they drove off in my car, which I had lent to Steven, but it stalled on the steep drive and could not be started again.

One robber ran back to Steven and, with a gun pointing at his back, told him to follow him to the car. He was ordered to get in, start the car and drive where they directed him. Naturally Steven thought he was going to be killed, but when they reached the gate he was ordered out and the bandits drove off into the night.

He rang me at about 5 am telling me that the car had been stolen. I thoughtlessly replied, 'How silly of you, Steven, to hand the keys over,' and felt foolish when he replied, 'I could not very well do anything else with a gun at my head.'

Next day our men from the hospital organised a search party and found the car in the market area, minus hubcaps, tools and spare wheel, but otherwise intact. We later retrieved the stolen parts from the Somali Terra in the usual way. After they ransacked several other houses, the robbers were caught and sent to prison.

We built a house for the Arrowsmiths on what was our cow paddock, with money supplied by the Australian Government, and they settled in and seemed happy. Jan bought a horse and loved riding, and soon the whole family was keen. They joined pony clubs, went on riding picnics and attended all the gymkhanas.

I imagined Steven might one day take over as medical director, but it was not to be. Relationships with the staff became increasingly strained as he tried to introduce ideas of American efficiency and, I think, failed to understand the Ethiopian culture. I, too, began to feel strained. I knew in my heart that he was not the one to run our hospital, and at the time I was certainly not prepared to hand it over to anyone else. So one day when Steven told me he was going to resign I accepted his decision.

Many were sorry to see him leave. He and his family had an emotional farewell at the airport. He is now working among American Indians in New Mexico in a big group practice, doing all the urology. Jan has visited us and other friends in Ethiopia several times since they left.

Even with Steven's departure we were not short of doctors. Dr Mulu Muleta and Dr Ambaye Wolde Michael were already gynaecologists on our staff – two young women who, after completing their medical training in Addis Ababa University, had done two years compulsory work in provincial hospitals. Both then joined a four-year arduous and well-taught postgraduate course in obstetrics and gynaecology. They graduated near the top and became specialists in this field of medicine in Ethiopia.

Reg and I picked them both out when they were with us for three months of postgraduate training. Mulu was the first to join us and has now been with the hospital for ten years. She was officially assigned to work at the Fistula Hospital by the Ministry of Health.

Later we noticed Ambaye as being talented and dedicated to her patients but when we asked the Ministry if she could work with us, they refused as they wanted to send her elsewhere. Without official permission she joined the staff anyway and worked for several months before being tracked down by the Ministry. With Reg's persuasion and Ambaye's charm, the minister gave in and allowed her to stay. I feel certain he could detect her love for the fistula patients and her dedication to their welfare.

Ambaye and Mulu are first-class fistula surgeons, and I can truthfully say they have had more experience of this type of surgery than anyone else in the world. Not only are they skilled surgically, both display a deep concern for each individual patient. Visiting doctors frequently notice and remark on this.

Once, when Ambaye was invited to a conference in America, the gynaecologists there tried to tempt her to stay, telling her that she would make a lot of money. But Ambaye would not be persuaded. She loved her country too much and the needy women she was helping – an unusual attitude when so many Ethiopian doctors have left and are making fortunes in America.

Both Mulu and Ambaye are content to devote their time and skills and indeed their lives exclusively to the cause of the fistula patients, and I am confident that in their hands the work will expand and diversify. Mulu undertook a year's postgraduate study in public health at the Prince Leopold Institute of Tropical Medicine in Antwerp, Belgium. She now has a further degree and is well equipped to start work on the prevention of these injuries. This is a huge undertaking and one that will need the co-operation of the government and the health bureaux in the provinces.

Mulu lives away from the hospital with her husband, who has a PhD from Sweden in teaching, and their two boys. It was terribly hard for her to leave her children for her year in Belgium – hard, too, for her husband to look after them without her.

Ambaye comes from a big family, some of whom she helps to support. Her parents died many years ago, her mother tragically from a post-partum haemorrhage. The baby survived – Ambaye's youngest brother – and is now a young man in his early twenties.

Ambaye was recently promoted to the position of medical director. She lives in a house in the grounds, and her life revolves around the hospital and her patients, but she has a family home to go to where some of her sisters and brothers live. There she grows beautiful roses and lots of vegetables. At the hospital she successfully raises chickens, and her hens supply all the eggs we need. Disaster struck on the first night we had them. There were 60 young pullets in a new tin shed, but by morning 48 were left, all the others lay dead as a result of an attack by a mongoose. The shed has now been made mongoose-proof, and we have not lost any more. I do not suppose there are many hospitals in the world where the medical director keeps chickens.

The most recent addition to our staff is Biruk Tafessa, who is a qualified gynaecologist from Addis Ababa University. I had noticed him while he was a student here, and so after his two years in Gondar, we were fortunate to make arrangements for him to join our staff.

Here I must mention a special friend, a gynaecologist who comes from the UK who has supported us for 31 years. John Kelly was the Assistant Professor of Obstetrics and Gynaecology at Queen Elizabeth University Hospital in Birmingham. In the early days when Reg and I were the only gynaecologists at the Princess Tsehai Hospital, John would come out and do our work while we had our annual Kenya holiday. He has continued to visit ever since, whenever we are short of doctors and need help. He retired two years before he needed to. This was mostly, I am sure, to be free to work for the women of Africa. He helps fistula patients in Somalia, Uganda, Tanzania, Zambia, Nigeria, Ethiopia and, recently, Pakistan. Another reason was that he did not agree with the Birmingham hospital's policy of doing abortions. John's conscience and Christian faith were against the practice. I greatly admire him for his courageous stand and for his commitment to patients who are the poorest of this world. He restores them to a new life without any expectation of financial gain for himself.

John is one of the foundation members of our charitable trust in the UK and is now a trustee. The charity, the Hamlin Churchill Childbirth Injuries Fund, was set up to care solely for women injured in childbirth.

Although we are able to help most of our patients, there are some who go away still sorrowful because their hopes of a cure have not been fulfilled. This sad 10 per cent of patients is, for our surgeons, a cause of disappointment and discouragement. Some are able to be helped at a second or even third attempt and are given an appointment to return in two or three months. It may only be a small residual fistula remaining, which can be mended next time.

Most often the breakdowns occur when the original fistula was difficult, perhaps because of scar tissue, or with a urethra totally destroyed by long labour. A small proportion, perhaps 1 per cent, have a bladder that is too small and contracted, having been so damaged during the long labour. Because of the fistula it has not been expanding as normal. It can no longer act as a reservoir and is unable to hold any urine. For these women no vaginal surgery will cure the incontinence, even if there is just enough bladder remaining to close the hole.

The best solution for them is to do an ileal conduit. The other is to transplant the two ureters into the colon so that urine is passed through the anus. Although the patient is dry, with the anal sphincter able to control the passage of urine, we do not recommend this operation. We rarely do it, as the incidence of kidney infection is high, and life expectancy is reduced.

So even among our 90 to 93 per cent of cured patients, there are some who are still incontinent. This is due to what is medically known as stress incontinence. The woman may be dry when lying down but as soon as she stands up and walks about, the urine runs out, or perhaps only when she coughs or laughs or lifts heavy objects.

There are various grades of severity and there have been many and various procedures invented to try to solve this distressing problem. When we first encountered it many years ago at the Princess Tsehai Hospital, Reg wrote to one of the world experts in the field – an Australian from Melbourne, Dr Robert Zacharin. He suggested he might pass through Ethiopia on one of his many overseas lecturing trips and give us some advice. This was in 1967. Dr Zacharin was a gynaecologist at the Alfred Hospital. He and his colleagues at the Alfred had written many papers on stress incontinence and were at the forefront of their field. Bob had developed a special operation for the condition.

Being a man full of energy and enthusiasm, he readily agreed to make the trip, thinking it was a wonderful idea, even if he was not quite sure exactly where Ethiopia was! He wrote back giving us his arrival date and Reg duly went out to the airport to meet him.

I don't think Dr Zacharin was prepared for Reg's enthusiasm. Instead of taking him to the hotel to recover from the long flight, he bundled him and his wife, Tricia, into our VW and brought them straight to the hospital, where they had to stand in the middle of a circle of women demonstrating their stress incontinence by jumping up and down to see if there was any urine on the floor.

Dr Zacharin was pessimistic about being able to help. What he was seeing in Ethiopia was different from the problems he dealt with. He told us, 'This is true incontinence because the mechanism has been wrecked.'

In Melbourne Bob rarely encountered fistulae and almost never saw those caused by obstructed labour. Sometimes he might see one after radiotherapy treatment of cancer or after a surgical procedure had accidentally damaged the bladder. These cases were usually referred to urologists, who mostly operated from the abdomen.

Our hospital was an eye-opener for him. On his first day he counted 54 fistula patients in our ward and the hostel. He soon became fascinated and was able himself to carry out many fistula repair operations. When he returned to Melbourne he became known as an expert, and cases were sent to him from all over Australia. Bob followed the method he had seen us use and not the urologists' abdominal approach. He ended up writing a textbook, *Obstetric Fistula*, which was widely acclaimed. It is the definitive modern work on the subject.

Bob and Trisha Zacharin were tireless in fundraising for us in Australia. Bob returned to Ethiopia several times, often bringing with him medical supplies and equipment. He went to a great deal of trouble to collect slightly used medical supplies from hospitals in Melbourne, which otherwise would have been thrown away. He always managed to talk his way through customs, once jokingly declaring that a bag full of Foley catheters was a new type of spaghetti.

Although the operation for stress incontinence pioneered by Dr Zacharin was successful in Australia and other countries, it was not suitable for our patients. Often they had the added complication of scar tissue formation, especially involving the urethra – the tube from the bladder to the outside. This stiff, scarred urethra mostly makes the standard procedures a failure. In spite of the disappointment, we learned a lot from Bob, and he was one of our greatest friends.

Stress incontinence continues to be a vexing problem for us, but we are now beginning to have new hope. In January 2000 we were fortunate to have a visit from a uro-gynaecologist, again from Melbourne. Dr Marcus Carey was introduced to us by Dr Judith Goh, a Brisbane gynaecologist who has been a regular visitor for about five years. At first she came to learn the techniques of fistula repairs. Later she helped out when we were short of doctors. She also goes once a year to operate on fistula patients at a mission hospital in Tanzania. Through her work she became deeply sympathetic to the plight of patients with stress incontinence.

Marcus heard about our hospital in 1998 when he met Judith at a conference in Cambridge. She mentioned her concerns to him, and he was immediately intrigued. Together they decided to devote time to finding a solution.

When his visit was confirmed, a group of patients was collected to be assessed as suitable candidates for a new operation that Marcus had thought out. We fortunately had a urodynamics machine, which is essential for sorting out the type of incontinence that might benefit from surgery. Marcus had with him a specialist nurse in the use of these machines, Christine Murray.

The patients all had the same symptoms of urinary incontinence, but the condition is not always due to the same cause. We found that about half our women had significant bladder problems. Because they had had fistulas for some time, the bladder was grossly contracted. Operating on them would be of no benefit. Marcus operated on this select group. Then in January 2001, another group had the same operation.

The procedure is relatively simple once the technique has been learned. Following Marcus's second visit our doctors are now able to carry it out, and I am sure in time they will become thoroughly adept.

The women who have had the operation have been asked to come back in a year and we gave them money to ensure they do. Eight of those treated in the first year have returned and are still dry. This gives us hope that the procedure really works, although this year the results have been rather disappointing. Out of 22 women only seven went home dry.

Perhaps our selection of patients was not so good this time.

I am optimistic that even the wet ones will eventually improve, so we shall persevere, as this is certainly the best operation for our patients that we have seen.

Ambaye has begun an outreach program, which involves trips in the hospital Land Rover to distant provincial hospitals to operate. Usually two nurses go with her – a trained nurse and one of our theatre-trained nursing aides. The Land Rover is loaded up with all the equipment they will need, such as surgical instruments, operating clothes, gloves, catheters, and spinal anaesthetics.

The particular provincial hospital's operating theatre is used, and the doctor from that hospital will already have collected patients needing fistula surgery. As many as ten or fifteen may be waiting. This is something we plan to do regularly with our other doctors, too. At the same time we will train the local hospital staff and even do some teaching in the villages about harmful traditional practices, such as early marriage, that contribute to fistula injuries.

One of Ambaye's first outreach trips was to the north-western province of Gojam. This is the province where a Channel Four documentary was made recently by an Ethiopian producer, Eleni Mekuria. It is called *The Child Brides of Ethiopia*. In this film, Dr Ambaye and Dr Brink are both interviewed by Eleni.

The people of this province and adjoining Gondar are deeply traditional. It is a joyous occasion if a boy is born, but there is not so much excitement if it is a girl. Often there is a shortage of money even for food, let alone to send the children to school. If they can afford education, boys get first preference. Girls stay at home to help their mother with cooking, weaving and looking after the livestock. A girl learns her status early when she sees her brother studying while she cooks for him. Children are taught to obey their parents, so if a father says, 'You are to be married,' this is what happens.

They may be betrothed at eight or nine. Negotiations are made between the two families, and money and goods exchanged for the young bride. She, unlucky child, is then escorted, usually sitting on a donkey with a brother or her father holding her, to the village of the young man who is to be her future husband. Here she lives with her in-laws, learning the ways of the household and getting to know her husband.

Pregnancy may occur at the age of fourteen, seldom before, as puberty is late in Ethiopian girls, who are often undernourished and of small stature.

Unfortunately, the Ethiopian Orthodox Church, which is the most powerful institution in the country, particularly in Gojam and Gondar, rarely speaks out against child marriage. In fact most priests encourage it as a means of retaining the virtue of young women. Their message is for her to be obedient, virtuous and fruitful.

Some of the priests out in the country are not well educated and have ideas based on centuries-old traditions. The outreach team met one who declared, 'At fifteen the girl shouldn't stay at home. Her body will mature, and her imagination will develop, and her parents will have no peace of mind. At fifteen she should marry and set up home and have children. These days, with Western ideas spreading everywhere, girls stay unmarried as late as 30. It's all very scientific and modern, but our Church prohibits it. Such girls aren't clean or blessed.'

We are hopeful that change may gradually take place, especially as education spreads out into the remote areas. There is a rider in Ethiopia's constitution that states that provinces are allowed to follow their traditional practices, so this rather negates any legislation the government might introduce to improve things, as it has recently tried to do. Perhaps the most effective incentive for change will come through the Church. The Patriarch has recently shown a willingness to use his influence to reform these long-held attitudes. In the meantime my heart goes out to these girls. They hardly have time to enjoy childhood before they are married and pregnant. Because they are still not sufficiently developed, childbirth can be a traumatic experience.

In Gondar province most people live at least two days walk from a road. Although in the ancient capital there is a medical college and a big hospital, elsewhere in the province there are few hospitals and these are poorly equipped and staffed – quite inadequate for the five million people. So for a girl in obstructed labour there is not much hope of getting skilled help.

Ambaye visited several villiages on an outreach trip to Gondar. In one, she and the team were led to a dilapidated hut away from the others. At first glance it seemed to be derelict. The whole structure was leaning to one side and looked as though it was about to collapse. Inside, crouched in the dark, downcast and listless, was a young woman, Amawa. She told them she had been married at twelve and was pregnant at thirteen. After a long labour her child was born dead, and she was left with a double fistula, incontinent of urine and bowel contents.

'What about your husband?' enquired Ambaye.

Tears welled up and trickled down her cheeks. 'He destroyed me and then he left.'

Amawa's mother looked after her until she sadly died, leaving her daughter to endure her affliction alone. She had been told there was a hospital in Addis Ababa where she could be cured, but she did not have the bus fare. When the outreach team found her she had been in this condition for twelve years. They arranged for her to go to a local hospital, where Ambaye operated successfully.

The team went to another village, where they had heard there was a woman living in a hut by herself. They followed directions and came to a *tukul* with a little room built onto the side.

'Is there anyone here leaking urine?' Ambaye asked.

The people said no. It seemed to Ambaye that they were hiding something so she asked them again. Still they insisted there was no one with that condition.

Ambaye persisted, and in the end they reluctantly showed her into the side room. The door was the only opening. Inside it was dark, and the smell was almost unbearable. In the far corner, against the wall was a raised platform. Peering through the gloom they made out a woman lying on her side with her legs drawn up in a flexed position. Her bladder and bowel contents were leaking into a pool underneath. Because she had been in this position for five years the joints had become stiff and ankylosed, and she could no longer walk. Her plight was pitiable beyond description. Ambaye arranged for her transport to Addis Ababa, where in our hospital we were able eventually to cure her.

On another trip Ambaye, Mamitu and Tenadem, one of our nursing sisters, drove 500 kilometres to Harrar, the most important Muslim city in Ethiopia. They had to take an interpreter with them because the people in those parts speak a different language to Amharic. A few kilometres outside the city, on the road to the Somali border, they came to the village of Babele, where they had heard there were some women with fistulae.

It was easy to find Hawa. She was sitting forlorn and alone – the only isolated figure in a landscape of people caught up in the busy comings-and-goings of village life.

Hawa had had a fistula for twenty years. Her husband was dead, and she collected firewood for a living. She told Ambaye, 'When I want to see my neighbours I do my best to wash myself clean. It is difficult. The only time I see people is when I collect water from the well, but I feel they have contempt for me. I can't hold my head up. There's nothing I can do about it.

'Once I went to Harrar hospital and paid a lot of money, and they gave me some tablets and an appointment paper. They told me to return on a certain day. I wrapped the appointment paper in my clothes. When I washed the clothes I forgot the paper. I couldn't go back for another because I had no money.'

Ambaye warned Hawa that she had a very big fistula, which they might not be able completely to cure.

The next woman they found was Mahjo. She thought she was between twenty and 30, but looked years older. She spent most of her time sitting alone in her hut and had been like that for about ten years. Like so many fistula patients, Mahjo was terribly depressed. Her eyes were downcast, her demeanour sad and hopeless. Her posture and every gesture demonstrated her wretchedness. She told Ambaye she had borne six children, but only one was alive. She added, 'The neighbours weep for me. They knew me when I was young and beautiful. They say, "Now she has this illness in her old age, may God cure her." I don't have any money. My child brings me food.'

Mahjo had quite a small fistula. Ambaye assured her, 'We can do an operation and mend the hole completely, then you can be a normal woman. You will be able to sit with the people without any smell.'

As Mahjo heard this, tears began to trickle down her cheeks. 'I would be so happy to be with people again,' she said.

The team made arrangements to take Mahjo and Hawa into the Harrar Hospital. The operation was watched by the resident gynaecologist in the hope that in future he would be able to do easy cases on his own. Hawa's operation turned out to be easier than first thought, and Ambaye, with her skill, was able to cure both women completely.

The lack of good medical care in rural areas is a deeply entrenched problem. Although all graduating doctors are obliged to serve in the country for two years, they find the conditions so frustrating and the pay so poor that they drift back to the city as soon as possible. Many hospitals have no gynaecologist or surgeon on their staff. I know this situation can only change if doctors have more incentive to work in the countryside, such as better pay and housing and even education for their children.

Mulu and Ambaye have plenty of good ideas on how we can help to educate the village women, especially relating to the occurrence of obstetric fistulae. One idea is that the cured fistula patients could educate others when they return to their villages. But really, a whole new attitude to marriage and childbirth needs to develop. Parents have to change their minds about the worth of their daughters. Teachers and religious heads have to show a lead, and the girls themselves must somehow learn that they do not have to marry when they are still children.

Others, such as the Minister of Women's Affairs, Wozeru Tadaletch, and Eleni Mokuria, who made the Channel Four documentary, are ardent campaigners for change to these entrenched beliefs. It is only through education that these harmful practices will be abandoned, not through government legislation.

Chapter Twenty-Three

It costs US$300 to cure an average fistula case. This includes everything – surgery and medication and about three weeks in hospital. In Australia I suppose this might be the cost of one day in hospital. Every cent we spend is donated by charities. Some have been helping us for decades. World Vision is a loyal supporter, especially the Australian and Canadian branches. They, with another wonderful charity based in England, Ethiopiaid, give us our annual running costs, and the latter organisation has promised to continue this aid for as long as we need it, increasing it if necessary. Others that help frequently are the Archbishop of Sydney's Overseas Relief and Aid Fund, Rotarians, the Zonta Women's Clubs, Inner Wheel, for wives of Rotarians, and others, too many to enumerate, including many faithful individual donors.

We have had a long relationship with Rotary clubs in different parts of the world, which have donated much equipment. We owe our extremely useful Land Rover to clubs in Australia, Canada and Spain. New theatre lights came from these same clubs. An X-ray machine came from Holland, while other clubs in different parts of the world contributed water tanks, a generator and an anaesthetic machine, to name just some.

The Rotary Club at Terrace End in Palmerston North,

New Zealand, is one of our champions. The association began through a member knowing Reg and following his career in Ethiopia, and has continued ever since. Such was the club's concern for our patients that they put together a submission for the Rotary International Award for World Understanding. The submission included supporting letters from people all over the world, a copy of the BBC documentary, *Walking Back to Happiness* and an extract from Dr Robert Zacharin's textbook on obstetric fistulas, in which he devotes a chapter to the hospital.

I was flattered that they were going to so much trouble but I did not hold out much hope of winning. Previous winners had included the International Red Cross and Fred Hollows, the great Australian eye doctor who dedicated his life to curing blindness among Australian Aborigines and people in the developing world, especially Eritrea.

As I expected, I failed to win. But the following year the determined Rotarians in New Zealand put together a bigger and better submission. The award that year was won by Nelson Mandela, the President of South Africa. I thought, Well, that will probably be the last I'll hear about it, but the New Zealanders were not daunted. Towards the end of 1997 I heard they were busily preparing another submission.

The committee decided that previously they had not been graphic enough in portraying the stark reality of our patients' condition. Their submission opened with this introduction:

> It is most unlikely that you will ever be injured in such a way that you have a permanent opening between your bladder and rectum (i.e. fistula) so that the urine and faeces trickle down your legs 24 hours a day! Add to this the difficulties of living in a remote village in a poor country, with an inadequate water supply and not enough money to buy rags as diapers. You would smell greatly and be totally ostracised.

This must have struck a chord with the judges, because in 1998

I found myself travelling to America to receive the award and a prize of US$100,000.

I do not enjoy speaking in public but I have had to steel myself to do it since Reg's death. My husband was an eloquent orator. I frequently saw audiences reduced to tears as Reg described the plight of the fistula patients. I was always thankful that he could do all the public speaking, never imagining that I would have to step into his shoes. I know I have received God's help whenever I have had to speak. Before these big Rotary conferences I spend time praying that I will not be nervous or my mouth become so dry that I will be unable to speak.

It was to Indianapolis that I went to receive the Rotary award. The ceremony was to be held in an enormous circular hall with a sort of fabric roof, evidently quite an architectural feat. As always there was a rehearsal the day before. Suddenly in the midst of this a loud siren sounded, warning of a typhoon. This precipitated a mad stampede for the doors. Fortunately the all-clear sounded a few minutes later, and we were able to continue, albeit somewhat shaken. I often wonder what would have happened to this sort of building if the typhoon had struck it.

The following day, with my heart pounding, I stood up before a huge audience. I thanked them for the prize, told them about our work and how this money would be spent. At the end of my speech I was amazed by a standing ovation. After Glen Kinross, the President of Rotary International, presented me with the award, people rushed up onto the stage to shake my hand. As always the story of our sad patients had touched the hearts of the audience.

The year before I received this award I had experienced the same overwhelming response at a Rotary International Conference at Annaheim in California. This was the first time I had spoken publicly in America, and it was another experience of the lavish way Americans look after their guests.

On the journey there I spent a few days in England with

Richard and his family and also had a chest X-ray, as I was recovering from a chronic cough. The X-ray showed a lesion in my lung which needed investigation. So I agreed to have it done on my way back from America.

I flew across the Atlantic and arrived at Los Angeles airport in the evening, where I was met by a man holding up a notice with my name on it. Outside he ushered me into a huge, long limousine. Naturally I asked if I could sit beside the driver but was told that this was not allowed, so I found myself sitting in solitary state in the back seat with a bar beside me in case I needed a drink or a sandwich.

It was almost dark, but I could see we were travelling down a wide motorway at high speed with probably six lanes of traffic all going in the same direction and at the same hectic pace. The interior of this amazing vehicle featured a thin glass tube with fluorescent lighting inside, running around the cabin and changing colour every few minutes. I was in another world and rather longed to be back in the one I knew and loved – this was all so different and intimidating.

I was too far from the driver to ask him where we were going, but it seemed a long journey. Finally we drew up in the driveway of an enormous, brilliantly lit hotel next to Disneyland. I was struggling to undo my seatbelt, which somehow seemed more difficult in America, when the door opened and a uniformed attendant reached over to help.

I felt foolish and unnerved as I was guided to the reception area and then, thankfully, to my room. But really everyone was kind, and it was only my nervousness that made things seem strange and rather daunting.

I am sure my room must have been one kept especially for VIP guests. It was extraordinarily large and had a magnificent view of Disneyland nearby, blazing with myriad coloured lights. I was asked if I would like something to eat. As it was now about 10 pm I suggested a bowl of soup would be nice. About twenty minutes later a table was wheeled in set with silver and laden with more food than I could possibly consume in 24 hours.

I could not sleep well after my meal and lay awake worrying about my speech the following day. I rose early to rehearse it again and to spend a long time on my knees praying. These prayers were wonderfully answered, for I felt calm as soon as I started to speak. As I described the desperate plight of our patients I could sense the sympathy of the audience, which later showed in a wonderful response and many generous donations.

With this ordeal over I felt able to relax and enjoy my luxurious surroundings. Before I left London, Richard had suggested that as I would be in Anaheim I should visit John Wimber's church and try to hear this world-renowned preacher. Next evening I took a taxi there. Inside it seemed more like a theatre than a church and would certainly have seated thousands.

I had telephoned during the day and knew there was no service that evening, but I was invited to attend a smaller meeting being held in a side room. There were other overseas visitors there too, and we were all asked to introduce ourselves and say why we were visiting. We sat and listened to a man expounding on a passage from the Bible. After this we had a time of prayer. Imagine my surprise when a woman came over to me, put her hand on my shoulder and prayed that my lungs should be healed. I said to her when she finished, 'How did you know I had anything the matter with my lungs?'

She replied, 'I was prompted by God's Spirit to pray for this healing.'

Then I told her about the tumour which had recently been diagnosed and that I was to have it investigated on my return to London.

Later when telling friends about this incident some were sceptical and said, 'You were probably coughing all through the meeting.' But this was not so, as my cough had got better.

Going back to the hotel in the taxi I was thinking about this prayer when I noticed a neon sign outside a factory building. Part of the sign was not working – only the words, 'I believe, I believe, I believe,' flashing out at me three times.

I knew then that God was surely affirming the prayer that

had been made for me at the meeting and asking me to believe. This was hard to do as I knew a lymphomatous tumour could appear anywhere in my body where there are lymph glands and that I could have such a tumour in the mediastinum between my lungs.

As soon as I got back to London I was admitted to the Hammersmith Hospital, where a biopsy was planned. Before the biopsy the head of radiology decided I should have a CAT scan. As I lay in this big tube after having the serial scans done I could see a group of radiologists behind a glass window studying the results. I could tell there was some sort of conference going on because it was such a long time before anyone came out to see me.

At last the head radiologist approached and said, 'I'm very sorry, but we can't find anything the matter with your lung.'

Perhaps she was apologising for the inconvenience, but whatever the reason, I was delighted and told her so. I also told her I believed in the power of prayer.

'Oh,' she said. 'Do you?' But I could tell she was not convinced.

I was taken back to my room, where I got dressed and went home. I have had no recurrence of lung trouble since.

One of our greatest benefactors has been the Australian Government's overseas aid organisation, AusAID. When Dr Arrowsmith moved to Addis Ababa, we needed to build a house within the hospital compound for him and his family. The head of the Hamlin Fistula Relief and Aid Fund Trust in Australia, Stuart Abrahams, asked AusAID for assistance and they gave us a contribution of AUS$50,000. Later they financed our laboratory wing and also a small extra ward, which was opened by Princess Anne during a visit to Ethiopia.

The Princess had expressed a wish to see our hospital while on an official visit as patron of the Save the Children Fund, UK. During the Emperor's reign we had been quite accustomed to state visits by royalty from many different lands. They were a rare occurrence under the communist regime, and Princess Anne's visit had been privately arranged by the British Embassy.

The staff lined up to meet her as she emerged from the leading vehicle in a cavalcade of Land Rovers. I think the staff were expecting to see a princess wearing pearls and lots of gold, so they may have been disappointed when a tall, slim woman, simply dressed in slacks and a casual top, greeted each of them in turn. One of our dogs, Saba, must have sensed that Her Royal Highness loved animals, as she, too, welcomed her by licking one of her shoes. We then gave her a full tour of the hospital. The Princess lingered beside the beds of several patients, asking questions, obviously concerned about all that she saw and heard.

After taking her to see a recently completed ward, which had not yet been occupied, she kindly agreed that we could name it after her. It now has a notice over the door, 'The Princess Anne Ward'.

At the end of her tour, with a crowd of officials trailing behind, I invited her to have tea in the gardens. It was ready on borrowed tables and chairs, under trees and umbrellas for shade. Before she could answer, the British Ambassador chipped in, 'We are late for our next engagement at the British Council, Ma'am.' But Princess Anne firmly decided she would like to have tea and, smiling assent, walked down the steps to the lawn.

Each year the number of fistula operations increased until, by 1995, we were doing more than a thousand per year. As well, the demand for training local and overseas surgeons had stepped up markedly. We were also hearing news of some heartening results from other countries. From Katsina in Nigeria, Dr Kees Waldijk had come for training in 1984. He had subsequently set up a special ward in a leprosy hospital and had treated over 4000 patients. In the Sudan, Dr Abbo of Khartoum, who trained with us on a WHO scholarship twenty years ago, was running his own private fistula clinic. We had also trained doctors from Nigeria, Niger, Sudan, Malawi, Benin, Tanzania, The Netherlands, India, New Guinea, Northern Pakistan, Bangladesh, Kenya, Nepal, Zaire and Ghana. As well as these doctors from developing countries, others from Australia, UK, USA, Norway and Sweden often came as visitors. We had to develop a policy of only giving training to doctors who were or would be working in countries where obstetric fistulae were common.

These increased demands were straining the hospital facilities to the limit. On every level there was overcrowding, and the old buildings, which had been added onto over the years, needed to be upgraded into a more efficient complex. The most serious problem was water. The erratic supply could not be relied upon to keep up with the cooking and laundry needs of 150 people a day. Sometimes we had no water at all and had to arrange for tankers to come from the Water Board to fill our tanks.

The water supply had become so critical that we even began looking around for possible sites to relocate the hospital. While considering that drastic step we consulted a hydrogeologist and a water engineer working at the Ministry of Mines, who had maps of Addis Ababa and surroundings showing where the water table was.

We were told there should be water under our area. An expert came to select the best spot to drill and informed us that we would have to go down below the level of the Akaki River, which ran at the bottom of our steep hillside. So we knew we would need a particularly deep bore. We were fortunate that the only suitable drilling machine belonged to World Vision and had recently returned to Addis Ababa after many months in the provinces drilling wells. Just when we needed it we found it was available. At the same time a friend of Steven Arrowsmith's was in Ethiopia for a visit. He was a well driller from Texas, so he and the World Vision team set to work bringing in the rig and all the machinery needed to drill our bore.

We watched day after day as the drill went down deeper and

deeper. Once it struck water, but it was contaminated, so they pressed on until they had reached a depth of 109 metres. We were then told to be ready with our cameras as there was only a layer of rock to go through before the water table would be reached.

I never found out how they were so certain, but we believed them. All the staff came and stood on the hillside, watching with expectation. Suddenly there was a noise like an explosion, and an immense spout of water shot up into the sky. Everyone cheered and clapped.

The bore was capped, and a pump was installed that sends water into two big tanks high off the ground, so that we always have good pressure. The water proved to be pure when tested, so we can safely drink it. Every six months it is re-tested at the Pasteur Institute and so far has been free of any contamination. The bore has been a tremendous blessing and has solved all our water shortage problems.

Although the water problem was remedied, our hospital urgently needed to expand and be upgraded. In 1995 Stuart Abrahams again bravely asked AusAID if they could help, in collaboration with the Archbishop's Fund. They were friendly but made no promises, telling Stuart firmly that they could no longer consider the sort of funding they had been giving in the past, supplying money spasmodically for specific needs. 'Work out your needs,' he was told, 'and come to Canberra and present the plans.'

When we looked at our needs in detail, it became clear that we practically needed a new hospital. The primitive kitchen and laundry, which had been there since 1974, were now inadequate. We lacked an administration building. The pharmacy was too small and did not meet the Ministry of Health requirements. We needed all-weather covered pathways between the kitchen and wards. The main ward was so crowded that the beds were half a metre apart. The operating theatre was too small and badly in need of modernising. There was nowhere for visiting doctors to stay. In the waiting hostel often two patients were sleeping in one bed . . . the requirements seemed endless.

Stuart was an assistant minister at St Andrew's Anglican Church in Wahroonga, Sydney. The organist was a prominent architect, Ridley Smith. One day after Sunday service Stuart told Ridley he was involved with a hospital in Ethiopia and they needed someone to take a good look at it and advise on a master plan. Would he be interested? Without a moment's hesitation he said he would love to be involved.

Ridley had an ideal background for the task. He was brought up in China, where his parents were missionaries, and had spent part of his schooling in India. He had travelled and worked in many countries and had a deep interest in designing projects for the developing world. He had done some similar projects before, upgrading schools and hospitals, so he was used to deciding what was worth retaining and what should be replaced.

In late 1995 Stuart and Ridley came to Ethiopia to see our hospital for the first time. Ridley had done some reading about the country but he was not prepared for the size of Addis Ababa or what he described as the 'oasis garden' of the hospital. Being a landscape architect and a keen gardener himself, he was captivated by the gardens that I had lovingly nurtured for twenty years. The buildings were another matter. They had grown up at random, and some were poorly built. For instance, in the lab the wastepipe from the sink went into a wall and simply stopped. The builder had not bothered to connect it to any plumbing. We had wondered for years why we had a drainage problem.

For two weeks Stuart and Ridley surveyed the site, took photographs, met with local builders and architects, and discussed ideas with the staff. Ridley was firmly of the view that everything should be done in consultation with the people who were actually working at the hospital. He wanted to have a friendly village feel. In his first design he drew the nurses' quarters and a little chapel as round buildings, to look like *tukuls,* with thatched roofs. When he showed this to the staff, they vetoed the idea. Thatch was too much of a maintenance problem and, despite being a traditional building material, it is expensive, as it has to be replaced every fifteen years. Ridley was disappointed but accepted their decision.

Ridley worked with a firm of local architects, Abba Associates. If he had searched the world he could not have found better people to help him. I know he enjoyed working with them and was grateful for their contributions, which often added an Ethiopian touch to the designs. Their knowledge of local conditions was invaluable.

Finding a builder was complicated. We were certain AusAID would ask for at least three quotes and that the cheapest would undoubtedly be the worst. There was one builder who was reputed to be the best in the city but also the most expensive. He was an Italian, Luigi Varnero, whose father had set up the firm and built most of the early city buildings, including the huge municipality complex that still dominates the city.

Stuart, Ridley and I went to see Mr Varnero in his office on the seventh floor of a run-down building in Addis Ababa. We scrambled through a congested yard to a back entrance and into a rickety lift that stopped dead at the sixth floor. Climbing the last flight of stairs we noticed several windows had glass missing. On being ushered into Mr Varnero's lavish suite, the contrast could not have been greater. We sat on comfortable chairs around a polished table and drank coffee, admiring the indoor plants and art on the walls.

Despite our project being much smaller than his usual ones, Mr Varnero seemed keen to help us and agreed to quote for the construction. While a little more than the others, his price was in the same region. We decided when we approached AusAID, to ask for Varnero to be the builder.

We now needed to submit plans and gain approval for an enormous sum of money, so Stuart again went to Canberra and presented the design document – a 60-page book containing every last detail about the project. Then we waited.

What happened next was partly linked with a previous trip to Addis Ababa by the Minister for Foreign Affairs in the Labor government at the time, Gareth Evans. Mr Evans had visited our hospital and was impressed by what he saw. He told me that when I was next in Australia I should come to see him as he might be able to help. It happened that I was due for leave the following year, 1996, so taking him at his word, I made an appointment to see him in Canberra.

Imagine my surprise when, after seating me on a sofa in his office, he said, 'Do you know you are our pin-up girl? I want to help you, so just say what you need for the hospital and I'll do my best to get it for you.'

I mentioned the running costs, but he replied, 'Please don't ask for running costs. I can't get that for you.'

So then I told him about our plans for upgrading the hospital. He immediately picked up the phone and made a call, then took me off to another building to see the head of AusAID.

I don't know if being Mr Evan's pin-up girl helped, but soon after that meeting we were told we would get the money we needed in instalments over the next three years. It would be distributed through the Archbishop of Sydney's Overseas Relief and Aid Fund, which had helped us regularly in the past and which would administer the use of the funds. They also approved Mr Varnero as the builder.

The hospital needed to keep functioning while the alterations were being done. Ridley adopted a 'musical chairs' solution. First he built the new kitchen, then knocked down the old one and put the new laundry where it had been. Then they knocked down the old laundry, and so on.

The new operating complex was one of the last additions to be completed. It adjoins the old theatre area but is bigger, more spacious and better designed. Now we have room for four operating tables in the one big room, which has new lights and a most interesting and exciting area for scrubbing up. Ridley designed this very like a ship's bridge, with a semi-circle of glass looking onto the trees and gardens. As it is high up off the ground it gives the feeling of being suspended in space. As we scrub our hands at the basin we gaze out through the glass at weaver birds making their nests or the kites floating effortlessly in the sky. It is a place where nerves are soothed and spirits calmed before we operate.

The old theatre was converted into an immediate post-operative ward of ten beds which continues into the main ward, separated only by two attractive arches that replaced the original theatre wall.

It was impossible to upgrade the main ward with patients there, so we stopped surgery for a few weeks. Patients unable to be discharged were crowded into the Princess Anne ward and our hostels, including the new one just completed. Mr Varnero's men then set to work. The tiles on the floor were buckling here and there and had become a hazard. When we pulled them up we discovered that there had never been a proper slab laid. They excavated and poured a new one and relaid light colonial tiles to replace the old, cracked grey ones.

When it was finished the new ward looked beautiful. Light streaming through the windows was reflected off the pale floor, the curtains and bed covers were blue, and all the woodwork was painted a darker blue colour. There was a separate room for the ward sterilisers, with a special ceiling that repelled the growth of mould, which had been a problem in the past. The ward was extended, and new bathrooms with showers and lavatories were built. There was a new outpatients' department and reception area for patients arriving.

Most of the new buildings were connected via paths, covered walkways and paved areas. There was a new home for three trained nurses and a small house for doctors visiting from other countries for training. The nursing aides had an attractive new home built on what used to be our cow paddock. It contained twenty beds, ten on each side of a central dining area, and had bathrooms and a laundry.

The car park was enlarged and paved, with a covered area where the cars could be parked in the rainy season. From there steps lead down to a new administration block hidden behind a row of tall trees and a high retaining wall. It contains several spacious offices and a conference room.

A covered walkway between the main ward and the Princess Anne ward is a great boon, not only for the nurses, who previously had to trundle across a rough car park pushing patients on trolleys and getting soaked during the rainy season, but also for waiting patients, who can now sit on benches under shelter and gaze across a colourful flowerbed to watch the comings and goings in the car park.

All the buildings are whitewashed and surrounded by lawns dotted with shrubs and trees, which Ridley was careful to preserve. I value each one, having planted most of them myself. There has been extensive use of local granite, which would have cost a fortune in Australia. The entire project cost a little over one and a half million Australian dollars – the cost of a house in some Sydney suburbs.

When we first moved into the hospital in 1975, Mengistu was consolidating his position as the leader of a communist regime. Along with banks, businesses and private institutions, he was nationalising some hospitals, which is why we did not want to draw attention to ourselves by holding an official opening ceremony. In 1999 everything was different, and when the new buildings were complete we decided it was at last time for a proper ceremony.

We chose 21 January, but preparations began weeks before. Ethiopians excel at arranging such ceremonies and on this occasion they lived up to their reputation. The hospital looked beautiful and the grounds immaculate. A landscape gardener friend lent us lots of potted trees and shrubs, which we placed in strategic positions where the assembled guests would be sitting.

We were honoured to have the President of Ethiopia, His Excellency Dr Negaso Gedada, the Minister of Health and the Minister of Women's Affairs as guests. The Patriarch of the Ethiopian Orthodox Church, Abuna Paulos, had declined our invitation as he had a previous engagement. The Archbishop of Sydney, Harry Goodhew, flew over from Australia with his wife and some of my family. Richard came from England with Sarah, my eldest grandchild, and the Australian Ambassador with responsibility for Ethiopia, Philip Green, travelled up from Nairobi with his Tanzanian wife.

The guests took their seats in the car park, the fortunate ones shaded from the blazing sun. A young girl was standing clutching a bunch of flowers to give to the President when he stepped from his car. This he handed to an aide-de-camp and then, with his German wife following, he was escorted to the place of honour behind a low table, on which was placed a bowl of red lilies gathered that morning from the garden.

Shortly after the speeches began there was a commotion. It was the Patriarch! His engagement had finished early and he had decided to come after all. We had already welcomed his assistant Bishop, who was now sitting comfortably in an armchair in the front row and probably rehearsing his speech.

The tall, white-robed Patriarch, adorned with several gold chains and crosses, made an impressive entrance. Everyone stood and bowed, and there was a shuffling of seats to make room for him. We placed him next to the Archbishop of Sydney where, in his regalia, he seemed to dominate the assembly.

Although he arrived late and was the last to speak, it was worth the wait. We were excited to hear him condemn the practice of early marriage and promise to use his influence to bring about its eradication. I only hope that the message is filtering through to his diocese in the northern provinces. The speeches ended with the Patriarch giving his blessing in English and Amharic.

On a tour of the hospital, trailed by security men and reporters, I had an opportunity to enlarge on a need I had mentioned briefly in my speech. This was to provide for the small percentage of tragic patients we are unable to cure through normal fistula surgery. Unable to return to their village communities, they need a home not too distant from medical care, and work that will give them some quality of life.

When I spoke of these matters to the President he tapped his head and said, 'I have in mind land that may suit you for this purpose.' He then instructed the Minister for Social Affairs, who was standing nearby, to follow it up.

The President and the Patriarch departed, leaving the rest of us to relax and enjoy a delicious lunch in the garden, shaded by trees. So ended a great day in the history of our hospital, such a contrast to that other day, 25 years earlier, when Reg and I alone cut a ribbon in our drawing room. I was sad that he was not here to enjoy the celebrations and to see his vision fulfilled.

Every day, as I walk along the covered pathway between the two wards, I pass Reg's memorial – a rough-hewn granite rock with a brass plaque set into it. On it are written those words of Jesus from St Matthew, chapter 25 verse 40, 'Whatever you did for one of the least of these brothers of mine, you did for me.'

Every time I read it I think of how Reg loved his fistula pilgrims and how he would have rejoiced at the continuation of his work.

Chapter Twenty-Four

The new government which came to power in 1991 has brought some relief to the long-suffering citizens of Ethiopia. From 1991 to 1998 there was a period of peace and economic growth. But then the war with Eritrea flared up again, and to cap it all there was another famine in the year 2000. As I mentioned earlier, the two sides have recently agreed to cease hostilities, and hopefully this time the peace will last.

In Addis Ababa new roads, hotels and private hospitals are being built and the supermarkets are well stocked, although everything is very expensive. While the rich seem to be getting richer, the lot of the poor changes little. In the provinces poverty is still widespread and pockets of famine remain. The 1990s saw a huge increase of patients from those parts of the country which had been cut off by the war.

Nearly every day new patients arrive at the hospital – a little group will be sitting patiently on bench seats, under cover, beside the entrance to the reception area. The weak ones may have been carried. Some are in ragged clothes with bare feet, holding perhaps a plastic or cow-hide bag, containing what may be their entire worldly possessions in some instances. Most come with a father, equally poorly clad, but as they greet you one forgets the poverty and the smell of urine. Little faces light up with hope when we tell them they are going to be cured. The fathers, with dignity, bow deeply, or even forgetting their dignity for a few moments, try to kiss our feet in gratitude.

Birru's son, Getahun, the hospital clerk, interviews them and fills in their cards with the details we need. After this they are taken into the outpatient's clinic and examined.

Sometimes it is not possible for them to be admitted straightaway, and then we have the heartbreaking task of telling them there is no bed. With the extra beds since the hospital was rebuilt we can take in more patients than before, even if it means sharing a bed with someone else. This is impossible to imagine in Western countries – two incontinent patients in one bed, but it is better than lying in the street at a bus-stop or in a churchyard.

My husband always greeted new arrivals before he started any other work. I vividly remember him standing in his white coat, giving them a kind word of encouragement and often enacting the little scene that he imagined would take place when they returned to their village. Shading his eyes, he would pretend to be one of the villagers spying a girl coming along the path. 'Who is this looking so pretty and happy? No, it can't be Hirut who went away only a few weeks ago so wretched and sad. Why, it is her, but how changed she is.' Then he would describe her reunion with her family just as vividly.

Although we are not such good actors as Reg, we try to continue this routine of welcome – so important to women who sometimes for years have known nothing but rejection, loneliness and humiliation.

Let me take you on a tour of the ward. We enter at one end of a long room divided by a waist-high partition down the middle. Each section has a row of beds along both sides. There are windows down the entire length of two walls, so the ward is airy and light. At the far end is the recovery section of ten beds and the nurses' station, and beyond that you can see the doors leading into the operating theatres.

The first bed we come to as we enter is permanently occupied by our dear friend and long-time nursing aide, Lete Birhan. It is empty during the day, neatly made up and covered with her patchwork quilt, which distinguishes it from all the other beds. Lete is usually to be found moving about the ward, unhindered by her wheelchair, helping and encouraging those who need special exercises to strengthen their leg muscles. Or else she may be working with patients in the physiotherapy department.

Walking along the ward we come to a young woman called Elfinesh, clad in a blue nightgown like all the other patients but wearing a brightly coloured scarf – her own touch. Elfinesh lost her baby four years ago and was left with a fistula in both bladder and rectum. She tells us she lived with her old mother, mostly just sitting in a corner of the small *tukul* and only going out after dark to try to wash herself with the limited supply from the water pot. She was afraid to go to the river at night and too ashamed during the day to face ridicule and rejection by the village girls. She was dependent on her mother for food and drink and never went herself to the market or to draw water.

'What was the worst thing about your life?' I ask her.

She replies without hesitation. 'The loneliness, never being able to mix with others, and the smell and wetness which were with me constantly.'

Elfinesh needed extensive surgery as we had to rebuild her whole urethra, which was totally destroyed during labour. She shyly asks if she will be cured. I tell her confidently that she will. Already it is ten days since her operation and she is still dry.

Further down the ward is Wude. She has had three babies, all of whom died. She was in labour for four days before the last one was stillborn. Wude had her fistula for two years before she came to us. Her husband left her and married another woman.

'Never mind,' I reassure her. 'Now that you are cured you can marry again and even have another child if you go to hospital next time.'

But Wude shakes her head and says she does not want another husband. Her village is three days walk from the main road and the hospital another day away by bus. No, she does not want to marry again, but only to be dry. We are confident she will be.

Next to Wude is Tabote. She had been operated on ten years ago for a fistula, complicated by scar tissue formation in the vagina. We repaired her then, and although she went home with some slight dribbling on walking, she was able to manage. Gradually, over a few years, the scar formed again, causing her incontinence to increase.

These are tragic cases, which cause us the most heartache because of the difficulty they present. Nevertheless, we operated again on Tabote, removing scar and lengthening her urethra, but with no improvement. So once again she has returned, for a third operation. It is too early yet to see if this time we have been successful. Despite all she has been through, Tabote is stoical and uncomplaining.

Wubayehu is in the next bed – an older woman who has had twelve children, six of whom are still alive. Although we have closed her fistula, she is still incontinent on walking because her bladder is contracted and thus not able to fulfil its function as a reservoir. We hope that with some bladder training this will improve. Wubayehu is trying hard and is already showing some improvement.

There is another woman next to her, about the same age, whose four children were all stillborn. The last one caused her uterus to rupture. Although Edjigayehu managed to reach a hospital it was not possible to save her uterus, so she will never have another child.

Today she is smiling because her catheter has been removed, and she is dry! It may seem a paradox to call this patient fortunate, but I do so because to have survived the most lethal and dreaded complication of labour is so rare in Ethiopia. Most succumb quickly to internal bleeding and shock from such a catastrophe.

At the end of the ward is a bed over which two coloured balloons are hanging. A little girl is lying nursing a rag doll. Only six years old, Fariha Ali was brought to us from neighbouring war-torn Somalia, where she was caught in machine-gun fire. The bullet caused a fistula in her bladder and rectum.

Fariha is such a brave child and a great favourite with all the staff. Soon Ambaye, who did her operation, will take her back to the theatre to remove the stitches and make sure her extensive injuries are completely cured. She will, of course, need another anaesthetic but because she will have so many people in the theatre who love her she will have no fear and will only know the tiny prick of a needle.

Her mother sits beside the bed for most of the day, and although we cannot speak her language we know she is happy by her smile.

Not far away is another beautiful child, for although Kongit is sixteen years old she is small and still looks a child. Her mother is very poor and carries water for the village to earn money. Her father is dead, and there is also a little boy to support, so Kongit was sent to the house of a merchant. She had to work long hours for a pittance, but at least there would be one less mouth to feed at home.

Her life was one of slavery and abuse. She was raped and became pregnant, then endured six days of labour, after which she was left with a stillborn baby and a fistula.

When Kongit arrived at the hospital she was weak and debilitated and also had a 'dropped foot' from nerve damage, so it was many weeks before she was fit for surgery. Now she has had her big fistula repaired, and we are confident of success. I wonder about her emotional state, though. She is very timid and seems still shocked by what happened to her.

'Can you take this man who raped you to court?' I ask.

She shakes her head. She has no money and no father to act for her. So there is no hope of justice for this girl.

We walk on past rows of clean, neatly made beds with patients lying quietly until we come to a young woman with vertical lines tattooed on her chin and a row of dots running down her jaw line. Fetenesh is 25. She has one live baby but lost her second after three days of labour. Her husband abandoned her. She begged money from the village and left her child with her mother-in-law while she came to Addis Ababa. Fetenesh had an extremely large fistula, which we have repaired. We are hopeful that she will be cured as, despite the size of the fistula, there was no scar tissue to interfere with healing.

She lies placidly, looking up at us with large, trusting eyes, and never complains.

Workenesh is 35 and has had three children, all of them dead. She begged for six months to get enough money to come to the hospital. She had to walk for a day to the bus, then travelled 120 kilometres to Addis Ababa. Workenesh had never been away from her village before and had to pay a man 104 birr (about US$13) to bring her to the hospital. That doesn't sound much but for a peasant in the countryside it is a fortune.

Each patient is different, with a distinctive character and appearance, only the symptoms are similar, as is the longing to be cured. When this happens they emerge like a butterfly from the chrysalis. The tragedy is that some of these women have been so terribly damaged and oppressed, that it seems as if all hope has been extinguished and the transformation will never take place.

One such is Dabousie. She is lying in bed curled up with the sheets pulled up around her head, peeping out at the world with wounded eyes. She is almost jet-black, and comes from Wollega where the Oromo people live, speaking their own language. The Oromo people are widespread throughout Ethiopia and form the largest ethnic group, but for centuries they were dominated by the Amharas.

I remember once years ago inadvertently insulting an Amharic patient in the labour ward by mistaking her for an Oromo. She gave me a withering look and retorted, 'I belong to the ruling race.' All this has now changed, and officially there is no distinction between these peoples. The Oromo language, unlike Amharic, can vary in different areas of Ethiopia, and for some of these patients there is nobody on our staff who can translate.

Fortunately, several people here can talk to Dabousie, and so we have been able to hear her sad story. Fifteen years ago she suffered an obstructed labour, ending with the delivery of a dead baby and also causing a fistula in the bladder and rectum. Her husband abandoned her, and until recently she had hidden in her *tukul*, afraid to face anyone. She was close to starvation when a farmer found her and kindly gave her some clothes and maize to eat. He even offered her a job working in the fields, promising her a small share of the profits.

She was discovered by missionaries and brought to us. Her injuries were of such magnitude that her operation lasted for over five hours. Ambaye has taken a special interest in Dabousie, trying to encourage and stimulate her, but she lies passively in bed, barely responding. I think she knows we care for her for she said to Ambaye one day, 'Don't worry about me. I am happy the way I am.'

Having been by herself for so long she has forgotten how to respond to normal human kindness. But we have all seen the transformation in similar patients and so we are hopeful that this will happen to Dabousie and that she will emerge one day as a beautiful butterfly.

Sureen is from Gojam and hence an Amhara. We could almost tell she was from Gojam without asking because of her close-cropped hair. We are told Gojam women wear their hair this way so they will not waste time preening themselves when they could be working. Although she looks young, Sureen says she is over 30 and has had nine deliveries, with four children surviving. She has been convalescing for about a week following surgery.

Sureen begins to cry as we approach and says she wants to go home. Her daughter is fourteen and pregnant with her first child, and she is worried that she, too, may end up like her.

We have quite frequently had a mother and daughter in the

hospital together, both with a fistula. Once I remember there were three sisters from a northern province where early marriage is common. When we asked why they got married so young they answered, 'We can't go to school so there is nothing else for us to do but marry.'

If we could alter this tradition we would indeed reduce the incidence of injury.

Bedria, in the next bed, is a pretty young woman of nineteen. She had a fistula for two years before coming to the hospital. When her husband decided to abandon her, the two families met and divided the assets. Her share was 200 birr (about $US25), which she spent getting to Addis Ababa. She is recovering well, and we are sure she will be cured.

Moving down the ward we pass two nursing aides who are mopping the floor. This goes on throughout the day, and we are proud of the cleanliness in our hospital. Visitors remark on this constantly, and although we are treating incontinent women, there is seldom any smell in the wards. All the pessimistic predictions of so many when we first planned to build a fistula hospital never came to pass.

Quite by accident, when I was putting in the garden, several shrubs were planted near the verandah which in the evenings give out a powerful, exotic scent. They are called daturas, or commonly, trumpet flowers, and for most of the year are covered with huge, trumpet-like blooms. Often as I walk up through the garden at night to see the patients, their wonderful scent fills the air and wafts into the hospital.

In the ward today there are two patients who have been with us a long time and who will continue to need much treatment. Ajebu is sitting on the bed with her feet dangling over the side. Although it is a warm day she is wearing woollen socks and a scarf, also of wool, around her head. She is terribly thin and feels the cold.

Ambaye found Ajebu on one of her outreach trips. She had been a fistula-sufferer for ten years. She lived in a hut with no sunshine and a poor diet, away from all contact with friends.

Her sister gave her food but did little else to help her. She lay on a goatskin bed, usually curled up, so that when she came to us she was crippled, with contracted knees and hips, and wasted, stick-like legs. Because of the poor diet her pelvis had become grossly deformed through loss of calcium so that it was impossible even to do a pelvic examination.

We consulted with radiologists, orthopaedic surgeons and urologists before deciding how best to treat her. Every doctor who saw her was baffled by her condition, especially the cause of her pelvic deformity. It obviously must have come after her delivery, following six days of obstructed labour, as even a dead, macerated baby could never have negotiated such a pelvis and been born vaginally.

Ajebu is now convalescing after an ileal conduit operation, similar to the one with Letekidane I described earlier. We only do this operation two or three times a year when it's essential because it means the patients can never return permanently to their villages. They need constant medical care and have to be able to regularly replace the bags and seals for the collection of urine.

Ajebu is learning to live with her disability, and we have even seen a smile beginning to lighten up her formerly sad face. Every day she walks with her two sticks to the physiotherapy department, where she does exercises to try to improve her crippled legs. Her progress has been slow, but now that her mental state has improved she is being diligent about her exercises, and eventually we expect her to have normally functioning legs. She will, I am afraid, become one of our permanent hospital community. Lately I have seen her helping others with similar disabilities.

Yezina has also been with us for over a year. Her father carried her on his back to our hospital. When she arrived it was impossible to comfort her, and she cried continuously for many days. Her history is sad indeed. She was at a country school in the seventh grade when her mother decided she should be married for she wanted a grandchild. So she found Yezina a husband, and she was duly married. At fifteen she gave birth to the wanted grandchild, but it was a stillborn baby after a long, terrible labour. Her mother had died in the meantime.

Soon her husband deserted her because she was incontinent of both urine and stool. Her plight was pitiable as she lay in her soiled bed for months, curled up and hoping the holes would mend. But there was no hope of this ever happening. Lying in this wet state, bed sores developed to add to her pain and misery.

Yezina's injuries were extensive. A colostomy has been done to divert the bowel contents away from her birth passage, so at least she is clean. She has learned to manage this temporary colostomy until we are able to cure her rectal injury.

For this operation we are waiting for our friend, Dr Brian Hancock, a colo-rectal surgeon from England. The injury in her rectum needs to be tackled through an abdominal approach, with possibly one of us working from below (that is, vaginally) at the same time.

Brian is a regular visitor, and we save up such cases for him. He also helps in Uganda at a Catholic mission hospital there, allowing the nuns to take a much needed holiday. He has also been to West Africa, where he does fistula operations as well.

In the interim Yezina goes regularly to have physiotherapy and is now walking with only one stick.

Next to Yezina is Shube. She is from the province of Arussi in the south, where a group of Oromo people live. They have a distinctive hairstyle and often facial scars which are put there for cosmetic reasons.

Shube has three vertical scars cut into each cheek and stained with a dark dye. She is 37 years old and had had her fistula for twenty years before she came to us. During that time the scar tissue had completely blocked her vagina, and so it was a difficult repair. However, when the skin was cut away, it was possible to close the fistula behind it.

Her circumstances are familiar; she describes them in a few sentences. Her husband abandoned her, and she left the village to live alone and eke out an existence by begging. One day she met a man who told her there was a hospital in Addis Ababa where she could be cured. It is hard to imagine such an existence. Twenty years of misery, with none of the comforts that would be her due in the West.

Now we come to a very special young lady. Minsera is eighteen, but she is so slight that she looks like a child. One Sunday in 1998 I came back from church and found her lying on the couch in outpatients with a man standing beside her. She was frightened and in agony. Her left hip was completely dislocated, and this leg was lying across the other one. It was impossible to examine her as I could not move her legs without her screaming with pain.

Minsera was from a village outside Harrar. She had been in bed for five months and had bed sores right down to the bone on her back. The kind man who brought her told us she had an aunt and some relatives who fed her, but they didn't know what to do. He must have been a relative, I think. When he saw her he felt such pity for her that he decided to take her to Addis Ababa.

It is an all-day journey on the train from Harrar, and he carried her in his arms all the way. I don't know how he did it. He told us how, during her long labour, Minsera had been heaving on a rope attached to the roof of the hut to try to get purchase to push the baby out. The rope broke, and she fell down, dislocating her hip. We were surprised that such a simple fall could do so much damage and were to discover the reason later.

Minsera was in a pitiful state – emaciated and dehydrated, her clothes soaked in urine and soiled with bowel contents. The smell in outpatients was overpowering. To lift her caused acute pain, so we gave her a very small injection of morphia and, when she was sedated, cut away her ragged clothes and put her into a hot bath.

To see her lying in a clean bed in her blue nightgown, with a bed cradle to keep the heavy blankets off her injured leg, brought tears to my eyes. Our nursing aides took her to their hearts and gave her loving care in the following weeks. She was dreadfully anaemic and needed blood transfusions to correct this. So thin was she that I could easily place her upper arm in the circle made by my thumb and index finger, with space to spare.

It was many weeks before we sought advice from the orthopaedic department at the leprosy hospital on how to treat her dislocated hip. They attempted to pull the head of the femur back into its socket by traction, putting a pin through the lower end of her femur to which weights were attached. But everything failed because her bone was diseased. Very soon an abscess formed and pus drained out. We cultured the discharge in our laboratory and grew the tuberculosis bacillus. So now we knew why her bones had been so fragile.

Later she developed ascites, an accumulation of fluid in the abdominal cavity, and from this we also grew the tuberculosis bacillus, thus confirming that Minsera had disseminated TB. Fortunately her lungs remained clear, and chest X-rays were normal.

Our physician, Dr Amha, prescribed five different anti-TB drugs which, after eight months, completely cured the disease. As time went by her condition improved dramatically. Her appetite returned, she gained weight, her hair, which was thin and sparse like a soft down when she arrived, became thick and shiny. Her eyes sparkled and lit up her pretty little face as she now greeted everyone with a smile. We were able to do a colostomy once the ascites disappeared, and she quickly learned to manage this and keep herself clean.

As soon as Minsera was strong enough, we started physiotherapy. I shall never forget the first day she got out of bed. We were all nervous about her taking this step, wondering what would happen to her hip. We were encouraged by Jenny Bassford, the physiotherapist who comes regularly, and happened to be over on one of her annual visits from England to help in the newly established department.

It was marvellous to see Minsera standing by her bed with the help of two of her devoted nursing aides. Before long she was taking a few steps with a walking frame then with just two sticks.

Minsera's left hip has been completely destroyed, but it has become stable and is now ankylosed, which of course greatly restricts mobility. We have had her left shoe built up so that both her legs are the same length, and she no longer has a limp. Now as I write, two years after she arrived, she has just one stick and she does not always use even that. She is again a beautiful young woman with a winsome personality and hope in her heart. Her youth, her resilience, and her courage have enabled her to weather this storm of disease and disaster.

Sadly, none of the vaginal operations have been possible yet for Minsera. Because of her stiff hip joint we are not able to turn her left leg outwards. Access to the injuries is at present impossible. However, she is persevering with the physiotherapy and making tremendous progress. We are hopeful that soon there will be enough movement in that hip to enable us to repair her huge rectal defect and close the colostomy. Later she will need an ileal conduit, as her whole bladder has been destroyed. There is no tissue to repair.

In the meantime, as Minsera waits for surgery she is an eager pupil, attending daily classes in our schoolroom, sitting out on the verandah with other waiting patients listening spellbound to stories of Jesus and His love, or just lying on the grass under the spreading thorn trees gossiping with her friends. Recently I have seen her in the physiotherapy room helping others with their exercises and encouraging those who, like her, have had to learn to walk again.

The last chapter of Minsera's story has not yet been written, but even so far the tale is remarkable. When I first saw her lying on that outpatients' couch I imagined we would just be trying to relieve her suffering for a few days until her death. Her recovery to this stage is almost totally due to the devoted nursing care given by our staff. Doctors give orders and prescribe drugs, but the daily task of looking after an emaciated, incontinent girl with bed sores and an excruciatingly painful hip has demanded nursing skills and compassion of the highest order.

~

I have sometimes been asked if these tragic cases ever test my faith. I can truly say that, if anything, my faith has been strengthened and my soul more firmly anchored to Jesus as the only one to whom we can turn. Jesus never promised us a smooth or trouble-free passage through life, but He did promise to be with us to share the sorrow and the pain.

The joy I receive from working for these patients is something for which I thank God every day. As the famous Dutch priest, Henri Nouwen, said in his book about spiritual life, *Here and Now, Living in the Spirit*, 'Ministry is first of all receiving God's blessing from those to whom we minister.'

This has been my experience and I know this is what Reg felt, too. I am sure that Reg and I were led here. At the time I did not know it, but in the end this is the place where we were meant to be. It hasn't really affected my faith. In fact if anything, it has strengthened my faith to know that we are doing something that is in His will, and the wonderful thing is that it is so enjoyable.

Chapter Twenty-Five

As I look back over my life with Reg and our work with the women of Ethiopia it surprises me sometimes to realise that I am 77 years old. Never for a moment have I felt like retiring, or wanted to change my life or my work. I still operate several times a week, and my hands are as steady as ever. Although most of my life has been spent working for fistula patients, the fascination and appeal has never palled. People sometimes express surprise that I could be satisfied doing the same thing for so long, but the work has never been a burden or a chore.

Professor Chassar Moir, the British expert, described so aptly the rewards of fistula surgery: 'Nothing can equal the gratitude of the woman who, wearied by constant pain and desperate with the realisation that her very presence is an offence to others, finds suddenly that life has been given anew and that she has again become a citizen of the world.' I look forward to every day. Always there are new interests, new challenges and new joys – perhaps just the smiling face of a sweet patient, the arrival of a group of new ones, a parcel of wool from some kind donor, a letter of interest, a bunch of e-mails from people wanting to help, or just the jacaranda trees in bloom.

I continue to live in the house we built 25 years ago in the hospital grounds. It was constructed in the traditional Ethiopian way, one which is now seldom seen in this expanding city. It is a *chika* house of mud and sticks.

Over the years it has sagged here and there. The ceilings are no longer straight and level, and doors do not always open properly. There is a quarry on the other side of the river, which perhaps has something to do with it. Often the blasting is like a small earthquake, and occasionally rock chips have fallen on the roof and in the garden.

Whenever the hospital architect, Ridley Smith, visits he is rather intrigued by the house and suggests all sorts of improvements. I admit that it could probably be made better with his ideas, but I fear that with any major construction it would probably fall down.

When he comes again to help with our village project he will see some changes. This year when I arrived home after spending Christmas in London with Richard and Diana, I was escorted down the hill to my home, with Birru leading the way. There was a new, shining roof in place, new ceilings in many of the rooms, and the whole house had been painted inside and out. Birru and Yeshi, with my elderly black labrador, Chips, trailing behind, proudly showed me around, and I was touched more by their smiling faces than anything else.

Birru and Yeshi look after me so well. Their devotion and loyalty never waver, and only when they have some illness, perhaps a headache or a cold, does their behaviour change in any way. Then I can always tell by their dejected looks that something is amiss, and how grateful they are to be noticed and treated, even if it is only giving them two aspirins.

We have many and frequent visitors, so Yeshi has become an excellent cook, able to produce a delicious meal in a kitchen that lacks the modern gadgets that most cooks depend upon. When five of our trustees from Britain were leaving after a ten-day stay recently, Yeshi produced a magnificent Sunday dinner for their last night – two farm chickens, which are bigger than the local ones, stuffed and roasted, and bread sauce as well. Yesterday she produced a tasty curry for four guests for lunch. One of them was an Ethiopian who has returned from America, where he went from being a taxi driver to owning a small fleet of taxis. He then studied at Bible college and finally returned here to look after street children with the money he has made.

Perhaps before Ridley comes again I may even buy a new stove. He tells me my old gas one should be in a museum, but this would have to be done without Yeshi's approval. She is so attached to this antique piece and would hate cooking on anything else.

Little has changed, really, since Reg died, and this is how I want it to remain. Here we spent the best years of our lives. I have kept his study as it was. His books on Churchill and the great heroes he so admired and his medical textbooks are still on the shelves. Birru dusts them every day. The administrative records that Reg kept meticulously all his life are filed properly as he would wish, also his correspondence with doctors and benefactors all over the world. I have thrown little away, only some of the numerous copies Reg used to make of every important document.

The best and biggest room in this, my home, is the drawing room. It has always been my domain and, I hope, reflects some of my mother's tastes and home-making ability.

Although the illiterate builder we had was dubious about the size, saying he had never built such a large room, it has stood for a quarter of a century and is where I spend most of my time. It is furnished with comfortable sofas and chairs – as well as some uncomfortable ones! There is a grand piano in one corner with a photo of Reg on it – a young Reg with kindness showing in his eyes. Against a wall is my desk, permanently littered with correspondence. It is always untidy, no matter how much time I spend trying to clear it. Every day it piles up with papers and letters. There are newsletters to write, fundraising activities to arrange, invitations to speak at various functions, correspondence with doctors wanting to visit or train, and letters from friends all over the world. Now, of course, there are also the inevitable e-mails. At times I wish they had not been invented – one has no breathing space between letters, decisions have to be made with little time for thought, and letters so composed are often lacking in literary skill.

Behind all the litter stand some photographs of my nearest and dearest – Richard and Diana with their four children; one of my mother looking serene and well, despite its being taken two weeks before her death; and another of Reg, looking out from a headland in Mombasa to the sea he loved. These give me comfort and inspiration as I struggle with my correspondence. Another source of comfort and inspiration radiates from three pictures of the Australian bush, still so dear to my heart. On other walls hang Ethiopian landscapes, and the similarity of the scenes from these two countries is uncanny.

On most days I get up at about six, just as it is getting light, make a pot of tea and take it out onto the verandah. Here I spend time praying and reading the Bible. I started this routine many years ago, and now it is something I treasure. I look forward to a time of peace and meditation when I can begin the day with God, where there is no noise from the horrid quarry across the river. The only disturbance is my *sebanya,* or guard, walking past occasionally, and Chips, who hates me reading and every now and then gives me a nudge seeking attention.

We also have a short time of prayer and Bible reading in our chapel soon after 8 am every weekday before we start work. It is a small hexagonal *tukul* in a corner of the garden away from the other buildings, overshadowed by two spreading acacias. Any of the staff can come and they often sing as well. The Ethiopians have a lovely way of singing from the heart in worship and praise, and some of their tunes are beautiful. It is appropriately named Bete Mesgana, or House of Praise. During the day it may be used for many other purposes, teaching, sewing, recreation or even for parties.

In the evenings I usually go to the hospital at about 6.30 to do a short round – often meeting Ambaye. As she also lives in the compound, she generally comes over to check the women who have had surgery that day and to see any in the ward who are sick.

Tonight I was there to see a small five year old whose rectal injury I repaired yesterday. She was raped by a drunken man in a distant village six months ago, suffering the injury as a result. Letekidane was able to find in the store a soft rag doll, which we gave her, and she was soon asleep with this in her arms. She is a lovely child, and we pray that this experience has not troubled her psychologically.

At night it is quiet in my house. No noise of traffic reaches me or radios from neighbours – only the occasional hooting of an owl in the garden or the distinctive whooping call of a hyena on the river bank below. Last year there was some excitement when one of these animals was found nesting in a drain below the hospital. The men smoked it out and killed it as they were afraid it might get into the hospital grounds. Years ago one was found roaming in my garden, to the terror of the guard, who shut himself in the laundry for the night.

During the rainy season, the noise I love to hear as I lie in bed is the sound of the river in flood. This reminds me of the distant roar of the surf on an Australian beach and takes me back to childhood holidays or to more recent holidays in the cottage on the beach at Malindi.

I keep in touch with news of the outside world through *The Weekly Telegraph* from London and if I ever get an aerial for my television set I shall be able to see the BBC News late at night. This is a recent addition to our TV broadcasts. Because my house is so far down a hill, the aerial needs to be very tall to see anything clearly. I always seem to be too busy to get one installed. The truth of the matter, though, is that I certainly do not miss television and am rather glad not to have it.

As I look ahead and think about the future, there is much still to accomplish. One great need that is always at the back of my mind is to ensure the financial security of our hospital and a second one, just as important, is the continuation of a dedicated and skilled medical staff. Also, we want to expand the work so that more women can be helped and to at least make a start in trying to prevent these maternal tragedies.

If we could have enough money invested to bring in interest to cover our annual running costs we would not have the worry of continual begging, depending on kind donors to keep things going. This is my aim before I die.

We have been told by our investment advisers that at our present rate of spending we would need US$5 million, but this could be more if we expand or the cost of living rises, as there is every indication it will.

So although our British trust is doing all it can towards establishing such an endowment, there is still a need for me to make fundraising trips and to try to break the hearts of millionaires. I feel I could do this if only I could get interviews with such people of wealth. But this is virtually impossible, as they are always well shielded from beggars.

Medical continuity is also important. There are few gynaecologists who are willing to devote their lives to fistula patients but these are the sort of doctors we must have. At present we have a wonderful team but none of us is immune to the passage of time. People often remind me of this – as if I need a reminder, a mirror is quite enough.

Dr Ambaye has now been appointed by our Trustees as Medical Director at my instigation. Ambaye was at first reluctant to accept the post when I offered it to her. She came to me with tears in her eyes, saying that she did not want to take my position. But when I assured her I was not leaving and still would be working, but needed an Ethiopian and somebody young to take over from me, she agreed. And what a good appointment it has been. Ambaye is dedicated to her patients and she is a truly skilled and careful fistula surgeon – certainly one of the best in the world. She is popular with the staff, has a vision for the future and along with all her ability, she has a charming, attractive manner. Her Christian faith and love for God are also attributes I would want my successor to have.

As yet Ambaye has not had experience in fundraising but I feel sure that in time she will become as good at this as she is at all her other duties. It will take time for her to become well known, and for her name to be associated with the hospital. I was reminded recently of 'what's in a name' by a long-time donor. The words he used were, 'There's magic in the name Hamlin.' It will take a little while for Ambaye's name to become magic, too. I know it is already happening in Ethiopia.

I sincerely hope Ambaye will not have to do too much fundraising, especially if the hoped-for endowment fund can be amassed in my lifetime. For the moment fundraising is far from Ambaye's thoughts as she focuses on the exciting event that is soon to take place in her life. She has at last decided to accept the marriage proposal of Mekuria Lakew, a very nice man whom she has known for some years. He is kind, gentle, accomplished and good-looking. As I write, the wedding is to take place in two months and then we hope the couple will move into Ambaye's spacious flat here and become part of our fraternity. He is a lecturer in biology and immunology at the Addis Ababa University and is also studying law at night school. They are both very happy, and everyone at the hospital is delighted.

Despite the many medical advances made and all the thousands of women completely cured of their fistulae, there remains a small group whom we can never make completely normal again. These sad patients have injuries so severe that they are unable to be cured by regular surgery. They require special operations which, although curing their incontinence, make it impossible for them to return to their villages. Many need to have a permanent urostomy and consequently constant medical care.

Imagine what a disaster it would be to send one of these patients home to a country village, where water is usually in short supply and hygienic conditions non-existent. They need to be near a hospital – some already have diseased and damaged kidneys, and are all subject to urinary tract infections.

Over the years these patients have increased in number until they are becoming a burden to the hospital. We were able to send a few to a government home so we can keep an eye on their medical needs, but recently this institution told us we could not send any more because our patients are young, and the home is for old people.

Some, like Letekidane Gebre Yohannes, are now full-time members of staff. Most permanent patients are not idle. If there is a shortage of staff in the wards or the kitchen or laundry, we call them in to help. We have a regular teacher who takes classes every day in the schoolroom or sitting in the garden. Often, as I pass the schoolroom, I hear the women reciting the Amharic alphabet. Or they may be learning words from the blackboard and writing them in their exercise books, listening to a teaching tape or watching a video.

Some learn to read and write quickly, and how proud they are. A group of friends and some churches in Australia have devoted money for this work and for buying Bibles that we distribute to all who can read. Other friends from overseas send knitting wool and embroidery cotton so patients can learn to knit and do handicraft work. Most countrywomen know how to make baskets, and this, too, is a popular pastime for our permanent patients.

We are hopeful that soon these permanent patients will be provided for and not have to live at the hospital. Earlier I mentioned that our President, Ato Negaso Gedada, had hinted that he might have some suitable land for a rural village where our special women could lead useful and happy lives.

As good as his word, some months later he promised us a gift of 24 hectares of beautiful land, 25 kilometres north-west of Addis Ababa. This was a truly fantastic gesture. It is almost unheard of to be given land and not just a lease. It is a lovely area with a steep hill behind and a gently sloping basin-shaped valley below, dotted with acacia, juniper and eucalyptus trees. This flattens out into a broad meadow suitable for grazing or cultivation.

Ridley Smith, our Australian architect, visited the site and was excited by what he saw. Soon he will come again to confer with our Ethiopian architects, Abba Associates, and draw detailed plans for the homes. There will probably be ten of them, each housing ten women.

Ridley's preliminary plans show the village nestling below the hill in a semicircle. One day we hope to build a teaching centre, but so far the funds available are not enough for this, or indeed for all the homes. Already the boundary fence is being erected, a water bore has been sunk and plentiful water obtained at a depth of 97 metres. We will soon buy an underwater pump and erect a storage tank.

There are some dilapidated sheds on the land, as there was once an orphanage on the site. We have mostly demolished them and used the foundation stones to make retaining walls and channels to carry the enormous amount of water that pours down the hill during the rainy season. A few of the sheds may be good enough to house agricultural equipment or livestock.

The women almost always come from a farming background, and we want to make them feel as much at home as possible. As he did with the hospital upgrade, Ridley has discussed every little detail with the staff. Ever hopeful, he again suggested thatched roofs and mud bricks, but both these ideas were quickly vetoed. Concrete blocks would be more durable than mud, and thatch is too expensive, and also houses vermin and insects. Ethiopians are not nearly so impressed by things that Westerners regard as rustic and charming.

The houses will be simple with two bedrooms, five women in each. There will be a central lounge and dining room, a kitchen and bathroom and an outside area for washing clothes. Perhaps a front terrace with a bench for the favourite pastime of sitting and chatting or, if the women are industrious, doing basketwork, knitting or sewing.

The village will provide a safe haven for these women who would otherwise be outcasts. As part of a community, they will regain a measure of self-respect and dignity. Eventually they may become self-supporting through light agricultural work, growing vegetables, keeping chickens and a few cows. We hope they will be able to supply the hospital with produce. Everyone who has seen this beautiful site is excited, and their enthusiasm has stimulated our thoughts and ambitions for this project.

As I write, our hospital has never been so overcrowded, so this village could help by taking our patients who need long rehabilitation before they are fit for surgery, thus releasing beds for those who are able to be quickly treated and cured. The village would then become an extension of our hospital, enabling us to admit and treat more of these women.

The outreach program will continue to be an important part of our work. As I write we have a team in Tigray, in the ancient town of Axum, which in the fourth century was the centre of Christianity in the Axumite kingdom. Many believe the Ark of the Covenant is kept there in St Mary of Zion Church. Ambaye, with two nurses and a driver, set out on an arduous journey of 1020 kilometres in the Land Rover, packed with equipment. They will be operating on twenty patients, who are already waiting in the local hospital.

Grass-roots community education programs are on the drawing board. Dr Mulu and Sister Ruth Kennedy are putting a great deal of energy into these. Working through local women's associations, health centres, schools and farmer associations, their aim is to prevent fistula injury. They know that they need to involve the men of the village, as unless they co-operate and are convinced that women often need help during labour, there is nothing the women can do on their own. All the decisions in the family are made by men.

We know that we would see a huge reduction in the number of fistula patients if the government could build more hospitals and well-equipped health centres, and just as importantly if they built new roads and provided better public transport. In the meantime our greatest challenge is to train gynaecologists and equip them to set up fistula repair centres in the regional hospitals. We need to fire them with enthusiasm, encourage them by improving their working conditions, and somehow provide the special instruments, suitable operating tables and good lights required for fistula surgery. As ever, we face the need to contact men and women of goodwill and wealth to provide this equipment.

It is a challenge we tackle with optimism and hope – optimism because of recent awareness in the developed world that mothers are suffering. There are organisations being set up to try to decrease maternal deaths throughout the developing world. The founder of Microsoft, Bill Gates, and his wife have put aside huge sums of money for 'averting maternal death and disability'. We pray that some of these funds may come our way.

Already in some provinces there are gynaecologists who have trained with us who are performing simple operations. It is happening in Gondar, in Mekele, Yirgalem and Arba Minsh. A doctor in Adigrat, Dr Kassahun, has done about 200 operations. Ambaye visited him to help with the more difficult cases. Unfortunately he recently left to pursue his career in Addis Ababa. We hope there will be another gynaecologist with surgical skills and a similar concern for fistula patients to take his place.

Recently doctors in England have contacted me about a plan to do fistula surgery on a mercy ship, soon to be working off the coast of West Africa. We are keen to help and even have plans to send one of our own surgeons on such an exciting mission.

All this is encouraging, but only a beginning if we are one day to see our beloved Ethiopian women able to have safe deliveries and live babies as in Europe, America and Australia.

There is still much to be done for thousands of women who every year suffer the agony of obstructed labour and its horrific consequences. I could never imagine just living here and not working, it would be unthinkable. Unthinkable, too, to walk away when I know the problems would be even worse. I have therefore made no plans for my retirement.

One plan I have made for the future is to reserve a plot in the British War Graves Cemetery where Reg is buried. These plots were becoming scarce, so I wrote to the British Ambassador, whom I happened to know well, as he and Richard were at the English School here together, and asked for one of the remaining spaces. The request had to be referred to the War Graves Commission in England but was duly granted.

Now I have come to the end of this story of the fistula pilgrims – a story that I leave others to continue and finish. Eventually, I hope they will be able to write that there is no longer any need for a fistula hospital, as Ethiopia will have become a country where every woman can be assured of a safe delivery. The fistula hospital will then become just one of hundreds of maternity hospitals scattered throughout the land.

This task I bequeath to my young doctors and nurses, to pursue with all their strength. Hopefully one day pregnancy and labour will no longer be something women dread, and the shame and suffering of the fistula pilgrims will only be a memory.

Reg often used to say, 'A mother is a family's richest possession, a being of priceless value.' And I know that for him working with Ethiopia's brave young mothers, so tragically damaged, was a labour of love.

I – and those who have helped me – have written this book in the hope that the torch lit by Reg for the fistula pilgrims of Ethiopia, and indeed of the world, will burn even more brightly, and that others will become inspired to stamp out this long-neglected and shameful maternal tragedy.

Postscript

In this postscript I wish to acknowledge the work of my senior staff, most of whom I have not mentioned by name in this book, but without whose skill and devotion the hospital could not function as a place of sanctuary and healing.

Our matron, Sister Ejigayehu, is one of our nursing graduates from the Princess Tsehai Hospital nursing school, so grew up under our eyes. I could not have a better matron, with her firm, wise and kind management. Under her are our trained nurses – all with special jobs – Sisters Tenadam, Azeb, Ruth and Genet, and our pharmacist Sister Metasabia, who is also a graduate from the Princess Tsehai Hospital.

When writing about hospitals the administrative staff is often forgotten, and so I especially want to mention our financial manager, Woizero Genet Kifle, who has been with us for the last thirteen years, making an enormous contribution in all matters financial. No praise is too high for her. Our auditors once told me she could not be faulted!

Our trustees contribute much with their wisdom and special knowledge. Two of the senior trustees are Geoffrey Wetherell and Ato Nardos Lemma. Geoffrey is a coffee exporter and businessman whose home has been in Ethiopia since he was discharged from the British Army after the Italian-Ethiopian war, so his love for this country and his knowledge of it are great. Ato Nardos is an Ethiopian lawyer whose wise advice and help we so often need. All our five trustees have the welfare of the women who come to the hospital as their first priority, and keep us from making decisions that would jeopardise this.

There are many friends and organisations here that share our concern for the injured women and girls, and who contribute towards their welfare – not only by donations of money, but with much else, thus bringing some joy into their lives. One such is Hazel Maunsell, who gives up one day every week to visit the patients, talk to them, comfort them and teach them of God's love. Hazel and her husband have worked with a mission in Ethiopia for many years, and have a special understanding and rapport with the patients. Hazel's love for them is deep and true. Our staff also enjoy her teaching and look forward to her weekly visits. I thank all my friends for what they do for this hospital.

But more than anything else, my heart is uplifted in thanks to God our Father, and our Saviour Jesus Christ for all He has done for us. The future I leave in the hands of an Almighty and all loving God – what could be more secure, as God is faithful. May we too, be faithful.

Dr E. Catherine Hamlin

For further information, please visit https://hamlinfistula.org/

Hamlin Fistula Ethiopia
Addis Ababa Fistula Hospital
PO Box 3609
Addis Ababa
Ethiopia
Email: enquiries@hamlinfistula.org
Phone: +251 (0) 113 716544

Afterword

by John Little, March 2016

Since it was first published in 2001, *The Hospital by the River* has never been out of print. It's easy to understand why it has become such a well-loved book. It seems to me that even the hardest heart could not fail to be moved by the story of traumatised, abandoned women being transformed from utter wretchedness to joyous new life. And who could fail to be inspired by Dr Catherine Hamlin AC and her late husband, Dr Reginald Hamlin OBE, who decided, more than half a century ago, to forsake affluence and ease, and devote themselves to a cause which few cared about.

When the book came out, there was one fistula hospital in Ethiopia. At that time it had treated some 20,000 women. The hospital was well established. And there were good people to help run it. But money was always a problem. Everything the hospital did was absolutely free of charge to the patients. It still is. It has to be, for the women who make those arduous journeys seeking help are generally destitute.

Catherine was 77 years old, an age when most people have long been retired. But she could not yet afford to sit back and bask in her achievements. The Hamlins always spent their holidays abroad wooing wealthy donors when possible. 'We're beggars,' Catherine would say. After Reg died, in 1993, someone had to keep raising funds, and Catherine was the only one who could do it. By then there were other good fistula surgeons to help, however, at 77 Catherine was still doing surgery, overseeing administration, dealing with donors, the Ethiopian government and all of the day-to-day concerns of a busy hospital. She often told me that she loved what she was doing and had no desire to stop. Her hope, though, was that one day there would be enough money to set up a future fund, where the interest would fund the hospital. That fund has now been established in Switzerland. Money is being channelled to the hospital but the expansion has been so great that it falls far short of covering all costs.

So in the last fifteen years Catherine has worked harder than ever. The number of patients treated now exceeds 44,000. There are now six fistula hospitals in Ethiopia. She has built an entire village on the outskirts of the capital to accommodate those, fortunately few, patients who are seriously injured and need long term care. Her crowning achievement has been the establishment of the Hamlin College of Midwives, for it is only through proper obstetric care during pregnancy and labour that fistula can be prevented. After completing a rigorous four years of training, graduates go into the field to areas which have never had midwives until now. They are able to diagnose when a patient is in obstructed labour, or is at high risk of obstructed labour, and get her to a hospital where a caesarean section can be done. In the areas where they are working the incidence of fistula and maternal mortality has been dramatically reduced.

Catherine is now 92. Until just before her 90th birthday she was still operating on patients. Every day she would make her way up the 67 steps and winding paths which link her house with the hospital. Hazardous enough for any 90-year-old, but Catherine needs walking sticks. She has a neuropathy in her legs. The nerves are dying and she's losing her balance. A year or so ago she told me that when she had last been in Australia she had visited a neurologist and asked for a prognosis.

'He said I would probably end up in a wheelchair one day. I can't live here in a wheelchair, how would I get up to the hospital?'

This last line was delivered in a matter-of-fact way, which was entirely typical. She never dramatises, no matter how dire the subject. 'It's not hard to get up and down, I hold onto the rail and just walk up. Don't worry about me, I don't want people making a fuss.'

She gave up operating, not because her hands were unsteady, but because of her balance problem. 'I could go on doing it because you mostly sit to operate, but sometimes you have to stand up to open the abdomen for some reason. Well I couldn't stand up and operate without my sticks. And now we have capable fistula surgeons who do all the surgery.'

Fifteen years ago the problem of obstetric fistula was practically unknown to the western world. That has changed. The United Nations Population Fund, UNFPA, in 2003 launched a $75 million global campaign aimed at eradicating obstetric fistula by 2015. They have been working in partnership with Non-Government Organisations (NGOs) in over 40 countries in Africa, Asia and the Arab region. Fistula hospitals and fistula wards have been opening up in developing countries, many of them staffed by doctors who were trained in Addis Ababa. Still, here we are one year past that deadline, and obstetric fistula has not been eradicated. The UN estimates there are two million sufferers still in the world. No one really knows with any accuracy how many are in Ethiopia. Some estimates put it at 10,000. All we know is that there is a certain percentage of women in the far-off countryside who suffer an obstructed labour with nobody to help. Many die undelivered; others survive but with a fistula – often wishing that they had died. On the positive side, the developed world has certainly been waking up. About ten years ago large aid providers started asking Catherine if they could help with medical equipment, building programs and money. This was very welcome. But one of the most dramatic changes can be summed up in one word: Oprah.

In late 2003 Catherine was asked to go to America for an appearance on *The Oprah Winfrey Show*. It was an invitation which charities dream about. America's talk show queen had a weekly audience of 49 million viewers, plus millions more in over a hundred other countries. A few minutes with Oprah had been known to change fortunes forever.

Despite Oprah's celebrity, Catherine had only the vaguest idea who she was. She flew to Chicago in January 2004 with her assistant, Ruth Kennedy. After being whisked from the airport to their hotel by limousine, they worried that they might not recognise Ms Winfrey when they met her the next day. Neither of them had any idea what she looked like. They solved that problem by buying a copy of *O Magazine* which had a picture of Oprah on the cover. When she welcomed Catherine in typically flamboyant style, they realised that there would have been no mistaking Oprah.

The segment began with a film explaining obstetric fistula. Then they showed Dr Ambaye Wolde Michael on one of her outreach trips patiently teasing out the histories of two fistula sufferers. Hawa had been living alone in a small, dark hut for 20 years. Majo was in labour for six days before her child was born dead, leaving her with a fistula. Typically tragic cases. Both cured.

The American audience of mainly women was visibly shocked. Then Catherine came on, answering Oprah's questions quietly and with grace. No dramatics, no hand wringing. The story is so powerful it doesn't need any of that. By the time the interview was over most of the audience were shedding tears.

At one stage Oprah asked Catherine, 'How much does it cost to run the hospital for one year?'

The answer at that time was $450,000. When the show finished she invited Catherine to come to her office for a chat, where she pulled out her chequebook and wrote a personal cheque for $450,000. That was only the beginning. Oprah's viewers later donated a further $3 million.

You could not imagine two more unalike people than Oprah Winfrey and Dr Catherine Hamlin: the extrovert, billionaire celebrity and the doctor working in near obscurity in Africa. Yet they became instant friends. In December 2004 Oprah came to Addis Ababa to open the new wing which had been built with her contribution. Oprah wanted a low-key occasion, but her concept of 'low-key' is rather different to most people's. She arrived in a cavalcade with a motor cycle police escort, accompanied by a host of producers and film technicians. She spent the day touring the hospital, listening closely to patients' stories. When the film of the visit was shown on American television, once again the hospital was inundated with donations.

Catherine and Ruth had plenty of ideas about what to do with this unexpected money coming from several sources. They inspected some government hospitals in outlying parts of the country with the idea that they might spend a little to upgrade some of the facilities, so that fistula patients or women in labour would have somewhere to go within reach of their homes. In the end they decided that they'd be better off building their own new hospitals in the grounds of the existing government hospitals in roughly the north, south, east and west of the country. The hospitals that they approached all had extensive grounds and all welcomed the idea with enthusiasm. The last one, at Metu, in the west, opened in 2010. These regional hospitals have greatly reduced the arduous journeys that patients used to make to get to the capital.

It has taken a while for people to realise that they are there. When I was visiting in 2007 the new hospital at Yirgalem in the south had just opened. A Norwegian obstetrician, Dr Einar Lande, was in charge. Einar had given up a comfortable practice in Norway to come there. He was full of enthusiasm for the task. The trouble was that few patients were presenting. Einar took heart from the experience of the first outreach hospital in Bahir Dar in the north. After opening in 2006 it took a year or so for people to realise that the hospital was there, and to trust it. Einar's optimism was well placed. In 2016, Yirgalem is now one of the busiest hospitals, always full of patients.

A small number of patients are so badly injured that they cannot be cured. They have to live the rest of their lives with a stoma, a small surgically created opening in the abdomen which allows urine to be directed into a collection bag. The bag is worn outside and can be emptied and changed when necessary. It is practically impossible for these women to return to their villages as they need to be near a medical facility where they can obtain a supply of bags and have help if they need it.

In the first edition of *The Hospital by the River*, Catherine wrote of her plan one day to build a village where these unfortunate women could live. That idea has become a reality. The village is called Desta Mender, or Joy Village. It was built with a grant from the Australian government and the land was a donation from the Ethiopian government.

The village is a semicircle of simple, small houses where ten can live in each house. In the centre is a community centre built like a *tukul.* The village nestles at the foot of some hills. Flagstone paths link the various buildings, and you can see Catherine's touch in beautifully kept flower gardens bordering the paths, reminiscent of the hospital in Addis. A long grassy, timbered expanse runs from the houses to a little man-made lake, beside which is a small cafe open to the public: the Juniper Cafe. A teaching or conference centre built nearby can be hired out.

In 2003 when Desta Mender opened, Catherine's youngest brother, Jock Nicholson and his wife, Louise, took a year off from their farm near Tamworth, New South Wales, to get things started.

Catherine's vision was for the village to be a home for life. As Desta Mender was set in rich farmland 17 kilometres from Addis she thought it could be partly self-sufficient. With their farming skills, Jock and Louise were able to set up market gardens, a dairy, an apple and pear orchard, and put in place the beginnings of a basic education program. In the beginning there were eighteen residents, but with more and more people arriving in Addis and the new outreach hospitals, the numbers have increased rapidly. Within five years of the opening it was obvious that making Desta Mender a home for life would not be sustainable. Apart from the numbers, the cost of looking after a patient for a year was nine times the cost of one fistula operation.

Recently, a dynamic new manager, Beletshachew Tadesse, devised a new strategy where patients enrol in a program to learn the skills they need to live independently. This is not as simple as it sounds. Besides being deeply traumatised and often close to suicidal, the women who move to Desta Mender are invariably illiterate and innumerate. They've spent their lives in remote villages where a modern education is unheard of.

At Desta Mender they have lessons in literacy and numeracy. They learn basic accounting skills, such as how to calculate profit and loss; and life skills like hygiene and personal health management. They are taught what their rights and responsibilities are in the new world they will one day inhabit.

The new scheme seems to be a success. Some 70 patients have been reintegrated into society. Many have left to start small businesses including a dairy, a jewellery business and a popular cafe on the road from Addis. The Hamlin organisation has arranged employment for some. Seven patients found permanent jobs at a nearby orphanage.

There is a follow-up process to ensure patients remain in good health. Still, there are some who are simply unable to cope in the outside world. Many work in the vegetable gardens which for most of the year supply all of the needs of Desta Mender. The surplus vegetables are used in the hospital in Addis Ababa.

Beletshachew has great compassion for the women in her charge. But she doesn't allow sentiment to stop her making businesslike decisions. They used to have 400 chickens, which was a popular venture, but when they calculated profit versus loss they realised the chickens would have to go. Ditto for the dairy which had been there from the beginning.

The Juniper Cafe is one of the most successful enterprises. In 2007 Soroptimist International launched an appeal for funds to support the hospital. Soroptimist International is a women's organisation similar to Rotary. The appeal, 'Restoring Dignity,' was one to which its members had no trouble relating.

Six hundred thousand dollars was raised. A large portion went to build the cafe and adjoining conference centre. As often seems to happen when there is a need, someone turned up to run the cafe. In 2008 Rae Newman, arrived. She and her husband, Winston, had left their home in Canberra to do mission work in Ethiopia. Winston was teaching at a local mission college. Rae took on the task of teaching residents how to cook and run a cafe. She was like a mother to the girls she taught.

As Catherine has written, the Ethiopian diet consists almost exclusively of *Injera* and *wat*. *Injera* is a sort of pancake made of fermented *teff*, a type of grass with a fine seed. The *wat* is usually a spicy paste of chickpeas, or on special occasions it might be lamb, chicken, goat or beef. Ethiopians are happy to live on this diet year in and year out; in fact they prefer it to any other.

The erstwhile cooks of the Juniper Cafe had no concept of western food. The idea of decorating a cake, for instance, was an enigma to them. Nevertheless they have proved to be very good at following recipes, even if they wouldn't dream of eating the results. The Newmans had to organise a system for ordering and paying at the cafe, since none of the women knew how to receive cash and give change. Zuriash, the teacher at Desta Mender at that time, worked on this in class, devising a system of coloured tokens. The cafe is popular. It's especially renowned for its meat pies and chocolate cake. It's perhaps not surprising that expatriate Australians, in particular, are regular customers.

~

The Hamlins came to Ethiopia in the first place to set up a school of midwifery. They were delighted when they managed to persuade a world-famous midwife, Maggie Miles, to come for a few months to help. The school only ever trained half-a-dozen graduates before the Ethiopian Ministry of Health disbanded it. This was a terrible disappointment. Catherine and Reg knew that the only way ever to eradicate obstetric fistula would be to have trained midwives available to women living in remote parts of the country. The government didn't see why nurses couldn't do the work of midwives just as well. The Hamlins would have been happy to start a school themselves but there was never enough money available.

Catherine never forgot their dream. It seemed unlikely it would ever happen until, at the beginning of the new millennium, money began to suddenly come in from abroad.

While the hospital was expanding at breakneck pace, Catherine decided the time had come at last for her college of midwives. There were already government schools offering three year courses for a diploma of midwifery. But the teaching methods and curriculum were simply not adequate for the kind of cases that occur in a country like Ethiopia. Midwives can expect to encounter every possible complication. If they are in the far-flung provinces with barely adequate medical facilities, they have to cope by themselves. Not surprisingly, most graduates went on almost immediately to tutoring, became nurses, or else practiced in the big metropolitan centres. In the villages, where the need was so desperate, nothing changed.

To illustrate how critical the need still is, there are about 7,000 qualified midwives for a population of 100 million.

Two experienced midwives, an Australian, Annette Bennett, and an Ethiopian, Solomon Abebe, devised a new curriculum which was very clinically based.

The first course at the Hamlin College of Midwives was for three years. Later the government made midwifery for every school a four-year course. Ethiopian teaching methods rely a great deal on rote learning, with very little practical experience.

Under the Hamlin curriculum students are subjected to a rigorous clinical regime. By the time they graduate, many of them will have delivered close to 100 babies.

'We send them down to Atat,' says Catherine, 'which is a Catholic hospital in the south west. It has a wonderful turnover of abnormal obstetrics, so they see every abnormality before they graduate. They're able to handle breeches and turn babies around before labour if they're in the wrong position. They learn a lot of things to prevent the women getting into obstructed labour.'

The students are recruited in their final year of high school, from areas in the countryside where the need is greatest. Once qualified as midwives they are deployed back to the area where they grew up. Being familiar with the people and their language (there are 80 different languages in Ethiopia), they are more likely to stay.

The first eleven midwives graduated with their Bachelor of Science (Midwifery) degrees in 2010, and every year since the college has graduated more and more. At the time of writing there are 80 Hamlin midwives deployed in regional areas. They work in properly equipped clinics, consisting of three rooms in the numerous Government Health Centres. The Hamlin midwives are located within 70 kilometres of the regional fistula hospitals, so that they have access to an ambulance and hospital support. These three rooms can be set up as antenatal clinics wherever in the countryside Hamlin midwives need to be working. So far this arrangement is working well. Catherine is most grateful for this help from the government as it has saved the cost of building separate rural antenatal clinics.

In a few of the antenatal clinics the Hamlin organisation has built accommodation nearby where the midwives can live, or else they rent rooms for them in the nearby villages.

According to Catherine you can already see the difference. 'We're getting fewer fistulas because of the midwives. Some of them are doing over 100 deliveries a month. One near

Harar did 190 in one month, certainly a record.' At the time of writing, Hamlin midwives have conducted 22,500 safe deliveries in remote parts of Ethiopia.

In her speech at one graduation ceremony Catherine told the graduates, 'You are embarking on a great and ancient career. Midwives are mentioned in the first book of the Bible. You are a key person in the struggle to eventually eradicate fistula injuries, or even death, from obstructed labour. You are indeed on the front lines of the battle to prevent fistula. We have confidence in your ability and devotion to the hard task ahead.'

Catherine's ambition was to eradicate obstetric fistula in Ethiopia in her lifetime. She has resigned herself to thinking that probably won't happen. But in ten to twenty years? Possibly. When it does happen she would like the fistula hospitals to turn into maternity hospitals.

In 2012 a new Australian fundraising trust, Hamlin Fistula Ethiopia (Australia), was created. A series of gala events was planned to launch the new trust. Catherine was initially reluctant to visit Australia because, in her typically modest way, she worried that there would be no support for her. The first event was a dinner in Sydney. Four days before it was due all the tickets were sold out. When Catherine anxiously walked into the ballroom 700 people rose to their feet and applauded her. Afterwards, 300 queued up for her to sign the book. The warm good will in that room was palpable. The next couple of weeks were a whirl: breakfasts in several states, newspaper interviews, countless appearances on TV and radio, including the top rating *60 Minutes*. There was no doubt in anyone's mind about the public's affection for Dr Catherine Hamlin.

Remembering that time, Catherine says simply, 'I was overwhelmed with all the love and help given! I was so pleased that they wanted to support us, and so thankful.'

~

There is something about this cause which appeals to the generosity in us all. Heartwarming examples over the years are legion. Some gifts have been spectacular, like the man from South Australia who gave $200,000 after watching a TV program about Desta Mender. There was another donation recently of $100,000 to build two midwives' homes.

The most remarkable was a donation from Sonia Fenton, a businesswoman who lived in a very up-market apartment overlooking Sydney Harbour. Sonia read this book and kept having to stop because she was crying. She could relate to what the fistula sufferers went through. As a child she had had an ovarian cyst which required injections three times a week, from the age of eleven to nineteen. She had been too weak to live a normal life. She went to school each day but she didn't dance or swim or do any of the enjoyable things that teenagers do. 'Knowing how I felt in a suburban family with the best medical attention at the time I just couldn't imagine how it would feel for the girls to be ostracised from their villages and leaking urine and sometimes bowel contents as well. I just didn't think I could continue to live my lifestyle while this was continuing to happen.'

Sonia bought a ticket to Ethiopia. As with everyone, her visit to the hospital reduced her to tears. The most profound impact was when Catherine invited her to her home for tea.

'It was life-changing. Just the fact that Dr Hamlin was so articulate and humble to sit down and pour tea with somebody she hadn't met before. She of course had no idea that I was thinking about donating any money. At that stage I was thinking about $50,000 to do something.'

After talking to Catherine for well over an hour Sonia came away with a very clear idea about what was needed. She returned home and straightaway put her apartment on the market. It sold for $1.9 million, of which she donated $1 million.

For every spectacular gift there are hundreds and hundreds of gifts of $10, $100, $500 from people of modest means. It seems that there is something addictive and wonderful about being generous. Hopefully this will never change for it takes US$6 million just to run the main programs for a year.

It is a little over half a century since the Hamlins arrived in Ethiopia to begin their three year contract. In 1959, they could never have imagined where it would lead. After decades of operating hand-to-mouth, this little family-run NGO has now expanded into a global organisation, with a first class professional administration.

Catherine's long-term aim has always been to have Ethiopians in charge. And this has come to pass. The first Ethiopian CEO is about to be appointed; the regional hospitals are all run by Ethiopians; the Medical Director, the Manager of Desta Mender and the Dean of the Hamlin College of Midwives are Ethiopians. In 2013 there was consternation at the college when a cook and three students were run down by a car while walking home. The cook was killed instantly and the three students were seriously injured. One, Belaynesh Abese, had a ruptured spleen, requiring an immediate blood transfusion. The Dean of the college, Ato Zelalem, immediately gave blood as he had the same rare blood group. By this action he saved his student's life. The following year Belaynesh graduated and won the Hamlin Medal for the most outstanding academic and clinical results.

This little anecdote says much about the people who work for Catherine. The Medical Director, Dr Fekade Ayanachew, was trained by Dr Hamlin and supports passionately her vision to further improve patient outcomes and the quality of life for chronic patients. He firmly believes that fistula can be eradicated. 'When we are able to support our mothers to plan when to have their babies and convince them to seek a skilled birth attendant and ensure unfailing obstetric care services then we can stop the occurrence of fistula.'

When patients were discharged Reg used to tell them, 'When you feel the baby walking around inside you then you must start walking to the hospital.'

There is now a ten-bed ward at the hospital in Addis Ababa where caesareans are performed on returning patients. Dr Fekade performed the firstcaesarean in 2013, delivering a lovely baby boy.

Richard Hamlin, now in his early sixties, has spent his life in England working in the IT industry. He is divorced, and father to four children. Whenever Catherine visited England she used to take delight in spending time with her family. Whilst Richard was always a strong supporter of his mother's work, he did not aspire to be involved in the administration of the hospital. In the last few years that has changed. He has visited the hospital frequently and is an important support for his mother.

As I write this Catherine is having a long sabbatical in England with Richard. When she returns home to Ethiopia she can see out her days knowing that the hospital and all of its programs are in safe hands. Throughout her tumultuous life Dr Catherine Hamlin's approach to medicine has never varied. The patients have always been treated holistically, with much thought given to their emotional as well as their surgical needs. Catherine has trained her people to make each patient feel valued, respected and loved. That's why this hospital by the river will always be so special.

Acknowledgments

Special thanks are due to Dr Robert Zacharin. The authors have drawn heavily on his work, *Obstetric Fistula,* for the section about the history of fistula surgery.

Many old friends gave their recollections of Crown Street days. They include Dr Bill McBride, Dr Ian Cope, Dr Peter Crowe, Dr John Murray, Dr John Newlinds, Dr Struan Robertson, Dr Jim Roche, former sisters Pat Sparrow, Hazel Woolston and Billie Abrahams.

Thanks are also due to Dr Rowan Nicks, Dr Eric Goulston, Charles Sherlock, Richard Pankhurst, Princess Sybil Desta, Terry Asfaw and Yeshi Kassa. Sheila Adams, Sheila Thompson and Mary Walters shared their memories of life at Frensham school.

The authors have referred to the Channel Four documentary, *The Child Brides of Ethiopia.*

Dr Richard Rawstron in New Zealand helped with historical research about the Hamlin family. Thanks, too, to the former Archbishop of Sydney, Sir Marcus Loan, and to my family, especially my son, Richard, and to my sisters, Sheila Knox and Ailsa Pottie.

Bibliography

Casbon, Eleanor, 1993, *The Incurable Optimists: Chris and Dan Sandford of Ethiopia*, United Writers, Cornwall.

Collins, Jodie, 1985, *Code Word: Catherine*, Tyndale House.

Crown Street Centenary Committee, 1994, *The Women's Hospital (Crown Street) 1893–1983: A Family Remembers*, Ultimo.

Harker, Jack S., 1989, *HMNZS Gambia,* Moana Press, Tauranga, New Zealand.

Kennedy, Priscilla, 1976, *Portrait of Winifred West*, Fine Arts Press, Sydney.

MacGregor, Miriam, 1973, 1975, *Petticoat Pioneers*, Books 1 and 2, AH and AW Reed Ltd, Wellington, New Zealand.

Ryburn, H.J., *Te Hemara, James Hamlin: Friend of the Maoris*, John McIndoe Ltd, Dunedin, New Zealand.

Sims, J. Marion, 1884, *The Story of My Life*, D. Appleton & Company, New York.

Young, Florence S.H., 1925, *Pearls from the Pacific*, Marshall Brothers Ltd, London, Edinburgh.

Zacharin, Dr Robert F., 1988, *Obstetric Fistula*, Springer-Verlag Wien, New York.